Astrology for Sceptics

ASTROLOGY FOR SCEPTICS

Charlotte MacLeod

Illustrated by the author

TURNSTONE BOOKS

LONDON

© 1972 by Charlotte MacLeod

First American edition 1972
First British edition 1973

Turnstone Books
37 Upper Addison Gardens,
London W14

ISBN: 0 85500 011 2

Set in Linotype Caledonia
Printed in Great Britain by
Lowe & Brydone (Printers) Ltd,
Thetford, Norfolk

Acknowledgments

WRITING is a process of receiving and transmitting. Being merely the apparatus which channels thought into word does not exempt a writer from taking personal responsibility for collecting, organizing, editing, and presenting available data in the clearest, most readable form she can achieve. I am deeply grateful to those who have shared this work with me.

Pierrette DeLys has proved to be not only a superb teacher of esoteric astrology but also a most capable critic of her first graduate student's attempts to transmit some ideas about this fascinating subject to a wider audience. Her patience, understanding, and keen intelligence in grasping and explaining the sound common sense behind the obfuscation are a joy at all times. They are especially welcome when brought to the aid of somebody struggling to make a difficult subject acceptable to perceptive, educated, and possibly incredulous readers.

Alick Bartholomew is an editor both relentless and delightful. His zeal to extract the best book possible is combined with a warm and rare regard for an author's opinions and sensitivities, so that one is spurred to complete far more than one would have dared to attempt without such support and encouragement. His extreme care and attention to minutiae in editing have given this text a solidity and coherence which must inevitably enhance its value as a teaching device.

Nathan Miller has contributed far more than he realizes. He has allowed himself to be pumped for information about the

Hebrew language and the Jewish religion from which so much astrological lore is derived. He has given the stimulus of an agile mind to countless discussions which led to fresh insights and entirely new trains of thought, and he has most capably played devil's advocate in testing some of the admittedly controversial arguments here presented.

Josephine Rogers deserves special mention for having seen the possibility of turning a vague suggestion into a workable text and for setting in motion the chain of events which have brought it to the publishing stages. To her, and to all who have shared in its coming-to-be, I offer my loving and heartfelt thanks.

CHARLOTTE MACLEOD

Sudbury, Massachusetts

Contents

    INTRODUCTION / 1
1. ENERGY AND ORDER / 6
2. BALANCE AND GROWTH / 15
3. ASTROLOGICAL COMMON SENSE / 23
4. SATURN   Responsibility and Control / 32
5. JUPITER   Acceptance and Expansion / 47
6. MERCURY   Concentration and Motivation / 54
7. VENUS   Imagination / 62
8. MARS   Achievement / 71
9. MOON   Memory, the Subconscious / 81
10. SUN   Consciousness, the Ego / 88
11. URANUS   Inspiration and Change / 96
12. NEPTUNE   Reversal, Forgiveness / 104
13. PLUTO   Redemption, the Master-Builder / 112
14. INTRODUCTION TO THE SIGNS / 120
15. COLORS / 133
16. ARIES / 141
17. TAURUS / 160
18. GEMINI / 172

19. CANCER / 183
20. LEO / 193
21. VIRGO / 203
22. LIBRA / 214
23. SCORPIO / 228
24. SAGITTARIUS / 239
25. CAPRICORN / 250
26. AQUARIUS / 259
27. PISCES / 269
28. A NOTE ON THE READING OF CHARTS / 281
 APPENDIX: A Note on the Use of
  Computer Data / 293
 SUGGESTED READING / 296
 INDEX / 299

Astrology for Sceptics

Introduction

Of all the arts which have originated in ancient magian wisdom, astrology is now the most misunderstood. No one believes any longer in the universal harmonies of Nature and in the necessary interconnexion of all effects with all causes. . . . The restoration of astrology to its primitive purity would be, in a sense, the creation of an entirely new science. . . .

ABBÉ ALPHONSE LOUIS CONSTANT, better known by his pseudonym, Eliphas Levi, wrote these words perhaps a century and a half ago in a book called *Transcendental Magic*. At that time, intellectuals were diligently pricking the balloons of mysticism which had been blown up into ridiculous shapes by centuries of charlatanism.

Since then, Western thinkers have been more and more zealous in their rejection of anything that smacked of the occult. We have evolved philosophies of determinism. We have discovered psychiatry. We have developed technologies which leave us gasping, sometimes with horror, at our own achievements. And all these innovations have led us straight back to the need to believe in the universal harmonies of Nature. We are beginning to realize that the so-called occult sciences are not playthings for the idle and credulous, that behind the claptrap and the tinsel, the knavery and the gullibility, there may be something worth investigating.

Right now, we are involved with a fad of occultism, most of it bogus, almost identical to that which swept Parisian society in Eliphas Levi's day. The reason is the same. A detached, rationalistic approach to life is too chilling for mortal bones to bear. The more scientific "common sense" we hear preached at us, the more we yearn to warm ourselves by that spark of Nature's fire which only the poets and the magicians have remembered how to kindle.

Whatever name we choose to call it by, mysticism has always been part of our everyday lives. Read the Gospel hymns written during the past century. Compare them to ancient magian writings which the ministers who wrote the hymns would have anathematized from their pulpits. Apply those words to the current resurgence of the occult. On the other side of Jordan in the sweet fields of Eden, where the tree of life is blooming, there is rest for you and your mandala and your Tarot cards. Yea, verily, even unto your guitar.

Go to an evangelist revival, then a rock festival. Where lies the difference? What do all the soul music and the shouting and the primitive, insistent rhythms add up to but a raw emotional appeal to blow your mind and release the pent-up spirit? We're still begging to be washed in the same old blood of the same old Lamb, and let's not kid ourselves that Janis Joplin and Aimee Semple MacPherson Hutton weren't sisters under the skin, even as you and I.

Or perhaps it's Bach who turns us on. Why would these intricate tonalities give us such ineffable satisfaction, if it were not that they put us in touch with something we know but cannot otherwise perceive?

However satisfying these moments of contact may be, we can't spend all our time on the peaks. We need an ongoing sense of involvement with something outside the mundane, yet not too far outside, for us to reach toward and touch whenever we need reassurance. That's why the cultism which has always been such a picturesque facet of the American scene is spreading so fast. College students who would laugh themselves sick at a meeting of the Elks or the Moose or the Pentecostal Baptists are rushing off to join the Zen Buddhists or the Satanists or whatever fancy-dress cult happens along with an appealing sales pitch.

For some of us, this sort of thing won't do. We don't care to become either lamas or lamiae. Theologies, however orthodox or unorthodox, no longer have relevance for us. We need an everyday kind of mysticism, some belief which won't conflict too sharply with the ways of life we know and find relatively agreeable.

Even though not many people today understand astrology any better than Marie Antoinette and her little group of serious thinkers did, it's not hard to see why we're becoming so widely involved with the subject. It has a direct personal appeal. It has a wealth of pictorial imagery. It has new information coming along every day. And it can be reduced to a rigid formula.

Go to Mass, say your beads, make the Stations of the Cross, and you won't go to the bad place when you die. Read your daily horoscope, obey the Gospel according to Zolar, and you'll stay out of trouble here on earth. The mechanics are familiar.

Yet the Catholicism of Teilhard de Chardin or Pope John XXIII is a far cry from that of Mother Machree, and there's more to astrology than you find in the "My Stars" column on the newsstands. Pablum for the masses can also nourish the thinking individual.

Astrology can be a crutch, yes; but it can also be a handy probe with which to reach your inner self and lever you into a more viable relationship to the larger reality. It can be a halter to lead you blindly around and around the same old treadmill, or an alpinist's rope by whose aid you can scale peaks you may have seen from a distance or only hoped might rise above the clouds that block your view.

Properly understood and used, astrology is neither risky nor transitory in its effects. It can carry you to a far more satisfactory high than any drug. The difference is that you choose your route, you can be sure the trip won't turn into a ghastly nightmare because you're in control every minute, and you get where you want to go. You never come down unless you want to, and the whole thing doesn't cost a cent.

It does require a great deal of concentrated effort, however. In order to enjoy the real benefits of astrology, you have to acquire a knowledge of how it works. Practical training in astronomy is not necessary, but you must have some conception of cosmic order. You have to think in terms which transcend terrestrial boundaries. You must be able to posit the concept of never-ending life which is capable of renewing its tangible forms.

Of course we all accept this principle in fact, or we'd never try to plant a garden or make a baby. Since the Atomic Age has made us familiar with the laws of thermodynamics, we can accept the theory of spiritual immortality and physical reincarnation far more easily than could the intellectuals of our grandparents' day.

We realize now that all matter is composed of energy. We have learned that energy, though it can exist in any imaginable destructible form, is in itself indestructible. We are aware that mental energy and physical energy are one and the same, and that both forms of this force are equally important to the processes of physical existence. We can't move a finger without first sending a mental impulse through the nerve to the muscle which performs the act.

We know that bodies can be destroyed, not only by violence but by the very process of living. We accept the fact that we begin to die at the same moment we begin to live, and that some day our cherished mortal coils will have to be shuffled off.

But what happens to the energy which has been operating the body? What becomes of the spirit which impelled us to keep making the motions of living, to train our muscles and enrich our minds by developing skills and acquiring knowledge? What is the result of our lifelong search for understanding of ourselves and our relationships with people and things outside ourselves?

What about all the ideas, the emotions, the sense of being part of something vast, all the stored memories, all the experiences we have tried during our span of years to weld into a more satisfying concept of that entity which now becomes just another name in the obituary columns? What does the mind do with its acquired knowledge of how to build and use a physical body? Did we stop making automobiles when Henry Ford died?

Is it possible to prove to you beyond a shadow of doubt that you are in essence a continuum potentially independent of your present physical structure? Can you see an atom? Can you be sure the man at the bank won't run off with your money, or that the food you buy won't poison you, or that the laws of gravity won't suddenly be repealed and send you flying into the void?

We live by faith, all of us, all the time. No matter what great skeptics we fancy ourselves to be, we trust. We believe in the orderly workings of Nature even when we do our worst to disrupt them. We expect certain effects to follow certain causes. The more we learn about how things work, the more skillful we become at predicting outcomes. A gift of prophecy is no special distinction. We are all prophets. Some of us may see a bit farther than others, that's the only difference.

It's time we stop telling each other ghost stories and look at the facts. Astrology is not fortunetelling. It is neither an implacable ruling force nor a conjuring toy. It is a technique for visualizing and understanding our personal relationships to the cosmic laws by which the Life Force operates. It is a tool which can help us to remodel our minds and bodies into vehicles that can perform the work of the spirit.

1 · Energy and Order

WE cannot see atoms, but we believe in their existence because we have found out how they work. We may not care much for the idea that what our senses perceive as solid is in actuality a mass of electrical charges constantly in motion and capable of drastic rearrangement; however, we have to accept the theory because both experiment and experience have taught us that what we think of as being real is in fact illusory and transitory. Only the energy which creates matter is real, permanent, and predictable in its actions.

Scientists have uncovered what they believe to be fixed laws of molecular attraction. Working with these laws, we learn ways of altering material relationships. We can change the structure of a molecule. We can produce visual, audible, tactile changes which may be subtle or dramatic, beneficial or cataclysmic.

We can release the energy contained in an atom and rechannel it to perform miracles of construction or destruction. But we cannot make the slightest alteration in the nature of energy. We cannot change the laws by which it operates. Nor can we achieve any transformation except by working within the structure of those laws.

Energy and order, then, are the two realities. You may call them by whatever names you choose. You may swathe them in the trappings of theology, science, sorcery, any disguise that tickles your fancy. You may discuss them in any known language or invent a special language for this one purpose. You may refuse to talk about them at all, even refuse to admit that they exist. How you handle reality makes a great deal of difference to yourself and the world you live in, but it makes no difference whatever to reality itself.

We can understand astrology more easily by bearing in mind that both the mortal body and the immortal spirit, like any other aspect of reality, are composed alike of the energy and order which make up and regulate the universe and everything within it. How, then, can stars and planets be supernatural forces which have the power to pull our individual lives about in inescapable but seemingly irrational patterns?

Obviously they can't. In the sense that we share the same building materials and regulations, we are the stars and the stars are ourselves. If this notion strikes you as bizarre, walk out into the light of our own particular star. Feel the sunlight streaming down upon your skin. Recall your sixth-grade science lessons. This is solar energy warming your body. It is the same solar energy which creates the food that builds the cells which are at this moment being formed to carry on the process of life in your person.

Remember that as a cell is used up, its energy is given back to the Sun, to be used again and again in the endless cycle of creation and destruction and re-creation. It is not mystical mumbo jumbo but sober scientific fact that we live in the Sun and the Sun lives in us, in our mental, physical, and spiritual aspects of being.

The Moon's workings are as familiar to us as the Sun's. We know it controls the tides. Doctors are familiar with the ways its waxing and waning can affect women's menstrual cycles and the retention of fluids in the body. It is not superstition but experience which leads attendants in mental hospitals and policemen in big cities to brace themselves for extra outbreaks of violence each month on the night of the full moon.

Less dramatically evident but equally potent influences are acting on us all the time, so deeply and intimately that most humans never even notice what's happening. Astrology aims toward making us more aware of these forces and their actions, so that we may control instead of being controlled.

We know we don't have to get sunstroke. We don't have to turn into ravening werewolves under a harvest moon. We don't have to let ourselves be snapped around like puppets on strings by any force in the universe. Like the Sun and the Moon, all planets have both positive and negative possibilities in their functions, and these functions are no more occult or mysterious to us than the alternation of day and night.

We can't stop the tide from coming in, but we can decide whether to sink or swim or climb to safer ground before it gets to us. Making the correct decision in any circumstance is simply a matter of seeing the alternatives and understanding what the probable outcome of each choice would be. We have to begin as scientists did with atomic theory, by analyzing what we can't perceive through the senses in terms of what we already know.

No doubt you have at least a general idea of how a molecule works. Perhaps it would help you to visualize spirit, that indestructible directing force which is the essential *you*, as a molecular structure. Picture it like any molecule, highly complex and constantly active. Note the positive and negative polarities, the magnetic force which attracts energy-giving units and throws them off once they have made their contribution to the maintenance of the structure.

We know that the human body is continually throwing off dead cells and manufacturing new ones. Under a microscope we can watch our own cells dividing and re-forming in a drop of blood or a section of tissue. With every birthday, we become increasingly aware that our capacity for self-renewal is limited. No matter how well we take care of the physical shell which houses the spirit, we shall have to slough it off once its ability to utilize energy for rebuilding itself is exhausted.

However, that part of the creative process which we term death and decay will release whatever energy is still contained in the factory when the machinery stops working. The second law of thermodynamics teaches us that all forms of energy are derived from the destruction of some previously existing physical or immaterial energy structure.

Whether or not we accept as absolute the dictum that energy can be neither created nor destroyed, we can demonstrate scientifically that destruction is always a prelude to the formation of new life. Thus we begin to get an inkling of the cyclical nature of physical life and death in relation to the immaterial and therefore, at least hypothetically, indestructible spirit.

Now picture a tree in full leaf. Come autumn, it will discard the dead leaves it has worn out during a summer's hard work. A winter of dormancy will give the tree a chance to rest and repair its elaborate machinery for growth. In the spring, the tree will put out new leaves and get back to business. Next year, the cycle of death and rebirth will happen again. The parent structure will grow from a sapling to a bigger and more beautiful tree until its growth machinery begins to run down and the opposite side of the life cycle manifests itself in decline and decay.

The leaves are necessary to survival and function, yet they are certainly not the tree. Neither is the bark, nor the wood of the trunk, nor the sap which runs through its veins. Each of these parts can be separated from the others and converted into different forms. The entire plant, root to crown, can be fed through a chopper and ground to sawdust, then set afire and burned to ashes. But the essential *treeness* can be neither converted nor destroyed since in the material sense it never existed.

We can touch the bark, smell the leaves, admire the graceful sweep of the branches, but we could not attach any meaning to them and they would have no meaning for each other unless the *idea* of the tree existed first to give them a coherent form and function. Can we say, then, that the *pieces* of the tree are more important than the *concept* of the tree?

In the end, the tree will have weathered the storms and worshipped the Sun, drawn food and moisture from the earth through its roots. Its leaves will have done their job of photosynthesis on which all terrestrial beings ultimately depend for nourishment. It will have given shelter to birds and animals and scattered its seeds to renew its kind. Finally it will be cut down for timber or fuel, be blown over in a gale or burned in a forest fire, or fall down and rot into humus. In one way or another, its energy will be released to begin a new growth cycle.

"But that tree is immortal only in the sense that new shoots may grow from its seeds," you argue, "just as human beings live again only in their children."

Then what happens to all the accumulated experience of growth? The tree may have spent many years learning to express its treeness to the fullest possible extent. Since experience is intangible, we may assume that it relates to the tree idea rather than to the physical tree. Therefore, the growth experience is not destroyed when the visible structure dies. So where does it go?

We talk glibly of genes and chromosomes. We accept the most abstruse conjectures as Gospel writ, as long as they emerge with the ring of scholarly authority from some institution of higher learning. So we have no difficulty with the idea that an acorn knows how to become an oak tree instead of a birch because its parent plant learned the mechanics of oakness by carrying out the fundamental oak idea during its own life cycle and built the proper equipment into the acorn so that the oak process could be repeated.

But what about the oak idea which will be expressed by the new little tree as it was in the old? How will this particular oak manage to assume not only its proper form and function but also the individual oakness which will set it apart not only from all other manifestations of matter but from all other oak trees? Since growth knowledge is separate from physical growth, we can't reasonably expect the mother tree to cram that into the acorn on top of everything else. Still, this tree needs a determining tree idea, as all trees do. Where will it come from?

Well, let's consider all the other oak trees which have grown up, lived, and died. Each had its immaterial oakness, what we may call its tree spirit. Since the life of the spirit does not depend on the life of the tree, the essential oakness did not die when the oak died. But what good can it accomplish by itself? The tree concept only knows how to function through the structure of root-trunk-branch-leaf. Now, here's a sprouting acorn which is going to need a spirit and here's an oak spirit which needs a material form. Why shouldn't the tree idea enter the new plant and get on with the job?

Essentially, that's all there is to reincarnation. The spirit functions through a physical structure of the suitable type. At death it is released, carrying with it whatever growth experience has been accumulated during the physical lifetime. The spirit then finds a new physical structure in which it can go on doing the things it has been trained to do, hopefully improving on past performance and adding new skills to its repertoire. Such gradual improvement is known as "evolution."

This is such a simple idea that some people reject it as too dull. We may prefer the magical approach, that little Herbie shows "natural-born" musical ability in a nonmusical family because his mother was frightened by an oboe. We can serve up the popular hash of pragmatic scientism, that Herbie's talent comes from some fortuitous scrambling of genes and chromosomes. Would it not be more reasonable to assume that Herbie knows how to play the piano without having been taught because he has carried over into this life a subliminal memory of a skill he acquired during a previous incarnation? If an acorn can do it, why can't a human child?

But if we can be liberated and reborn into any body we choose, why do we so often come back as stupid, unattractive, unfortunate people?

We don't necessarily get any smarter merely by dying. We tend to bring back pretty much what we took out. While death may come as a release from mental anguish or physical pain and give us a welcome period of rest in which to regroup our forces for the next growing season, there's no cosmic guarantee that we shall use our vacation from Earth wisely.

Does the spirit of a demised gangster spend his enforced holiday strumming a celestial harp to the music of the spheres, or scheming how to hijack a new body fast so that he can get back at the son of a bitch who rubbed him out? Does he decide to become an honest laborer and give all his hard-earned wages to the poor, or will he reincarnate as a gorgeous blonde who'll play his rival for a sucker? His choice will inevitably be conditioned by whatever values and motivations have been attached to his essential self idea during previous incarnations. He is more likely than not to keep making choices which will keep him on the dreary treadmill of crime and punishment, incurring more and more drastic penalties until he at last makes a firm effort of will to become a decent person.

So it is with all of us. When we absorb information on what constitutes a truly happy and worthwhile life, we lay the groundwork for wiser choices in the future even though we may not fully attain our stated goals in this life. If we restrict our present thoughts and aims to petty revenge, self-pity, or unshared sensual satisfactions, we limit ourselves more than we realize.

For example, suppose you were a hypochondriac who constantly demanded but never received sympathy for your imagined ills. In the end, you might be so consumed by self-pity that you decide to be reborn as a helpless invalid, totally dependent on your nurses. You would now gain all the attention of which you had previously been deprived. Of course you wouldn't remember why you wanted it, and the penalties of such a position would be infinitely greater than the compensations, but you wouldn't think of this side of the situation until you were irrevocably committed to the crippled body.

This sounds ridiculous, perhaps, but how many equally irrational acts do we perform every day? We shirk our personal civic responsibilities, then snarl about rotten government. We break traffic laws, bribe some underpaid civil servant to fix the ticket, and demand that something be done about crime in the streets. We throw papers around and blow smoke into the air as we denounce ecological pollution. We act hostilely toward our families and our neighbors as we demonstrate for international peace.

If we fail to meet our responsibilities, why should we expect others to act responsibly toward us? If we restrict our approval to the chosen few who think as we do, what grounds have we to hope that men can ever be brothers? If we have no respect for life, how can life show respect for us?

Astrology deals with polarities. The life cycle brings back to us exactly what we contribute to it. If we fail to steer the life we are now living in a positive direction, we ought not to complain next time around that we haven't been reborn rich, handsome, brilliant, and universally beloved. We are what we are because we have been what we willed ourselves to be. We shall become what our present efforts lead us toward.

During the moment you read this sentence, your old self has died and a new one has been born. Cells have been used up, others created. Your lungs have expelled the breath which sustained your life seconds ago and taken in fresh air which your heart is even now pumping into your ever-flowing bloodstream. You have moved a step in time. Your brain is opening a new channel to accept or reject the idea which your eyes are transferring to your mind from the printed page. Countless functions are going on within you, each of them an end and a beginning.

We know enough physiology to be aware that even though our bodies are constantly changing, they function according to a fixed set of rules. We accept the fact that physical processes can be made to operate more or less efficiently in relation to the outside influences we bring to bear on them. Good food, adequate sleep, uncontaminated air, the practice of effective sanitation will keep the machine running longer with less trouble than will neglect and abuse.

Whether or not we choose to take proper care of our bodies is up to us, but the consequences of the choice are inescapable. If we want to be healthy, we have to develop habits of hygiene. So it is with a lifetime. If we desire to become wise and happy, we must start immediately to make choices which will lead to the attainment of happiness and wisdom.

2 · Balance and Growth

"The door," said Epictetus, "is always open." Freedom of choice is ours whether or not we consciously exercise it. Astrology does not open new doors. It helps us to notice which doors are open to us in any given circumstance, and where they are likely to lead.

A more modern philosopher stated, "It's the right of a modern tabby to choose the cats who shall father her kits; and she ought to make sure that their pasts are pure, and they're free from fleas or fits."

Mehitabel the Cat didn't always take her own good advice, and most of us humans don't choose much more intelligently than she did. Hence the growing popularity of Astro-Dating and Astro-Mating. Like the patent medicines which claimed to offer magic cures for all Grandma's agues and phthisics, these matchings-by-the-stars tend to claim more than they deliver. By oversimplifying highly complex patterns of relationship, astrologers have gotten together some remarkably strange bedfellows.

"You're a Libra and I'm a Capricorn, therefore it can never be"; or "You're a Libra and I'm a Capricorn, so let's make beautiful music together," depending on which service you subscribe to. Snap judgments based on scanty information make it easy to reject the whole concept of astro-mating, especially if you happen to be a Libra happily (or unhappily) married to a Capricorn.

Suppose, however, that we were to make a careful comparison of two people's charts sign by sign, analyzing all their aspects. Could we then uncover harmonies and tensions that would give a coherent overall pattern of possibilities for compatibility? Research on charts of existing conjugal relationships has, in fact, pinpointed areas of agreement and stress which would take psychologists many hours of prodding to bring out, and which the partners themselves might never have fully understood by the trial-and-error processes of living together.

Rightly interpreted astrological data can make reliable analyses about the likelihood of success in any sort of partnership. It now appears that we can even carry the preplanning of a relationship from man-woman to man-woman-child. Some fascinating research has been done, notably by Dr. Eugen Jonas of Nitra, Czechoslovakia (see Ostrander and Schroeder, *Psychic Discoveries behind the Iron Curtain*) on the possibilities of controlling not only fertility and sterility but also the sex, health, and personality characteristics of a wanted child by means of astrological data taken from the would-be parents' charts. Briefly, his theory is based on the ancient one of auspicious and inauspicious times.

The Catholic Church has long allowed its followers to practice a form of birth control by selecting their dates of intercourse by a "rhythmic calendar" which is intended to reveal the woman's fertility cycle. This system is popularly known as "Vatican Roulette." Any Catholic mother of seventeen children can tell you that the calendar isn't infallible. However, Dr. Kurt Reichnitz, former director of the Budapest Obstetric

Clinic, has worked out a system of astrological birth control which apparently does determine the fertile times with accuracy.

Dr. Jonas, Dr. Reichnitz, and others have done research on many mother-and-child charts that gives repeated indications that it would have been wiser to abstain from conception when the fertility period coincides with certain planetary configurations, and that healthy, intelligent babies are the result of intercourse under more favorable aspects. Parents who have followed up these theories are said to be finding the results eminently satisfactory.

If this is so, getting the child you want might soon become a simple matter of talking things over with your friendly neighborhood astrologer and feeding your husband a beefsteak on the right night, or merely selecting the appropriate test tube at the Embryo Market.

Although we do not believe that one incarnate spirit can determine the life pattern of another, we can see that it might well be feasible to refuse to give birth to a baby who's going to attract a spirit we won't like. Why should we give birth to a fool or a crook? Why should souls bent on revenge or cold-blooded exploitation be allowed to materialize at our expense? By begetting children with the capacity to live up to our loftiest ideals, we can change our social patterns, create a world where our offspring can formulate still higher goals for children yet to come. Imagine being reborn into a "Peaceable Kingdom" for which we ourselves have laid the groundwork!

Family planning at the cosmic level may sound like an overwhelming task. But we do it, whether or not we perform intelligently, and we follow stringent regulations which have been the same since time began. Can we have the slightest awareness of the wondrous complexity, the beautiful order of the life cycle, and still think its continuance depends solely on haphazard fertilization? Why do some ova get fertilized and others not? Why do some organisms abort or die young, while others, apparently no better equipped, reach maturity?

We can see that balance exists in nature. When animals breed too prolifically for their habitat, they either emigrate or starve off to workable numbers. Trees growing thickly together choke each other out. Cells which subdivide too fast become a malignant tumor that kills the parent body unless growth is checked. Only the ceaseless struggle toward equilibrium, the endless chain of checks and balances keeps the life cycle going at the primitive level.

But how does the idea of balance evolve? Why this prodigal waste of life, this eternal potlatch, unless physical being is a much more easily transferrable state than we have supposed?

It is in this prodigality of the primitive state of being that we learn one of astrology's most important lessons. Nature unaided always fails. Without the intervention of a superior intelligence, the growth process tends to turn upon itself and defeat its own aims.

Let's go back to our symbolic tree. Left untended in the forest, how many lives and deaths will it have to go through before it evolves into the perfect specimen of its kind? How much damage from insects, wind, lightning, bark-chewing animals, and other natural enemies will it have to endure? In its fight for survival, what crimes may it commit? It may steal the sunlight from other trees and plants, grab all the available nutriment from the soil. It may develop poisonous fruits, grow cruel thorns, or learn to throw off a noxious odor.

Now, suppose a competent forester takes that tree under his care. He can give it breathing room by cutting away choking vines and underbrush or transplant it to a more favorable location. He can treat its wounds, improve its shape by pruning and training. He knows how to protect it from insects and other damage. By grafting, he can breed out its undesirable qualities, increasing its beauty and utility. For any major change, he will have to guide the tree through several growth cycles, but the rate of growth can be speeded up from cycle to cycle.

Raising sheep or cows or pedigreed cats, we follow this same process of gradual improvement through intelligent care and selective breeding. When we give the rearing of human children the same attention we do to pugs and poodles, we can expect to improve bipeds as well as quadrupeds.

From visible evidence we can deduce the feasibility as well as the necessity of spiritual cultivation, that is, conscious application of effective methods for living up to the best that is in us.

"You're only going through once" may serve as a convenient excuse for taking a second helping of pie or making love to your neighbor's wife, but it doesn't stand up as a guide for living. What makes us so cocksure we shan't have to come back and pay the piper after we've had our fling? How can we dismiss a world full of evidence in one silly catch phrase? Does the thought of having to go on living scare us all that much?

We ought not to belittle anybody's fears. The amount of courage it takes to carry on human existence must fill our hearts with reverence, each for all the others. We don't have to turn on the Late Late Show to catch the thrill of bravery in action. We can see housewives keeping their kids clean and their husbands happy while making one dollar do the work of three. We can see men tired to the bone, riding home from work on the subway and having the guts to go back and do it again the following day. We can see pretty young girls pinned to a key punch for seven hours, still able to giggle in the elevator at quitting time.

Don't we realize that every breath they take is a triumph over death, every laugh a victory over despair? Can't we see how worthy of our love and respect is every one of our fellow beings? Don't we know that we, too, are marching with the heroes? When are we going to stop moaning over our sore feet and share in the joy of the life experience?

If we clear the underbrush out of our lives, give our minds and spirits room to breathe, we see that there are more things right than wrong with our world. Eventually, if we work at it, we are able to perceive our lives as an ongoing cycle. By hard work, we can lift ourselves out of the ruts we've dug through many lifetimes of futilely chasing our own tails. Reading the signs which astrology makes plain to us, we start climbing the upward-spiralling road to the state where the finite part of our being coexists in harmony with the infinite.

We don't know how much of our climbing will be done on this planet, nor do we know whether the human race began somewhere else in space. As we explore the planets in our solar system, we find that none seems to be adapted to any form of existence now known, but can we be sure that the life we know is all the life there is?

The type of body which we are accustomed to build is a surprisingly frail vehicle for the tasks we set it. In fact, it is so apt to break down under stress that no manufacturer on Earth would put up with such inefficiency in his factory. He would set engineers and technicians to work designing machines that could do what he expected of them without requiring such costly maintenance as we do. How, then, can we be sure that no better equipment than ours exists, or that man will not one day be able to build a more workable shell around his spiritual self?

All bodies in space are composed of certain elements which are found in the Sun. We know what these elements are, and we can measure their proportions by breaking down light and observing those intriguing runes in the spectrum which are known as the Fraunhofer lines. If we were able to read these well enough to determine what combinations of elements would work best in terms of each planet's atmospheric, climatic, and geographic positions, why should we not be able to build vehicles that could adapt to each different environment?

Ample evidence that this is possible exists on our own planet. We know there are creatures living under the sea, at pressures which would crush any body not designed specifically for this mode of existence. Others live in high mountain regions, having developed outsized lungs to cope with the scarcity of oxygen. By equipping himself with appropriate removable shells, man has been able to explore both the heights and the depths. If we could learn to regard our bodies as temporary vehicles for the spirit, we could better visualize our ecology as being not only local, national, and planetary, but also solar, galactic, and universal in scope.

We ought not to be discouraged by the difficulty of grasping this concept. We already know that our present forms of perception aren't very good; they may be even poorer than we realize. Any dog can hear sounds and detect odors which the most highly developed human organs can't pick up. A cat's whiskers may be more effective sensors than many people's fingertips.

Doubtless we have good reasons for making our sensibilities so blunt. If we were aware of supersonic vibrations, like some other animals, we might suffer too acutely from their results to perform the mental tasks for which our brains are particularly fitted. We know that even a slight noise can affect concentration; imagine how distracted we might be if we went frantic every time a fire engine passed the house, as we see our pet dogs do.

Human eyes are at present not built to handle intense light vibrations. Ultraviolet and infrared rays which we can't even see without special apparatus cause us to develop cataracts unless we screen them out with ophthalmically correct sunglasses. If we look directly at the Sun, even through tinted lenses, we can be permanently blinded. But we don't try to claim these phenomena do not exist on the grounds that we ourselves are not physically equipped to cope with them.

Now that scientists have confirmed what Hermes Trismegistus told the alchemists long ago, that everything is a variation on the same theme, it seems irrelevant to keep asking each other, "Is there life on other planets?" We know the whole universe is life, so we might better phrase our question, "What does life on other planets have to do with life on Earth?"

Having established that every body, everywhere, is made up of energy taking different forms, and that energy charges are constantly being bounced back and forth throughout our solar system, we may logically assume that planetary interactions might all produce certain effects depending on the relative positions of reflector and reflected; as getting a suntan or freezing to death depends on where our bodies are in relation to where the Sun happens to be at a given moment.

Whether we could ever actually go and live on Saturn is interesting to think about, but right now it would be more useful to know what happens when radiations from Saturn come and live in us. Do they really affect our daily lives? If so, how?

Astrological concepts are easier to grasp once we learn to step outside our self-imposed limitations and realize that, while Earth happens to be the planet on which we live, we are in fact working to improve a solar ecology. As far as we know, the quality of human life at this moment may be the most important thing in the entire solar system because, in a real sense, we are that system.

3 · Astrological Common Sense

WE started this book with **Eliphas Levi's** observation, "No one believes any longer in the universal harmonies of Nature and in the necessary interconnexion of all effects with all causes." The present ecological crisis has shown us how dangerous it is not to believe.

To take an everyday example: a factory dumps mercury-laden waste into a stream. Fish in the water are contaminated by it, and humans who eat them get sick. Children swimming in the stream may absorb enough mercury to cause permanent physical damage. Gradually the stream becomes so polluted that all the fish die. Swimming is now forbidden. Useless as a recreational or food source, the watercourse is nothing but an open sewer carrying pollutants many miles from the factory and eventually out to sea.

This one selfish, easily prevented act has created a chain of events which downgrades first the neighborhood, then the adjoining areas, eventually the entire global ecology. By taking notice of the simple fact that *nothing in Nature stops*, anybody could have foreseen the outcome of such a beginning.

Psychiatrists have taught us something about cause and effect in the human psyche. We now are aware that an apparently trifling trauma can be enlarged by the subconscious mind into a stumbling-block huge enough to disrupt a whole life experience. We see how such disruptions affect our culture and our economy. The amount of money spent every year to support and treat mentally sick persons is enormous but nowhere near adequate to the need. The suffering caused by such illness, not only to the patient but to his family and to society in general is incalculable. Insanity is costing us too much on all levels. The only way we can improve our mental ecology is by becoming more aware of causes and effects.

For one thing, we are learning that noise pollution is causing not only increased hearing problems but also nervous tension which leads to both mental and physical damage. Think what noise can do. A singer can shatter a goblet with a single note. Sonic booms break windows and crack walls. Supersonic devices drill holes in teeth, cook a dinner in seconds, and wash the dishes afterward. We don't have the faintest idea of their potential. Since the world began, sound vibrations must have been affecting existence in ways that are going to surprise us very much when we find them out.

We still know next to nothing about the interrelationships of tangible and intangible factors in our lives, but we are beginning to catch a glimmer of what a vast lot there is to explore. Is it reasonable to discount the importance of the spiritual as well as the conscious and subconscious aspects of personality?

When Margaret Fuller made her grand declaration, "I accept the universe," Thomas Carlyle retorted, "By God, she'd better!" Now that we are adopting so many of Miss Fuller's ideas about communal living, women's liberation, and whatnot, we ought to show equal tolerance toward the concept that the universe not only exists for us but that its workings are as integral to our personal life processes as we are to the universe, that is, that the macrocosm exists in the microcosm, and vice versa. The alchemists put it more simply: "As above, so below."

This is what astrology is all about, learning to handle our personal relationships with universal forces so that we can live more successfully. No doubt there have been almost as many quack astrologers as quack doctors, and we do well to look twice at what they try to force down our throats. Some of us refuse to deal with the medicine men, saying that illness is only a state of mind. Most humans, though, prefer to take the pills and the penicillin shots, to let the surgeons cut us up and make us over, on the assumption that trained men know more about our bodily workings than we do, and that there's no sense in our suffering whether the pain we feel is real or not. Mankind has endured horrible tortures in the name of medicine; yet we have kept on believing the doctors could make us well because we had a fundamental need to be healed.

So it is with astrology. We keep rediscovering the ancient lore because we need it. We have to learn where we fit into the ecology of time and space. We require information on how to adjust not only to the familiar world of things but to the vaster worlds of mind and spirit. We know there's a sound idea under the incense and the nonsense, just as we knew the barber and the horseleech could be turned into capable healers, if we only insisted long enough that they learn their trade.

We still don't know why it is the heart and not the liver that pumps the blood through our veins, or why we breathe with our lungs instead of our bladders; but this ignorance of *why* does not prevent our knowing *how*. By understanding the functions of each organ in relation to the system it works in, we learn how to adjust it when it gets out of order. For the practical purposes of living, that's really all we need to know.

We don't know why Saturn has one effect on the psyche and Jupiter the opposite, but we do know what these effects are. Therefore, we can learn to work with them in terms of our relationships to ourselves, our fellows, and our world.

Like medical language, astrological terminology lends itself far too easily to fantastical gobbledygook. We have to remember that its signs date from a period when allegory and pictogram were accepted methods of putting across abstract ideas to audiences who were usually illiterate and relatively unsophisticated. The symbols are occult only in the sense that we have to learn what they stand for. Wearing Aries the Ram on your sweatshirt or having it printed on your cocktail napkins has no magical effect in and of itself, no matter what they told you down at the gift shop.

Undoubtedly there are many natural devices by which we could interpret the workings of cosmic law. Celestial bodies happen to be particularly suitable for the purpose because they move in measurable ratios within predictable orbits and are observable anywhere on the globe. Earlier than we know, each of the planets in our solar system, together with the Sun and Moon, was assigned a specific value and function. Exoteric astrologers, dealing with effects, worked at first with only five planets; later six, seven, and eight; tacking on each new planet as it was discovered astronomically. Esoteric astrologers, interested in causes, were able to postulate the existence of Uranus, Neptune, and Pluto and work them into their conception of the zodiacal system many centuries before they were spotted by astronomers.

The zodiac we see on the cocktail napkins has no reality, of course. Like the lines of latitude and longitude on a map, it is purely a charting device and serves exactly the same purpose: to show you where you are in relation to your environment and to help you plan the route that will take you where you want to go.

Traveling to a new place, you may use a road map or not, as you wish. Refusing its help, you can follow your hunches and find your way by trial and error or pester others for directions. You can accept the map as a rigid control, not deviating a hair's breadth from what it says to do, even though you're missing the most interesting scenery and running into stretches of bad road that take all the joy out of the trip. Or you may investigate the geography of the area, learn what it has to offer for your instruction and enjoyment, then use the map to plot a route which will be a delightful experience from start to finish. You can do the same things with a horoscope.

Your natal zodiacal chart is unlike that of anybody else in the world. Even if you were a Siamese twin, your chart might vary slightly from your sibling's, since it's almost impossible for both infants to draw their first breath at precisely the same moment. To obtain a true reading, the correct time of birth, day, and year have to be computed with painstaking accuracy in terms of latitude and longitude. The mass-distributed "This Is Your Life, Taurus" sort of thing is not properly a horoscope at all and will not be a great deal of help in interpreting your individual assets and liabilities.

But what if you do obtain a true chart, accurate down to the minutes and seconds of degrees? It still shows nothing but a fortuitous distribution of signs and planets, doesn't it? How can any such pattern have relevance for the ongoing spirit which is the essential you?

Ah, but suppose the distribution were not fortuitous? What if the time and place of birth were carefully chosen to give you that particular chart and no other? What if all your rewards and debts, all the things you learned or failed to understand, all the good and ill of your previous life were weighed and balanced, and a judgment made as to the kind of life you should live next, to fulfill your wants or pay what you owe, to perfect a skill, finish a job, complete a relationship, to teach you the lessons you need most at this stage of your journey through time?

Who would do the judging? Who would select the birth time? Who else but yourself?

This is the logical basis on which we may accept astrology. And this is where many readers will run screaming from the room.

The reason so many of us humans are reluctant to subscribe to this theory is not that it doesn't make sense. It makes most excellent sense. But the concept of free choice places responsibility for every circumstance of your present life squarely on your own metaphysical shoulders.

The whole aim of astrology, as in psychiatry, is to make the individual accept full responsibility for living his life. To make this commitment requires even greater courage than any other act of being. Like it or not, however, this is what we have to grit our teeth and do if we hope to make a success of this life, and of our spiritual relationship to the never-ending processes of the life force. Nothing else makes sense.

What would be the use of stretching our intelligence wider and wider, of building elaborate cultural systems, of reaching out into the universe for greater understanding, if humans were mayflies to dance in the sun for an instant, then crumple into the swamp? Why should we be able to conceive of personal responsibility if we were never to assume it?

Let's get back to our molecular theory for a moment. We conclude from the evidence that magnetic energy works by polarity, the attraction and repulsion of positive and negative charges. Polarity is what makes us and keeps us what we are. Polarity is the key to our equally real nonmaterial existence.

Good and evil are merely opposite ends of the same principle, just as hot and cold are opposite ends of the same thermometer. Where we draw the line between them is the result of our personal, conditioned reactions. Which degree of which end we expose ourselves to is a matter for personal decision.

We see the evolutionary processes of Nature continually changing the faulty into the more nearly perfect, the lesser into the greater, the grosser into the finer. Therefore we assume that positive, creative use of the cosmic forces tends to put us in harmony with the upward-spiralling movement of the life cycle. Since ultimate destruction does not exist in Nature, we must also assume that destructive acts are futile, illusory, and contrary to cosmic law. If we perform a negative act, then, we throw our personal life cycle out of balance and the polarities have to make an effort to compensate, to steer us back on to the road which leads to a better life.

In short, justice exists. Nobody gets away with anything. If we fail to correct a negative act during one lifetime, we find its compensating punishment waiting for us in the next, and we'll keep on getting it in the neck until we see our error and mend our ways.

This notion of lugging a Sisyphean lump of guilt around and around the twelve houses through eons of time is enough to put anybody off astrology, or off living for that matter. But isn't it glorious to think that we can use our past and present mistakes and troubles as steppingstones toward a happier tomorrow! Various theologies have promised us everything from harps to houris, but the hope of someday becoming a human being gives even those of us who are neither male nor musical something we can look forward to with delight.

The horoscope for your time of birth in this life is basically a reminder of where you left off last time. Read with an understanding of what the symbols mean in relation to their positions and to each other, it can show you in exact detail what you already know about life and what you have to learn, where your strengths and weaknesses lie. It can reveal how you are likely to approach any given situation, what the situations you encounter are likely to be and how they will probably be resolved, *unless you make deliberate, conscious efforts to choose different approaches and different solutions.*

It is not true—indeed it is most viciously false—that every moment of your present existence is controlled by the positions of the stars at your birth or at any other time. All the horoscope does is to show you what conditions prevail so that you can adjust yourself to cope with them. You don't have to freeze to death just because the weather turns cold, and you don't have to fall down and break your neck because Saturn is in an unfavorable aspect. It is both stupid and cowardly to become a slave to any circumstance or any ruler.

Blind obedience to what somebody says the stars are telling you to do will not enable you to skim through to Nirvana unscathed. It will simply lead you back around the same old rut. You'll waste a life making the same foolish mistakes you made before, when you could be getting on with the fascinating work of improving your personality, your way of living, and the environment which surrounds you. You cannot let anybody or anything make your decisions for you. It is your job to make the choices and suffer the consequences or reap the rewards in precise ratio to the positive or negative impulses you generate by your acts and thoughts.

"You can't take it with you" is another of those untruisms

with which we suffocate intelligent thought. You certainly can and do take everything which is genuinely yours. You carry over not only the spiritual profit-and-loss figures but also whatever personality traits, whatever depths of understanding, mental agility, and motor skills you have attained, whether or not you intend to use them in a coming life. No effort at self-improvement is ever lost. No bad habit or wrong idea is ever lost, either, until you make a definite effort of will to get rid of it, so take care what you pack in your bag for the Great Journey.

Since the material body is so readily disposable and renewable, we don't have to worry much about flesh and bone, except to keep them in the best possible working order while we're using them. We tend to be overly concerned with the mechanics of physical being, hailing an organ transplant as a miracle of restoration instead of a rather ghoulish interference with the process of living. If we saw our bodies as miracles in the beginning and gave them the care they deserve, we shouldn't have to be so dependent on the repairman. How many of us would abuse an automobile the way we do ourselves? Why is it so much harder to get a driver's license than a marriage license? Why do we clutter ourselves up with so much excess baggage?

This tendency to put last things first is a characteristic of the Piscean Age. For the moment, let's concern ourselves with the first and second aspects of personal reality: spirit and mind, or superconscious and conscious. It might be helpful to think of mind as a computer and spirit as the programmer. Your computer can be as simple or as complicated as you choose to build it. As programmer, you have unlimited freedom to decide how many circuits you wish to employ and how you want to set up your programming sequences. Potentialities for changing the sequences or setting up additional ones will always be available to you in the subconscious, whether or not you ever choose to bring them up to the conscious level.

Psychiatry has shown us what a happy hunting ground the subconscious is, as it dredges up apparently forgotten materials to be used or exorcised through the agency of consciousness. Attempts have been made to probe memory back beyond the time of the present birth. You may or may not find any of the documentary evidence convincing. Whether or not we believe in Bridie Murphy and the rest, though, we have all seen enough science fiction come true to suspect that what man can imagine, man can accomplish.

If we care to make the effort, we can find out all sorts of interesting things about our past lives from our natal horoscopes. However, the time would probably be spent more profitably trying to determine a straighter course for the future.

To draw up a chart all you need are a knowledge of simple arithmetic, a little patience, and some easily obtainable reference materials. To understand one, you need a comprehension of the meanings attached to the individual planets and their combinations, which we will call the signs of the zodiac, and of the positions in which they occur. You need to know something about the elements, the triplicities and the various aspects. To be a competent astrologer, you have to acquire a good deal of technical knowledge. To be a successful one, you have to see the fun of it. This is above all a happy study, so let's start by renewing some fascinating old acquaintances.

4 · Saturn
Responsibility and Control

STRANGE indeed to Earth-trained eyes appears the planet Saturn, whose unique rings make it one of the most spectacular bodies in the solar system. Second only to Jupiter in size, this huge mass lies nine-and-a-half times farther out from the Sun than we do.

Most of us have got away from the idea that planets are perfect spheres moving in regular orbits; still, we are surprised how much Saturn varies from this concept. Because of a fast rotation period, only 10 hours, 14 minutes as compared to our 24-hour day, it is markedly oblate in shape. Its orbit is so eccentric that there is a 100-million-mile difference between perihelion and aphelion, that is, the points nearest to and farthest from the Sun.

Even the colors astonish us. Saturn's equatorial zone looks brilliantly white, its subtropical and temperate zones darker yellow, and the polar caps often appear green. Density of the planet is less than that of water, but its atmosphere may be extraordinarily deep and its internal pressure is estimated at approximately 50 million Earth pressures.

The impressive rings lie at the equatorial plane. Solid as they look to us, they must be extremely thin. Astronomers believe they are probably particles of frozen ammonia packed so close together that they create the illusion of solidity, revolving around Saturn in gravitationally stable orbits.

Saturn has ten known satellites. The largest, Titan, is actually bigger than the planet Mercury. Unlike our Moon, it seems to have an atmosphere similar to Saturn's. Phoebe, the outermost satellite, is also large and may be a captured asteroid.

If we tried to guess at Saturn's astrological function solely on the basis of known physical attributes, what conclusions should we draw? First, its influence must be enormous, because it's so big. It is capable of exerting tremendous pressures. It has the ability to catch and hold weaker bodies, even using them to create what appear to be impenetrable barriers around itself.

On closer inspection, we find that Saturn behaves very eccentrically. Its climate would appear to work in reverse to ours. In spite of the immense pressure, its interior density is relatively slight. Those apparently solid barriers are flimsy things which could be vaporized in no time, should the planet ever swing a bit closer to the Sun. At least two of Saturn's satellites could probably function independently if they succeeded in breaking the gravitational hold which the father planet has over them.

If even half our deductions are right, we can see why Saturn has acquired such a terrible reputation. "That dull and malevolent planet" has given us the word "saturnine," which means "sluggish, cold, gloomy in temperament." Its medical connotation, "afflicted with lead poisoning," is a heritage from medieval alchemists who equated the power of Saturn with the element lead, or *plumbum*.

At the mythological level, Saturn started life as a simple god of agriculture. His festival, the Saturnalia, was held in December, the tenth (*decem*) month of the Roman calendar. As we are going to see, astrology is largely a matter of simple arithmetic.

We still hold yuletide festivals which stem from that ancient rite. Our Christmas tree is a holdover from the Saturnalian custom of decorating a live tree with fruits of the harvest. Until recent times, its display was anathema to Christian churchmen, and still is to some sects. The Puritans refused to celebrate Christmas at all, because of the pagan association. Next time you deck the halls with boughs of holly, remember that you are observing the season to be jolly in honor of an ancient Old King Cole.

In classic times, Saturn ceased gradually to be merely a roistering old rip and became identified with the Greek Cronus, father of Zeus. (Zeus, of course, was the Greek name for Jupiter, ruler of all the gods.) As progenitor, Saturn thus became either directly or indirectly responsible for the entire Olympian family. *Responsibility* is the key word for Saturn.

To understand the function of Saturn, we have to associate him with Jupiter. It is in the relationship between father and son that we see the working of the cosmic law of polarity. Jupiter expands; Saturn contracts.

Every breath we take shows us the necessity of the Jupiter-Saturn polarity. We inhale, then we exhale. Alternate expansion and contraction of our lungs draws life-giving oxygen into our bodies, then expels waste gases before they can poison us. Neither intake nor outgo would be of any advantage to us if it were not immediately followed by the opposite impulse. What happens in our lungs happens all the time, everywhere. All motion, all life depends on expansion and contraction, on push and pull.

Picturing Saturn as a father figure makes it easy to understand his position in our lives. Traditionally it is the father who controls, punishes, instructs. The father provides a shelter which keeps hostile outside forces from attacking his child and also prevents the child from straying into danger. The father sets an example as a responsible adult on whom the child can model himself, gradually achieving a mature role in the tribe or in society.

This, in essence, is what Saturn does astrologically. Wherever Saturn appears in our charts, there is a lesson in responsibility to be learned. Until we can accept and master that lesson, Saturn will continue to keep us in our playpens no matter how lustily we yell that we're grownups and we want to get out.

Not all fathers are wise and kind. A shelter can be a jail. Saturn allowed to exert too vigorous a pull can be ruthlessly destructive. Cronus castrated his father and ate his own children. Learning to recognize and cope with one's responsibilities can be both frightening and heartbreakingly difficult.

We cannot defeat Saturn by avoiding responsibility. We can't stand in the road and avoid being run over by pretending we don't see the oncoming traffic. We can hope the drivers will see us and manage to stop or steer around us. Maybe one of them will have the kindness to pick us up and drive us off to a nice, safe padded cell where we won't get hurt. We can maneuver other people into making our decisions for us. Our mothers, our teachers, our wives or husbands, our friends, even our enemies may be willing to take on the job. But we'll pay for their services.

Electing to remain a child is no good. Even Peter Pan found that out in the end. It only frustrates us in one life and adds to our burden of unsolved problems in the next. The chain which Marley's ghost forged for himself out of money boxes is a perfect picture of how we can fetter ourselves tighter and tighter by always taking and never giving. The more often we fail to balance a contraction by an expansion, the more securely we bind ourselves to failure and discouragement.

Like it or not, we do better to face up to each problem as it arises. Even if we don't find solutions, we gain skill in balancing the Jupiter-Saturn forces by making the effort. "To fall face forward, fighting, on the deck" is no bad way to end a lifetime.

The Old-Time Religion promised rewards in Heaven for virtues which didn't seem to be getting us anywhere here below. When we entered the third decanate* of the Piscean Age, rationalists began to denounce this "pie in the sky" philosophy as being conducive to passive acceptance of miseries which we need not have tolerated. Now, standing on the threshhold of a hopefully more enlightened era, we begin to see that there's something to be said for both sides. If we act out of cowardice or blind obedience to self-proclaimed authority, turning the other cheek won't get us anything but another kick in the teeth. On the other hand, courageous, *aware* acceptance of trials as opportunities for learning can lead to that Promised Land where we shan't have to die to get our share of pie.

Never let anybody or anything trick you into feeling trapped. Find out where your problems really lie, learn your lesson, take your medicine, and move on to a happier situation. This is making effective use of Saturn.

Because we think of ourselves as living on one plane, we tend to forget how mobile we are. We speak of being alive and think only of physical aliveness, as though electricity didn't exist unless we flipped on the switch. We frequently act as though the body we wash, dress, feed, and train to perform the tricks we call living were all there is to us.

Even the physical body can move up, down, backward, and forward through every degree of the compass. When you look at a terrestrial globe, does it ever occur to you that you are not standing upright on a flat surface as you think you are, but clinging to the curve of a sphere as a fly clings to a vertical wall by the suction pads on its feet? A little girl skipping a rope is flying out into space at every skip, no less daringly than any space-walking astronaut. We live in space. We use Earth merely as a base of operations and move about, above, below its surface as we please.

---

*See pages 124-126 for a complete discussion of decanate.

"Not me. I can't go as I please. I have to stay here and take care of Mother."

See what happens when you don't say what you mean? "I choose not to go because my sense of duty (Saturn) has imposed on my physical being the responsibility for my mother's welfare" would be a truer statement.

If you go, you forfeit your self-esteem. Perhaps someone dear to you will die for lack of the food and nursing you can provide if you stay. These are perfectly valid reasons for curtailing your own mobility, but please face the fact that the curtailment is voluntary. If you wanted very much to go, you would try to find some nursing home, social service agency, or kindly neighbor to take care of Mother. Or you'd take her along.

There is always an alternative; usually there are several. You will accept the one which best suits your inclinations, whether or not you admit it. By staying, you may be neurotically punishing yourself or paying off a karmic debt. You may be preventing yourself from attempting something at which you're secretly afraid you'd fail. Whatever the motive, it's yours and not your mother's, even though Mom may be taking advantage of your unwillingness to face up to the facts.

Physically, we do have to work within certain limitations. Our bodies have to be provided with food and air, protected against extremes of heat and cold. If we were born with one leg, we probably wouldn't try to become professional hockey players. If the temperature dipped to zero, we might not care to go swimming. This is not to say we couldn't do these things if we wanted them enough to find a way. Determination and ingenuity can always overcome physical limitations.

Generally, though, we can accomplish more by working within the bounds of likelihood. A blind man turns his energies not to inventing an artificial eye but to developing his senses of touch, smell, and hearing to a degree where he finds the lack of sight no great handicap. A Norwegian learns to ski and a Hawaiian to ride the surf. The thrills and the skills are much the same. Snow and waves are both formed of water. Only the outward forms and circumstances differ.

Saturn does for the spirit pretty much what cold weather does for the skier or heat for the surfer. It sets a climate, a frame of reference which tends to steer us toward certain forms of activity.

We can't avoid weather, but we can find ways to cope with its effects. We learn to choose the right clothing for the season. We build dwellings appropriate to our environment and equip them with heating and cooling systems. We have the choice of sitting around complaining about the heat or the cold or of getting out and participating in each season's special opportunities for gain and enjoyment.

We can make ourselves as happy or as miserable as we choose to be, depending on how we handle the limitations of our environment. And if we don't like being where we are, we can always find ways to change the conditions or move somewhere else, *if we really want to.*

The trouble is, it often seems easier to stay put and moan about what great things we could be doing if only it weren't so hot or so cold, if only we weren't so poor or so sick or so burdened with obligations, if only *somebody* would listen to our pleadings that the laws of Nature be altered for our particular benefit.

Well, we might as well quit expecting the laws to be changed. Any alterations we want will have to be made by ourselves. We are, each one of us, both the controlled and the controller. Rewards and punishments, misery and joy, hope and despair, damnation and salvation are ours for the asking. The choice is up to us.

We have become aware that everything is composed of energy operating according to fixed laws of order. Ideas exist as truly as their physical manifestations. Saturn the cosmic force is as real as Saturn the planet whether or not we care to think of the two as having any relationship except in name, or even in name.

Saturn the planet continues to turn in its orbit only because it functions in accordance with the cosmic laws of order. To put your own Saturn in its proper orbit and keep it there, you also have to work with the laws of order. Handling responsibilities effectively is purely a matter of tackling each problem in its correct relationship to your whole being.

Obviously, then, one's first responsibility is to observe the cosmic laws. Notice that verb is *observe*, not *obey*. We obey whether we want to or not because the laws work with equal effect either positively or negatively, according to the polarities we set up.

A planet which strayed from its orbit would trigger the reverse polarity of the force which keeps it turning, and would disintegrate. A person who tries to run the world to suit himself invites his own destruction. A girl can't stop herself from getting pregnant during intercourse by refusing to accept the concept of motherhood. We can't keep from living and dying in accordance with the eternal laws by shouting, "God is dead."

By God I mean, simply, everything. I mean the Life Force. I mean the all-pervading Intelligence which directs the stars in their courses, Nature in its growth cycles, myself along the upward spiral of expanding consciousness. I know that a loftier awareness of life is available to me, because I find that I become more aware if I try. I assume that the possibility of greater awareness is infinite because the more I learn, the more I realize how ignorant I am. I see that many are ahead of me along the way to enlightenment and many behind, but that we are all on the same path, under the same guidance.

This is a childish explanation, but I am a child. So are you. We're always dying and being born again. Oliver Wendell Holmes's *Professor at the Breakfast Table* said he had "died out of his lodgings." He meant that he suddenly realized one day that his present apartments no longer suited his needs and that it was time to move. We die out of kindergarten when we enter first grade. We die out of bachelorhood when we get married, and too often we die out of wedlock when the honeymoon wanes.

Every little death means a rebirth in a new situation. We're always having to learn to walk all over again. And to get anywhere, we have to take first steps first. When we drive our cars, we must stick to the road and watch the signals if we expect to get where we're going without being wrecked. As above, so below. The great is revealed in the little.

Think of God as That Big Registrar of Motor Vehicles in the Sky, if it tickles your fancy. He's been called worse than that, and it really doesn't matter. The point is, first you understand how your vehicle works. Then you learn to work it. Then you head it in the right direction. Then you keep your eyes on the road and be ready to stop in the right place. Most ancient hidden mysteries of the occult masters boil down to something like this.

Your second responsibility is to yourself. Granted that your body is both destructible and replaceable, the physical form is a necessary vehicle for the expression of the spirit.

Since we are in fact talking about forms of transportation, we might picture a space ship traveling to the Moon. By the time it falls back to Earth, the stresses of the journey will have rendered the capsule unfit for any future trip. Of itself, it will have accomplished nothing, except to provide a protective shell for the men and instruments that carry out the actual mission. Yet the container has to exist, and it has to function at peak efficiency if the mission is to be fulfilled.

A sound, clean, suitably nourished body is an instrument which can be used in countless ways to make our present lives happy, useful, and productive of a higher and happier state on the next plane of existence. A sick, ill-kept body is a bore and a burden to its owner and to everyone around him.

The whole purpose of astrology is to help you understand and employ the best ways to increase your present and future physical, mental, and spiritual well-being. For you, for me, for everybody, anything that genuinely contributes to the joy of living is good. Dissipation is not good because it stems from despair instead of joy and leads to illness and deeper despair. However, mortifying the flesh by fasting, rigid sexual abstinence, or eating pigeon food is no way to feed the spirit. Failing to wash for weeks on end and then riding in a crowded train on a hot day doesn't tend to promote universal brotherhood, either.

Taking care of your body does not mean becoming preoccupied with every morsel you put between your lips, every twitch of a muscle, every momentary tummy pang. The hypochondriac, the food faddist, the muscleman are caught as tightly in Saturn's net as the drug addict, the sexologist, the alcoholic, and the compulsive eater. Anything which demands an unreasonable amount of your energy, anything which upsets the balance of your life is Saturn, whether it's a web of overdeveloped muscles or a slavish reliance on blackstrap molasses and brown rice. A tight girdle is Saturn. Jealousy of your neighbor, a job you hate, an unhappy sexual relationship you can't seem to break off—all these are Saturn.

The more you allow Saturn to dominate your life, the more its leaden weight will press you down and keep you tied to misery and failure. You can't remain the patient martyr making the best of a bad situation, at least not for long. Bad situations become worse unless we take energetic steps to make them better. "You owe it to yourself." How often do we hear that pleasant bit of advice applied to everything from getting an education to buying a chocolate bar? Well, you do. You the controller owe it to yourself the controlled to make your physical and emotional situation as comfortable as possible.

We're not talking about satin bedsheets here, but about the sense of well-being that comes from knowing you're where you want to be, doing the things you want to do, earning the love and approval of those who matter most to you by being the sort of person with whom they want to share their lives.

You can't expect to be loved unless you're lovable. You can't be lovable until you are capable of initiating love and returning love. You can't love anybody else until you've learned to love yourself.

This is not selfishness but simple logic. How stupid would a partner have to be to love a person who can't tolerate himself? How could one respect such a foolish lover enough to return such a stupid love?

Did you ever have a sore toe? Perhaps new shoes pinched,

or a sandal thong raised a blister, or you stepped on a piece of glass going barefoot. The hurt was nothing serious, but didn't it affect your entire state of being until it healed? Perhaps the pain kept you from walking somewhere you wanted to go. Perhaps it made you hurt someone by breaking a date or annoyed you into acting snappish without justification. Maybe your mind was on your sore toe when you should have been concentrating on more important things, so you made a serious blunder.

When you stop to think about it, even this minor, transitory ailment may have had far-reaching, harmful consequences in your life. How often has something equally trivial been allowed to disrupt your plans? How do you expect to carry on the business of living if you keep letting small physical upsets hold you back?

If you really love your body, you'll dress it comfortably. You'll protect it from accidents. You'll keep it clean. You'll eat sensibly and enjoyably. You'll balance work, play, and rest periods. You'll keep yourself in a pleasant frame of mind. Remember that Saturn has his fun side! You'll demand fresh air, pure water, clean streets; and you'll assume your share of responsibility in the ecological struggle. By using the Saturn force to get what is best for you, you'll be helping other people as well.

Responsibility toward others is third and last on Saturn's list. This is directly contrary to Piscean interpretations of duty and helps us to understand why so few of us in the Piscean Age have been able to practice what we've preached. But why should we think we're capable of running somebody else's life if we haven't first demonstrated that we can manage our own? What makes us so sure we know more about what's good for our neighbor than he does himself? Furthermore, if we all share in one universal energy source, why should some other entity be any more worthy of our best efforts at development than the one we can work on most effectively—the self we now inhabit?

Demanding equality is redundant. We *have* equality. Why

should we keep pestering each other for something it is not in anybody's power to give? All we need do is *feel* equal and *act* equal, bearing in mind that everybody else is as equal as we are.

You cannot be truly free until you acknowledge my right to equality. As long as I remain poor and ignorant and diseased and criminal, I am your jailer and you are my prisoner. You have to support me by paying taxes which provide jails and hospitals and mental institutions for me and my feeble-minded children. You have to give me welfare money so that I can stay alive and create more problems which add to your burdens. You have to carry the weight of my sufferings as you struggle to boost yourself higher in the spiral of life. Until you find intelligent ways to get me off your back, you're going to have a tougher climb than I am because you'll be aware of what's happening and I won't. Only when you stop treating me like a child, put me down, and show me how to walk beside you as a fully responsible human being will I claim what is mine and set you free.

On the other hand, my freedom leaves off where your nose begins. I have no right to impose my concept of the good life on you nor do you have any right to interfere with my carrying out my ideas unless they get in your way. This is anarchy, of course, and we have a long way to go before we can run a planet on no law but the Golden Rule. For the time being, we have to work within the framework of national government. Therefore, we have a responsibility to make that government as fair as possible for everybody. And that means everybody: rich, poor, middle-class; white, black, brown, red, yellow, assorted; male, female, undetermined; spanning every possible category, starting from ourselves.

The basic difficulty with taking astrology seriously is that it confronts us squarely from the outset with the need to accept full responsibility for our lives. It does not allow us to purchase self-approval by taking the woes of the world on our shoulders. Espousing a cause, acting the Great Father or the Great Mother or the Great Brother or the Great Sister or the

Great Friend or the Great Lover or the Great Anything achieves nothing whatsoever unless we first concentrate on making ourselves greater individuals.

On the spiritual level, nothing can be bought or bartered because we already have everything. Self-respect can be gained only by sorting out the positive from the negative, counting our blessings and buckling down to the arduous business of mending our shortcomings.

The advantage of dealing with our responsibilities in the correct order is that each solution tends to take care of the next problem. When we genuinely and sincerely work at understanding the cosmic laws and bringing harmony into our own lives, we find that we're having a more positive effect on others without even trying than we ever did by coaxing or coercion.

We can't give anything to anybody else, really. Our brothers and sisters have all potentialities for manifesting good and evil within themselves, just as we do. What we can do is set an example. We can make each life a continuing illustration of what happens when one honestly tries to live positively at all times, in all ways. And if this sounds like "Brighten the Corner," that's because it's meant to.

The urge to know and share love is our highest feeling. The practice of love is what life is all about. But do we know what love means? Can we love merely by wearing a button that says we do, or by making out all over the sidewalk with anybody who happens to be handy and willing? Can we profess to love our brothers and still hate the police or the Irish Republicans or the White Anglo-Saxon Protestants, or anybody?

Love implies a sense of unity. We've overdone the "this is bigger than both of us" bit into a low-camp cliché, but when the genuine feeling takes possession, any pair of lovers finds out that it's still the sweetest story ever told. Love is bigger than any two of us because it spreads to include all of us. Nobody is undeserving of love, and I have to include both you and myself in that statement.

If I set fire to my body to show you how much I hate the

injustice you're committing, I'm acting as silly as the child who pouts, "I'll eat worms and die, then you'll be sorry you were so mean to me."

I do not escape from the responsibility to love by committing suicide. I am only showing that I've failed in my primary obligation to make the best possible use of the life which has been given to me; and I'm going to have to come back and keep trying until I do better, whether I want to or not.

Loving everybody doesn't mean we shouldn't have our particular loves. Of course we care more deeply for certain people than for people in general. Of course we experience, if we're lucky, a sense of utter, sublime union with one soul more perfectly attuned to our own than all the rest. And accepting the fact of brotherhood certainly does not mean that we have to accept our brothers' standards. We may abhor everything they do, say, and think. We may find long hair and bare feet detestable, or we may be revolted by the sight of an elderly woman wearing a Shirley Temple wig and a size 10 shift strained over her size 16 flab. But if we have the right to do our own thing, so do they. If we learn to smile instead of sneer, we may find them smiling back. This is the only way revolutions can be won.

Now, at the end of the Piscean Age, tremendous upheavals are taking place everywhere. One of the most fascinating phenomena to an occultist is the mass incarnations which sociologists are calling the "population explosion." Instead of waiting to be reborn after what could have been a considerable interval in less dynamic times, we are forming new bodies almost before we've shucked off the old. Souls who have not reincarnated for centuries are hurrying to get in on the excitement.

Some of those who haven't been around for a while are visibly having difficulties in adjusting to the higher living standards which have evolved since their last incarnations. In many cases, this seems to be due to the fact that they have not acquired the technical ability to handle present-day situations. They may have different priorities, different inclinations than we. This does not excuse boorishness and it doesn't give the more evolved persons license to regress to their level. However, it may throw some light on why we now see such a divergence of types in the world, why we find it so hard to arrive at a consensus, and why we have such an unparalleled opportunity just now to observe and enjoy variety in human nature. This is perhaps a unique chance to exercise our faculties in learning and loving, to develop a real sense of responsibility and handle it intelligently.

To sum up, Saturn is *control*. We must use controls, but we must understand how they work and use discretion. When a car starts to skid, the driver can't just slam on the brakes or he'll precipitate the very disaster he's trying to avoid. Nor can he simply shut off the engine and sit where he stops. If another car doesn't hit him, the police will tow him away and fine him for obstructing traffic. He must check his momentum with judgment and moderation, then steer away from danger and get back on the right course.

Positive and negative polarities are involved with Saturn as with everything else. Saturn consuming you with hatred and envy is negative. Saturn controlling your hostilities to the point of frustration and martyrdom is also negative. Saturn applied to control your anger only to the point where you can divert it into constructive energy is positive. As we said in the beginning, contraction has to work in harmonious partnership with *expansion*.

5 · Jupiter
(power)

Acceptance and Expansion

JUPITER is not only the largest planet in our system, it is probably as big as a planet can get without beginning to radiate as a stellar body. Astronomer Peter Lancaster Brown suggests that it may, in fact, be "a unique example of a cosmic body halfway between a planet and a star."

Three-hundred-eighteen times as large as Earth and about 5.2 times farther from the Sun, Jupiter rotates much faster than Earth: 9 hours, 50 minutes at the equator and 9 hours, 55 minutes at the poles. This discrepancy suggests that the surface is not rigid, in fact, nothing about Jupiter suggests rigidity. Its mean density is even less than the Sun's. Apparently its outer layer is composed of various gases, although the core is probably solid.

Telescopic observation shows a complex system of cloud belts which are constantly changing in appearance. Jupiter's famous Red Spot, one of its most dramatic and so far unexplained features, alters in both color and size, although less rapidly than other atmospheric features.

Perhaps the most fascinating thing about Jupiter is its ability to emit radio waves of two apparently unconnected types. "A" source radiations occur near the poles; "B" source radiations seem to be emitted at times when Jupiter's inner satellite Io crosses the planet's strong magnetic field, which is similar to Earth's but ten times larger.

Io is only one of four major satellites. Ganymede and Callisto are larger than our Moon and the planet Mercury, Io and Europa about the same size as Mercury. These huge moons move around their parent body in a counterclockwise direction, while eight smaller satellites move clockwise. What a picture twelve moons going in different directions must present from Jupiter's surface!

There may be many other bodies too small to be seen by us in Jupiter's orbit. Such a huge planet could easily hold a whole family of satellites under its sway, as Olympian Jupiter ruled his turbulent clan of gods and goddesses.

To the ancients, Jupiter was *Optimus Maximus*, Hurler of Thunderbolts, Supreme Ruler, Great Father. The fathering propensities they ascribed to him, in fact, were both pronounced and picturesque. Although a much-married god, first to the Titaness Dione, then to the battle-axe Juno, he seduced Europa in the form of a sacred bull, Leda while disguised as a swan, Io as a cloud, Danaë as a shower of gold! In short, there was no game he wouldn't try. This unbridled enthusiasm for life and the fullness thereof is our clue to astrology's interpretation of Jupiter.

We can see why Saturn found his uninhibited son a problem. The stern, conservative parent, the rebellious, unconventional child—the apocryphal struggle between Saturn and Jupiter goes on and on between nations, in the home, in the streets, on campus, wherever an authoritarian figure can be pitted against the bursting virility of youth. There is nothing new about bucking the Establishment. We have always done that and we'll keep on doing it until we realize that we're only fighting ourselves, that the enemy stands not on the opposite side of the barricade but within our own beings.

We know from our discussion of Saturn that our responsibility lies first not with the world, nor our parents, nor our children, nor our troubled friends and neighbors. The balance we have to adjust is our own. We have to accept the positive, driving side of our nature and adjust it in correct proportion to the negative, holding-back side. The keyword for Jupiter is *acceptance*.

Before we can do much about improving ourselves, we have to accept ourselves. We have to care enough about ourselves to make the effort toward improvement worthwhile. We have to realize, matter-of-factly and with no attempt to butter up the old ego, exactly what sort of foundation we have to build on. We have to accept our virtues as well as our faults.

We must also accept not only the cyclicities of the seasons, the great, sweeping global movements, but also the private rhythms of our individual lives. Thoreau said it best: "If a man does not keep pace with his companions, perhaps it is because he hears a different drummer. Let him step to the music which he hears, however measured or far away."

Jupiter may spin the wheel more quickly or slowly for you than for your sisters and brothers. Maybe you already know this. You have had periods when nothing seemed to work. Then, as if by magic, your affairs took an upward swing and everything fell into place. If you have kept a diary (a most useful habit for an occultist) or have a good memory, you will find on checking the dates that your ups and downs tend to recur in cycles.

You may even have developed what people call superstitions. "Friday is my lucky day." "Five years in one place, then

I move on." "Nothing ever pans out for me in July." You make jokes about these ideas, but something down inside you knows they're not just funny.

If you have reached this stage of awareness, you have taken an important step in learning to handle Jupiter. We need to search out our individual time rhythms, to know when a thing is likely to materialize for us and when it's unlikely to succeed. In this way, we can plan our lives intelligently, using the downs as periods of relaxation and quiet preparation for the busy season to come.

This is not at all the same thing as the negativistic use of astrology which tells us, "Librans shouldn't make long journeys this week." It is the same calm acceptance of the growth cycle which moves us New Englanders to plant our tomatoes in June and expect to harvest them in late summer and early fall. We've found it sensible to move with Nature instead of trying to fight her.

This doesn't mean we have to deny ourselves all the joys of life during a downswing. We can bottle our tomatoes or raise them in a greenhouse and eat them all winter. It's a bit more fuss and they won't taste quite as good, but that very fact may spur us to improve our talents at cooking them into more exciting dishes. Down cycles in our lives are always opportunities to assimilate the lessons we've learned during the high periods now past and to develop an attitude of joyful expectancy to meet the better time we know is on its way to us.

Since everyone has his own life tempo, we must accept others not for what we'd like them to be but for what they are. This isn't easy. The urge to live someone else's life is as common a malady as the head cold, but much more uncomfortable in its consequences. Attempting to control someone else sets up Jupiter's opposite polarity and snaps back as a Saturn situation. The jailer becomes trapped by his prisoner.

If that sounds paradoxical, try to picture a prison without a guard. Is the keeper's confinement any less real than the inmate's, even though it may be voluntary? Is the too doting mama any less enmeshed in an unbalanced relationship than her overprotected child? Accepting doesn't mean grabbing everything you can get and yelling for more, and it doesn't mean being a doormat. What, then, may one reasonably expect from a fellow human?

Whatever he chooses to give. Only that, and nothing more. Remember, though, that you don't have to take it. You are as free to accept or reject as he is to proffer or withhold. Swallowing everything which comes your way, good or bad, wholesome or contaminated, is a ridiculous misuse of the Jupiter force.

This is one of the lessons we've learned the hard way. We know now that if we turn the other cheek too often, all we get is punchy. We have a right to protect our bodies from attack. We have a right to shield our minds and spirits from hostile influences.

Acceptance is not a sponge but a positive use of energy, a definite act which you perform. You have to hold your own bag, but you don't have to stand there like an idiot watching others fill it with whatever garbage they take a notion to throw in. Nobody but yourself is entitled to select the elements which you want to make up your life, nor do you have the right to select for anybody else.

You may offer to share what you find good. You may put all your powers of persuasion into the offer. You may hope with all your heart that your gift will be accepted, but you may not force acceptance. So there's no sense in being angry or disappointed if your good intentions fall flat.

One of the hardest things we have to learn is that we cannot live another person's life. Until we do realize this, however, we can't move along to the practical work of building a physical world where peace and freedom exist as truly as they do in the spiritual world.

Astrological concepts make acceptance easier. We begin to understand that like the stars and the planets, each of us has to move in his personal orbit. We may not approve of the direction another's life seems to be taking. We may see him headed for tragedy. We may try to steer him straight. But if he won't heed our cautions, there's nothing we can do but stand clear and let him go.

We don't have to be dragged into someone else's disaster, and we don't have to feel guilty because he refused to let us save him. Maybe he knows better than we do where his salvation lies. What looks to us like calamity may be a vital step forward in his progress toward a spiritual goal he has to reach, a barrier he has to cross before he can stand where we are now standing.

We must have faith in each other. Everybody has infinite capacity to increase his awareness, and every spirit moves at its own rate. If we try to teach what the other person is not yet ready to learn, we are in danger of assuming a superiority which we do not in fact possess.

Any teacher can tell us that nobody teaches anything. One can only create an atmosphere in which, hopefully, the pupil will open his mind and learn. This is the real service we can perform for others. Those who are willing and able to accept what we have to offer will seek us out if we make ourselves appealing enough as teachers. We do this by expanding our awareness through mental and physical self-discipline, not by making irrevocable demands that somebody set up a Department of Instant Understanding and award us a degree in Omniscience solely on the ground that we want it *now*.

As Saturn means contraction, Jupiter means *expansion*. Accept what the life force brings you, assimilate it into your store of experience, and you will inevitably grow. What you grow into depends on what you accept and how you handle the intake. You can expand into a wise, happy, loving adult or a fiend in human form or any kind of in-between. It depends on where you draw your lines, how you balance the seesaw.

Every impulse has both positive and negative sides. The electricity wired into our houses can keep us warm, cook our food, entertain us, work for us in all sorts of ways. It can also shock us to death or burn our houses down. We may elect to disconnect the current and do without its potential benefits. We may poke our fingers into sockets or grab live wires. Or

Jupiter

we may pay our light bills and equip ourselves with whatever electrical appliances will contribute most to our comfort and happiness. The force is there, waiting to be tapped. In itself, it is neither beneficial nor harmful. What it does for us depends on how we channel it.

Where Jupiter exists in your chart, you will see special opportunities for progress. You will see clues to furthering your career, to broadening your relationships with the material world. You will see ways to make money or to acquire skills to get what you want.

Of course you have to be selective. Try to grab too much, and Jupiter can blow your prospects up like balloons which burst into scattered fragments and have to be collected and painfully put back together before you can get on with the journey. Learning what and how to select is a tricky business, but Jupiter, like a good *paterfamilias*, has provided us with just the force to handle that problem.

6 · Mercury

Concentration and Motivation

LYING closest to the Sun, Mercury is hard to observe with the naked eye, except for brief periods around sunrise and sunset. The Greeks called our innermost planet "the twinkler," and we shall soon see how appropriate this name is from the astrologer's point of view.

Mercury is the smallest planet in our system, only 3,005 miles in diameter, compared with Earth's polar measurement of 7,950 miles. Yet this is one of the densest or most concentrated bodies in the solar system. We naturally expect it to have the shortest year, and it does, completing an orbit in only 88 days, even though its path is highly eccentric, swinging within 28.3 million miles of the Sun at perihelion and out to 43.2 million miles at aphelion. Its orbital plane is steeply inclined at only 7° to the ecliptic.

Recent radar findings have exploded earlier theories about Mercury's axial rotation. To our amazement, we have learned that each rotation takes 59 Earth days, or almost two-thirds as long as a Mercurian year. Apparently this is due to a resonance effect with the Sun's tidal forces. As a result, the same side of the planet is exposed to the Sun for 176 of our days.

If we explained the adjective "mercurial" as meaning "to blow hot and cold," we couldn't be more right. Temperatures on Mercury are said to vary from $+350°$C. to $-160°$C. On the whole, it seems this is rather a mixed-up planet. Perhaps a glance at Mercury's family tree will help us to understand his astrological personality better.

Astronomers have not yet spotted it, but one of this fast-moving little planet's outstanding marks is said to be a bar sinister. Olympian Mercury was one of Jupiter's illegitimate sons. His mother was Maia, oldest daughter of Atlas, the Titan who was thought to hold Earth on his mighty shoulders.

Perhaps because of her father's important position, Jupiter seems to have behaved toward Maia with unusual gallantry. He caused the month of May to be named in her honor and appointed their clever offspring messenger to the gods.

Mercury served so competently in this position that he soon acquired other duties. He conducted sleepers to dreamland and souls of the dead to Hades. He became the deity of roads, protector of travelers, god of doorways, of commerce and thievery, of good and bad luck, of treasure trove, of gain both honest and dishonest.

Using the nimble wit for which Mercury was noted, we can trace these diverse attributes back to his early pastoral character as the giver of fertility. In any event, we get a clear picture of an immortal go-getter, a god who gets things done. This is how we interpret the role of Mercury in astrology.

Think of roads and doorways. Think of a force which channels, directs, *concentrates*.

Mercury gathers together the energy we attract through Jupiter and balance through Saturn and compresses it into usable form. Mercury, we might say, is the wire through which the current flows. Mercury finds ways to get stored impulses out of the subconscious pool, so that they can be self-consciously put to use.

"Self-conscious" is an expression we often employ when we mean "unsure of one's ability to perform adequately." This is only one of the possible definitions, but it does illustrate how accustomed we are to equating consciousness with confidence.

It also shows us what a cheat Mercury can be. He cheats us if he keeps us thinking about the negative aspects of self-consciousness. He even cheats us sometimes by making us pay through the nose to learn what ought not to cost us a cent. The many "How to succeed through positive thinking" courses are all based on one thing: effective channelization of the Mercury force. After the trimmings have been stripped away, we are left with one simple instruction: know what you want. Concentrate your thoughts and efforts on this one specific goal and you're bound to achieve it sooner or later. The more effectively you pinpoint your efforts, obviously, the more surely you achieve what you've set out to do.

You don't have to be bashful about setting your goals, either. The only limitations you face are those which you choose to put on yourself. However solid the obstacles in your path look to you, always remember that matter is not what it appears to be.

We know that anything capable of being created is capable of being destroyed. We understand the physical laws which bring molecules together to form visible, palpable substances. We know that the motivation which assembles them is an idea, a mental impulse. Therefore, we conclude that the visible thing is capable of being organized, dissolved, and reorganized over and over *ad infinitum* by the invisible promptings of thought.

The power to separate and regroup positive and negative energy impulses in such a way as to bring you what you want and take away what you don't want is not restricted to magicians. It is available to us all and we are constantly making use of it, either consciously or unconsciously.

Mercury

Mercury, messenger of the Olympians, is working for you, too. Right this minute, he can turn about to bring you anything you ask for. He's been doing it all along, although you may never have heard the approach of his winged sandals. Every feeling of desire you have expressed, or experienced without bringing to consciousness, has set in motion a chain of reactions which ultimately affected your life. The process goes on continually, so take heed what you ask for.

The power of Mercury is charmingly illustrated in the old fairy tale about the peasant who was given three wishes. Being hungry, he wished first for a big, juicy sausage. His wife flew into a rage when she saw the wish come true and realized what an opportunity he'd wasted so foolishly. "I wish that sausage were on the end of your nose!" she screamed. So then they had to use their third and last wish to get the sausage off the man's nose. How often has each of us done something equally silly?

What do you want? Can you honestly and definitely formulate the dearest wish of your heart right now?

Think it over. Take pen and paper and write it down in one sentence of not more than twenty-five words. Don't content yourself with scribbling some vague generality like "world peace" or "brotherhood." State in simple, specific words exactly what you personally want for yourself. Don't put down what you think you ought to want, nor what you wish Civilization or Society or Man or whoever would do. Write what you wish to achieve by your own efforts, through your own mind and body. It doesn't have to be a big thing or a high and noble thing, but it must be a *real* desire.

That's a bit of a stinker, isn't it? Now do you understand why we try so hard to kid ourselves into wanting things we can see and touch, why we pacify our bodies with small, immediate gratifications, why we use drugs and drink to dull our frustration at not achieving some truly rewarding life experience?

It is this inability to focus on exactly what we want that leads to a sense of defeat. Because we're confused, we become liars. We never say what we mean because we don't *know* what we mean. We utter words of love even while we're performing acts of hate. We scorn our neighbor's bourgeois materialism, failing to see that we are caught up in exactly the same situation with different trimmings.

What's the essential difference between taking a trip to Miami or a trip to Tierra del Fuego or a trip on acid if all we're really trying to do is get away from our boring selves?

No matter where we go or what we wear or how much or how little luggage we take, we do not alter our personalities merely by shifting our locale. If we expect magic to happen as a result of transporting our physical and mental and emotional baggage to some other sphere of activity, we have to decide beforehand exactly what sort of magic we're looking for. Charms don't work unless we first wind up the spell. A miracle is strictly a do-it-yourself project.

Of themselves, material goals are perfectly valid. We are physical beings living in a physical world. It would be foolish for us to deny ourselves physical comforts and gratifications. It's only when we forget that we are also spiritual and mental beings that we run into trouble.

What's wrong, for example, with wanting a new car? Cars are rather fun. They offer convenience and opportunities for recreation. A new automobile is something big and shiny and socially approved in our culture (provided it's equipped with adequate pollution controls) on which almost anyone can focus his desire power without straining his intellect. Even though cars cost far more than we choose to admit, most of us think we can afford one. We may obtain the purchase price by practicing self-denial in other areas, working overtime, saving our pennies. We may feel that we've genuinely earned the right to enjoy what a car can give, and we may be absolutely right.

On the other hand, thoughtful analysis of our real reasons for wanting the car might tell us things about ourselves that we'd rather not know. We may be regarding the vehicle as a means of escape, entertaining the absurd notion that physical speed can carry us away from mental anxieties. We may be trying to prop a weak ego with an expensive status symbol which we hope will arouse envy and/or admiration among our peers. We may be saddling ourselves with an impossible financial burden in order to divert our attention from more serious personal problems which we can't summon courage enough to face.

We may even want the car for a weapon. We've all met meek little people who turn into raging tigers the moment they get behind a wheel. It doesn't take a psychiatrist to observe that they're venting their hostilities in a way they think will escape detection. Medical examiners have uncovered overwhelming evidence that many, possibly most, fatal wrecks are either suicides or murders or both. One can hardly drive two miles without meeting some driver who seems bent on mass slaughter. Doesn't it gall you to see a peace symbol on his rear bumper as he forces you off the road and hurtles toward his next victim?

Today, as in all periods of spiritual revolution, many of us are refusing to want the things our elders think we ought to have. Sometimes we overreact to a ridiculous degree. Sometimes we think we're rebelling when we're actually fighting to defend the status quo against the genuine rebels, who sometimes, believe it or not, are chronologically older than we. By and large, however, refusing to be drawn into the trap of materialism makes a great deal of sense.

Most of us have had enough experience with material things to know that mere possession of consumer goods does not bring inner contentment. Too often, possessions bring with them an excess of the constricting Saturn influence. We have seen that every exercise of the Jupiter force—acceptance—brings with it added responsibility to take care of what we acquire. Being poor is miserable, but being rich is no picnic either, unless we can direct the Mercury force to focus on desiring goals which don't depend on buying and selling.

Until recent years, the socially accepted method of avoiding getting caught up in this Jupiter-Saturn seesaw was to join some religious order and take a vow of poverty. That didn't work, and the cloisters are rapidly being depopulated. Eventually only the truly consecrated ones will be living the monastic life. To these higher souls, material objects simply have no meaning, not because they find poverty attractive, but because they are accumulating their riches on a plane we can't even visualize. The rest of us won't even know such beings exist until, perhaps, we go to join them.

For us, Mercury deals with the here and now. We need not fear to dip into his treasure chest. No material object can prevent us from leading decent, constructive lives. Even a hydrogen bomb is harmless as long as we don't set it off, though the kind of thinking which allows such things to be created is an active and present menace in our group consciousness.

We must be aware of such menaces, and we must cope with them by refusing to be controlled by the group. And that means *any* group, *especially* one headed by somebody professing to have higher spiritual powers. *Nobody* has higher spiritual powers than anybody else. Anybody who is actively using spiritual power more intensively than his fellows knows better than to make such a claim, unless he is using power in a way which will involve him sooner or later in a catastrophe far worse than any physical atrocity we can imagine. Make sure he doesn't involve you with him.

Motivation is what makes good or evil, positive or negative. Motivation is what determines result. You, like everybody else, have the power to achieve any goal which you can imagine yourself reaching. You have at your disposal the Mercury force, which can lead you along the road to success. You have the ability to develop that force in your life. You don't need any magic words, any talisman, any course in dynamic thinking. You don't need anything but practice.

You have to focus your attention consciously, consistently, constantly. You have to perform each step of your work with all the physical and mental ability you can command, never letting anything divert you from your target. You must put aside doubt. If you fear failure, you are forming a mental picture of yourself in the act of failing which can develop into manifestation.

Remember, though, that "Take what you want and pay for it, says God" is more than an old Spanish proverb. It is an exact description of what happens. Choosing a goal means sacrificing other possible choices. If what you want is worth more to you than the things you'll have to give up in order to achieve it, you have no problem. Just be sure you've studied the map before you start out.

Olympian Mercury was a notorious trickster, the associate of pickpockets and confidence men as well as honest merchants and travelers. Astrological Mercury works through the self-conscious mind, and we know from experience as well as from Freud how adroitly consciousness can deceive itself as to our true motivations. Mercury can lead us along dangerous paths if we don't use other cosmic forces to keep him firmly in hand.

7 · Venus
Imagination

LIKE the goddess for whom she was named, Venus is almost incredibly beautiful, reflecting the Sun's light more brilliantly than any other planet in our system. Astronomers who know exactly where to look can observe her even at midday, and many amateur stargazers have noticed the shadow she casts on her neighbor Earth during her brightest phase.

It is easy to see why early astrologers attributed influences of peace and love to the planet second closest to the Sun. Her orbit is remarkably close to being a perfect circle, so that during the Venusian year of 224.7 days we find relatively little difference between perihelion and aphelion. Through telescopes, her surface appears serenely smooth.

However, the recent Soviet space probes have sent back

radar signals which indicate that parts of the surface hidden by her dense cloud covering may be rugged, although the equatorial region seems quite smooth. In fact, Venus may be full of surprises. One astonishing find of the past decade is her rate of rotation, which astronomers had never been able to count because of the lack of distinguishing surface features. According to radar findings, her rotation is clockwise and takes 243 days. This means that each day on Venus is 117 Earth days.

As yet we have no idea why the rotation period is so slow. One theory is that Venus used to rotate at about the same rate as her sister planet Earth (the two are almost the same size) until she captured a satellite about twice the size of our Moon. The satellite would have acted as a drag, slowing down Venus's momentum and moving ever closer until the two finally crashed and were merged into one. The intense heat generated by such a collision could account for the surface temperature of over 450°C. as well as atmospheric pressures 100 times greater than ours.

To an astrologer, this is an intriguing hypothesis. A fierce impact changes Venus's physical structure and slows down her daily activity but not her overall revolution. She is not shaken out of her regular orbit, and whatever may be going on inside her seems only to have made her more beautiful than ever. Doesn't this make you think of a pregnant woman?

Like so many glamorous women, Venus has been consistently misunderstood in her Olympian role. Even her origins are cloaked in obfuscation. One theory was that she arose spontaneously from the sea, at the spot where Uranus's sex organ fell after he had been castrated by the son we know as Saturn. A more plausible, though less picturesque, explanation of her birth is that Venus was a legitimate daughter of Jupiter by his first wife Dione. This would make her a half-sister of Mercury, and therefore we might reasonably expect to find some working relationship between them.

We are familiar with Venus as the epitome of sensual love and physical female beauty, but she was a great deal more than that. She was worshipped as the embodiment of pure spiritual love and as the protectress of marriage and family life. With a child of her own to defend, she could at times become a war goddess. In addition, Venus was a sea goddess and the patroness of sailors, who still pay her homage in every port.

In other words, Venus is a woman. At her best, she is what every mortal female might aspire to become and every male to have as his mate. She is capable of any depth of understanding, every height of love. She is the ultimate in beauty of spirit as well as of body. She can show any tenderness, any strength in expressing her love.

At her worst, she's indescribable. The most vicious, screaming, clawing whore in the last stages of physical and mental ruin is an angel of light compared to what Venus can be when she gets wound up and headed wrong. Ask any psychiatrist what a devastating thing female hostility can be, and especially how much human agony is traceable to the mothers we sentimentalize over on the second Sunday in May.

It should be emphasized that our attribution of male and female characteristics to cosmic forces is deliberate but not to be taken literally. For example, Venus is related to the essential feminine principle, but this influence is not restricted to the female half of humankind. We are aware, of course, that all humans have bisexual characteristics, although most of us are able to define our physical proclivities in terms of our equipment.

The war between men and women wasn't started by male chauvinists. It has been going on since time began, inside each person as well as at the interpersonal level. Venus is a factor in the chart of every male as well as every female and may be the predominant force. This would not necessarily turn a man into either a homosexual or a ramping stallion, so don't start worrying (or hoping) until you've grasped the total picture.

In the Tarot, Venus (Key 3, the Empress) is shown as a beautiful, pregnant woman. Thus we see her not only as a sex object but as an actively gestating female.

What happens during gestation? A seed is fertilized. An

embryo begins to develop. Gradually, the fetus acquires organs of assimilation, digestion, and elimination; a respiratory and circulatory system; sensors of sight, taste, hearing, smell, and touch. Its form undergoes a progression of improvements until it is well enough equipped to emerge as a functioning creature.

A thought gets born much like a baby. Mercury opens the door to mentation and a seed idea enters. We mull it over, elaborate on the possibilities it presents, tack on whatever parts it needs to become suitable for our purposes, then bring it forth into consciousness so that it can be put to active use. This process is called *imagination*, the formation of images; and it is this power which we attribute astrologically to Venus.

Imagination is the continual, active, creative, and formative power of man. The pictures which Venus forms in and through us are the images we live with. Whether they represent truth or falsehood, beauty or ugliness, pleasure or pain, riches or poverty will depend on how capably we utilize our powers of mental gestation.

We recognize the fact that our beauty may be somebody else's ugliness. The steatopygous belle of the Bushman would hardly appeal to the bosom-conscious American, and what Bushman would give a chipped cowrie shell for one of our skinny fashion models? To the righteous down-east Yankee horse trader of yesteryear, the Levantine's fluency as a liar was deplorable; but how did the latter compare an artistic fabrication with the practice of swindling a purchaser without breaking the strict letter of the law?

Monogamy has been a virtue in some cultures and a sign of contemptible poverty in others. Chastity can be moral or stupid or anywhere in between depending on where you happen to live. We set up personal and social standards according to our images of what is desirable for us, regardless of what the rest of the world may do, and we change our values to fit the times. In America, for instance, homosexuality was outlawed for as long as the invading white men needed more babies to populate the land and secure their position. Now that overpopulation is threatening to use up our resources, we're suddenly turning homosexuality into a great American pastime. The essential nature of the practice has not changed. Homosexuals are neither better nor worse than they ever were. Only the frame of reference differs.

Oscar Wilde's statement, "Each man kills the thing he loves," has at least a germ of truth in it. Everybody creates the image of his adoration, therefore he is free to destroy it at will if he chooses. We fall in love not so much with an individual as with the dreams we are able to weave around him or her. The love lasts as long as the image-making power finds materials with which it can work. In a reciprocal love relationship, each stimulates the partner's imagination on a continuing basis.

The easiest and most usual way to commence a relationship is through mutual physical stimulation. Normally, this would progress from looking to hearing (conversation) to touching to sexual intercourse which could be an increasingly delightful experience spanning many years, a one-night stand that may end in tears and disgust, or just a gradual letdown. Physical copulation doesn't mean very much unless it leads to a sharing of the image-making experience at the mental and spiritual levels. Learning to practice the fifty-seven varieties is only a way of saying, "Look what I'm willing to go through to give you pleasure." One might get the idea across in less fatiguing ways by exercising the power of Venus at all three levels.

A writer knows he doesn't make a book but simply lets it happen through him. Mothers know they don't actually make babies. The life which develops within the womb is merely utilizing environmental growth materials. The child who emerges will keep growing as a separate entity. Soon he will be free to accept or reject parental ties, regardless of how tightly Mama tries to fasten the apron strings. The only bond which will keep them together must be fashioned in exactly the way the baby was made: by the multiplication of a seed idea into a total image.

If the mother keeps picturing her offspring as a helpless infant, she'll feed him only what she thinks a baby should eat, let him do only what she considers safe. She'll plan for him, try to think for him. If she succeeds in getting him to share her image, she will be helping him to turn into a monstrous caricature of what he was meant to become. It is such subversion of the creative function, such striving to reverse the life cycle, which shows Venus at her most horrible.

Conversely, if the mother accepts the child as a creative experience with a life of its own, she begins to picture him as something to be loved and then let go. Even in a face only a mother could love she finds infant charms. The slightest hint of intelligence is made much of, coaxed, and wheedled into fullest bloom. She pictures her tot growing up wise, kind, beloved, and successful, and shares her images. Because she makes no unreasonable demands but turns her affection outward, she creates within her own psyche a space the child can fill with reciprocal images of the mother as a dispenser of love and happiness.

Experiments are being done on the production of children *ex utero*. A recent article in the *New York Times* mentioned that of course mothers would stop bearing babies the old-fashioned way as soon as they could be relieved of this onerous chore. Sure they will, just as the *consolateur* replaced the live penis as soon as it was learned that the vagina could be stimulated by artificial means. How many little girls in the class know what a *consolateur* is? How many know what a little boy is?

Experiments in so-called free love have been going on since Adam met Lilith. Why stick to one partner when the world is so wide? Why not flit like a butterfly from flower to flower, sipping wherever the nectar is sweetest at the moment? Any ex-nectar-sipper has the answer. We're not butterflies.

As we attain maturity, we become aware that the only relationship which gives a sense of completeness is that which is conducted on a continuing, one-to-one basis with a member of the opposite sex. Inability to form such a relationship may be compensated for in various ways such as sublimation of the libido in work or in friendships with persons of the same sex. These have satisfactions which may be deep and genuine, but nobody ever truly and honestly believes they fully replace the primary and essential blending of the male-female polarities in human partnership.

This does not necessarily mean sexual partnership. Male-female polarities may work effectively in situations where no physical contact is involved, as between student and teacher, employer and employee, older and younger relatives, and especially between fellow-workers engaged in mutually satisfying projects. You may have many such contacts in the course of a lifetime. But if no genuinely pleasing male-female relationship of any kind exists in your life, you are almost certainly misusing the Venus force in some way.

You may be forming false pictures of what such relationships should be, thus provoking potentially satisfactory partners to produce false images of you and refuse to cooperate. You may be imagining reactions which no sensible person would give, and this is an extremely dangerous practice.

Psychic wounds can be inflicted only by ourselves. No matter what anybody does to us, only we can decide what effects these experiences will be allowed to have on our imaginations. Some of us can sail through the most terrifying ordeals without a scar, while others will be shattered by events so trivial that they soon get buried in the subconscious memory.

Our earliest opportunity to form a relationship, of course, is between child and parent, and it is often here that trouble starts. One tot muses, "Father saved me first when our house burned down. He must love me best. The fire was rather fun, after all."

Another broods bitterly, "Father saved me, but he let my teddy bear burn up. He knew I loved my teddy bear. Maybe he wishes I'd burned up, too. Maybe he hates me."

If the child persists in such perverse image-making, every cross word from his father, however well deserved, is going to be interpreted as "proof" of hatred. Any momentary inattention may be taken as a rejection. The youngster may become depressed and withdrawn or start "protecting himself" by hostile words and acts which provoke more drastic punishments and confirm his fantasies. He can drive himself completely insane and possibly neither he nor anybody else will ever find out what caused the psychosis.

We've all done this sort of thing, to a lesser degree. We may have fancied ourselves slighted or insulted when the alleged offender meant no ill-will toward us. Especially during the hypersensitive years between twelve and twenty, we can make ourselves miserable over nothing at all, if we put our minds to it. Unless we practice mental birth control, the Venus power which is constantly working within us can mess up our lives, even creating psychosomatic illnesses which are no less incapacitating for being wholly imaginary.

Once in a while we meet some happy soul who knows that all geese are swans at heart, that all his friends are wise and kind, that the world's forever young and every lass a queen, that words like "love" and "trust" have meaning, that wealth and health and beauty are largely a matter of rejoicing in whatever life brings one's way. If you want to be in their number when the saints go marching in, remember that what mankind can imagine, mankind can achieve.

You are, in your immortal soul, anything you want to be. Nobody but yourself has a key to the private storehouse of your mind. Nobody else can make selections from the limitless possibilities for ideation which are open to you. Only in you can the Venus power gestate the seeds which lead to the materialization of your personal goals, be they conscious or unconscious.

Even if others put your body in bondage, they have no way of getting at your mind unless you let them. You cannot be hypnotized or brainwashed or whatever unless you first think yourself into a mood of receptivity. You may not be conscious of doing this. You may see yourself as being caught up in a situation too big for you to handle, such as a war. But remember, it was you who chose to be born in the time and place which exposed you to this circumstance. No matter what is happening to you, you have somehow made it happen and no doubt you had what appeared at the time to be a good reason for setting this train of events in motion, whether or not you now understand why you did it.

Knowing that Venus works within us leads us to reject some cherished notions about neurosis and psychosis. It has been tempting to blame our parents instead of ourselves for our psychic ills. Hitler, according to some pundits, became the personification of evil because he had a harsh father. So who was responsible for the old man's meanness? The grandfather? The great-great grandfather? Some fur-bearing ancestor who was too free with his war club? If a rotten parent is all it takes to make a fiend, why was there only one Hitler?

Somewhere along the line, you see, we have to stop passing the buck. Hitler was evil incarnate because he deliberately and consciously opened his mind and spirit to the forces of darkness. He was destroyed because everyday human decency is greater than all the powers of wickedness. In the end the Hobbits always have to win, for the simple reason that love is stronger than hate.

Enemy and conqueror, then, are the children of Venus's womb, and that womb lies within each one of us. Venus the war goddess draws the lines of battle. Venus the mother brings forth the soldiers for our personal army. Venus piles up the carnage or sends forth the dove of peace, according to the directions we send her by Mercury.

Imagination is compounded of memory and emotion. What we draw up from the sea of past experience depends on how competently we use the Mercury force to locate the best fishing spots. What we make of our catch depends on how we feel about it. If we try, we can control our negative impulses and use our materials wisely, but Venus of old was known for letting her heart run away with her head. Now as always, a female force needs a strong male force to develop her positive polarity.

8 · Mars Achievement

WE have been so prone to embody Mars as a fierce, hairy-chested planet that it comes as rather a shock when we stop and think that our nearest neighbor is almost the runt of the solar litter. About 4,200 miles around at the equator, the red planet is not much more than half the size of Earth and our sister planet Venus, whose waistline measures only 200 miles smaller than ours. Furthermore, Mars is not that glowing ruby in the sky we like to picture. Usually he appears a rather brickish or terra-cotta shade, but atmospheric scintillation may cause him to flash all the colors of the spectrum.

So much is being discovered about Mars through space probes that today's certain knowledge may be tomorrow's exploded fallacy. The notion of canals on Mars which Professor Lowell and others believed in so thoroughly and publicized so effectively has been disproved, and it now seems doubtful whether the sort of life we know here on Earth has developed there.

Mars's surface seems to be cratered like the Moon's. What we thought might be primitive vegetation is more likely just variation in the colors of soil or rock. The polar caps are probably only thin layers of solidified carbon dioxide, the familiar dry ice which we use as a refrigerant in shipping perishable products. Polar temperatures are estimated at $-200°C.$ as against Earth's Antarctic temperatures of $-130°C.$ The atmosphere is much thinner than we had expected, equivalent to 100,000 feet above Earth's sea level and radically different from ours, with much carbon dioxide and little nitrogen.

A Martian year is 687 sidereal days, or almost two of our years, but its day is only about half an hour longer than ours and its axis is tilted at $23°59'$ to the orbital plane, almost the same as Earth's.

By the time we get to Mars, we become aware of a curious regularity of interval in the distances of the planets from the Sun. This is expressed in Bode's Law, named after a German astronomer who formulated the relationships in 1772, although Titius of Wittenberg made the discovery independently at about the same time.

The gist of Bode's Law is this: if you write down the numeral 4 (which, interestingly enough, the Tarot ascribes to Aries, where Mars rules* and the Sun is exalted**) as many times as there are planets, then add 3 to the second, 6 to the third, 12 to the fourth, and so on, doubling the amount added each time, then add the results and divide each total by 10, you come up with a series of numbers which represent the ratio of distances with surprising accuracy.

Thus, we might wonder whether the concept of order has anything to do with Mars's astrological function. The Mars of

* Has dominion
** Exerts a strengthening influence

mythology certainly shows a passion for law and order which seems at times to consort oddly with his other passions.

Mars was the legitimate son of Jupiter by his second wife and official Olympian consort, Juno. The Romans placed Mars second in rank to his father. They relied on him for victory in war and gave his name to the month of March, where his fiery planet rises to begin the zodiacal year.

Like soldiers of every time and nation, Mars had his tender side. He fell in love with Venus. Even after Jupiter married her to Vulcan in payment for the forging of the Jovian thunderbolts, and she had taken many other lovers, Mars remained faithful in his fashion.

His methods of keeping his mistress in hand were crude but effective. When Venus took to the woods with a handsome youth named Adonis, Mars turned himself into a wild boar and gored Adonis to death. Of course the young man should have known better than to go. Mars Silvanus was the clearer of forests, and either the wolf or the woodpecker, both sacred to him, would be sure to sound the alarm. Legend says it was the woodpecker who tattled and that Venus reddened the bird's head with the blood of her slain lover, shrieking furiously, "*Sanguis eius in caput tuum erit!*" Presumably, incidents of this sort merely added spice to the wooing, since the relationship between Mars and Venus is still as warm as ever.

The Romans knew Mars Silvanus as the reclaimer of farmlands, protector of crops and herds, the farmer's helper against disease and famine. Thus we see him, defender as well as aggressor, lover as well as fighter, clearer-away of the confusions which stand in the way of spiritual growth.

Mars is the general who lines up your personal army of thoughts and feelings which have been created through Venus and marches them off to win what he believes are your chosen goals. Like his ancient prototype, however, astrological Mars loves the battle for its own sake. He will fight on either the right or the wrong side with equal zest, so you can see why it is vital that you use Mercury to show him the road you want him to take.

Mars is the *achiever*. He can and will perform whatever task you set. In order to win your goals, you must let him know beyond any question exactly what you want. Venus must draw him a definite mental picture of the objectives he is to attain. The more details she puts in, the less chance he has of going astray.

When you build up a positive image of yourself as a certified public accountant, a prima ballerina, a perfect physical specimen, a helpless invalid, a millionaire, a bum, or whatever you honestly want to be, you set Mars in motion. This force will keep struggling to bring the desire into manifestation for so long as you hold the image firmly in mind and continue to work at it.

Please note that key word, *work*. Mars is no dreamer. Physical action is necessary in his operation. Your body must expend energy so that he can marshal each act into a further step toward your goal.

You can see why it is necessary to pinpoint your target. If you scatter your thoughts and aspirations in several directions, Mars won't have the slightest idea which way you want him to go. Your army of energy-charges will mill around in confusion, causing you to waste time and strength in getting nowhere. Should you tire of the struggle and start drawing pictures of failure, Mars will assume the plan of battle has been changed and fight just as fiercely to achieve your ruin as he would have done to win your success.

Often, especially during the first twenty or so years of a life cycle, we find it hard to focus on exactly what we want to do. While the Mercury force is ready and willing to map out a road, the confusion of available choices is so great that we simply can't make up our minds which route we want to travel. Here's where Mars Silvanus comes in. We can use him to clear away the mental tangles so that it will be easier to determine which paths are most appealing to us.

A simple method of setting Mars Silvanus to work is to begin putting our physical surroundings in order. Merely weeding out a few useless possessions can spark a train of thought which will result in decisions as to what we do and do not want in our lives. Arranging one's desk or workbench so that every tool or piece of material is in the most convenient spot helps us to use energy efficiently. Packing a knapsack or suitcase to carry everything we need in the least possible space and the most comfortable balance leads us to meditate on the relevance of where we're going and what we intend to do when we get there. The more habits of orderliness we form in our physical lives, the easier it becomes to concentrate on organizing our ideas into constructive actions. Disorder tends to confuse and frustrate, and who needs any more confusion and frustration than we have to cope with already?

The love affair between Mars and Venus is forever being revealed in the sensual beauty of order. Great artists are great organizers. Anybody who tries to tell you that his soul is too loftily artistic for such mundane things as neatness simply has not grasped the essence of art.

Granted, Michelangelo wore his dogskin stockings until the skin peeled from his legs when he took them off, but he didn't do it to be arty. He was preoccupied by the drive to complete a superhuman work in an incredibly short time, and he had the genius to complete it. If we have leisure to sit around chatting about our emotional reactions to Life and Art and whatnot, we have time enough to straighten our rooms and take a bath. The action may teach us more than the conversation. It will be a positive Martian action: a touching of objects, physical movement, sensual experience of water-on-skin, a stirring-up of nerve ends and blood vessels, a purification rite. It will be a change.

"God grant me the serenity to accept the things I cannot change, the courage to change the things I can, and the wisdom to know the difference." We have heard this prayer uttered by drug addicts in maximum-security prisons, seen it embroidered by sweet little ladies on samplers for their grandchildren. While we may or may not feel any need to badger the Almighty for what He has already given us the power to realize within ourselves, we respond sympathetically to the idea it expresses.

The wisdom to know the difference. The grace to confront a

problem squarely and say, "This is what is wrong. This is what I personally can do toward setting it right. The rest is beyond my personal sphere of responsibility. I will not waste my time and energy fretting about that part. I will do the task that lies at my own hand." Have you ever honestly tried to do that in every experience of your life? Have you ever entirely succeeded?

At bottom, every honest person is an anarchist. We know perfectly well that the only workable form of government is self-government. However well we organize our executive, legislative, and administrative departments of government, they cannot work any better than the collective efforts of the people who run them, and nobody can contribute more to the collective effort than the good, bad, and mediocre things he is able to express through his own personality. The government is not a thing apart. It is you, and you are it.

Let's not get any notions that any one of us can save the world, however. We can't save any part of it except ourselves. You are no more or less your brother's keeper than he is yours. The Mars force at your disposal is the same as everybody else's, no better and no worse, just as the energy which propels a bullet is the same for the good guy and the bad guy. Mars is only a soldier. A soldier does not assume single-handed the responsibility for winning or losing a war. His duty is to obey orders, to carry out the job assigned to him with every ounce of his strength.

We must fight if we want victory. We must strive to win the faith that we have the ability to become reasonable, honest, loving people. We must batter down every negative thought and impulse. We must overcome every apparently hostile circumstance that is blocking the way to a better life. We can't force others to fight along with us, but we can help them to fight for themselves. As a soldier can inspire his comrades by showing bravery and fortitude under fire, we can set an example to those around us by maintaining our sanity and good humor in situations which can provoke anger or despair.

It's not easy being both general and private in a one-person army, having to map out the campaigns and man the barricades, fire the guns, and patch up the wounds. Mars in our charts is a call to battle, and the war can be a long and tough one. However, we do not need to label every Martian aspect "malefic," as is too often done. Some astrologers still tend to overemphasize the angry, aggressive side of Mars, just as some members of the Women's Liberation Front are making a *grande histoire* about the brutal domination of the female by the male.

It is physically possible for a man to rape a woman, but not for a woman to rape a man. His sex organ is designed to give and hers to receive. Even if a female tries to force a male by threats and weapons to have intercourse with her, he can always plead impotence. He probably won't dare, though, because he has been brainwashed into believing that if he can't perform on command, he has no right to call himself a man.

That penis which all females were once supposed to covet may not be such an unmixed blessing as Freud almost succeeded in making us believe. Being a man can be infinitely lonelier, more difficult, and less rewarding than being a woman, not only in regard to sex but in every phase of human existence. One who has been trained to look questioningly behind the scenes may begin to wonder whether the current female uprising could be in any way related to the Momism which Philip Wylie excoriated in *Generation of Vipers*.

Could some of our latter-day Amazons be trying, whether or not they realize it, to become such blatant caricatures of the devouring monster Mom that humanity will laugh her out of existence and start afresh to create a truer and more beautiful image of what a woman should be? Is the cry, "Male chauvinist pigs!" really a ribald oink from the Old Sow herself? With a woman, it's always safer to listen to what she means than what she says.

This is not to ridicule the basic concept of the Women's Liberation Movement or the good faith of its members. Mutual respect between man and woman is essential to the balancing of the cosmic forces at the interpersonal level. When sympathetic understanding and sharing do not exist, the polarities go into wild fluctuation and everybody gets hurt. If woman castrates, man punishes. If she threatens, he defends himself by attacking. If she is confused as to her role, he doesn't know what to do in his.

We have learned that Mars depends on Venus to show him how his energies shall be spent. We note physical examples of this all through the usual man-woman relationships. The man earns the money to maintain the home and trusts that his wife will manage it wisely while he goes off to hunt for the next day's food. The male gives the female his sperm and trusts his mate will bear him a healthy son or daughter, but how does he know what's going on inside her? How does he even know it's his child that will be born? When we consider how much a man has to take on faith from a woman, we begin to have more tolerant insights as to why social and sexual taboos, repressions, and frustrations have loomed so large in our cultural history.

Mars *has* to act, has to give and keep on giving. Whether he gives a kiss on the lips or a poke on the jaw depends entirely on what Venus provokes him to do. What he gets back as a result of his act will depend on how she decides to accept it.

Venus is imagination, don't forget. If Mars punishes, she can always think of some interesting way to retaliate; and she has none of his masculine inhibitions about playing the game according to the rules. She may not be able to rape, but she can castrate and put him out of business. She can refuse to accept what he has to give, thus keeping him from doing his duty and forcing him to heap guilt upon himself. She can get along without him far better than he can manage without her, because she can use her power of fantasy to persuade herself that she's better off that way.

We talk of sublimating the aggressions, that is, of turning the Mars force-to-action toward some usefully productive or at least relatively harmless purpose. Normally, we do this by happy heterosexual relationships, by becoming absorbed in work, and by active sports. War has always been the most popular sport for young men because it channels the Mars drive at the time of life when it is most active into a form of violent action which has been pictured as the embodiment of all that is noble and courageous. Now we are beginning to understand that war is nothing but a bloody mess, with all the wrong people getting killed, so what do we do?

Mars must have an outlet for his tremendous drive, or he starts tearing the psyche to pieces. How much of the current craze for self-destruction by drugs is due to young people's realization that it is no longer fashionable to go out and take pot-shots at strangers for the glory of the Fatherland? How much is due to the fact that we've killed off so many animals that hunters now have nothing to shoot but each other? We've taken all the joy out of mass slaughter, so we're trying mass suicide and that's nowhere near so much fun.

It really should be possible to find adequate substitutes for killing. We might join a peace group, as many do, and pick quarrels with other peace groups, or stage bloody riots in the name of civil liberties. Better, we can stop fighting each other and start battling against poverty and ignorance, against diseases of our bodies, our minds, our environment. We need land armies like the Civilian Conservation Corps, which was one of the more tragic casualties of World War II. We need people to clean up our cities and our countrysides, to combat floods and forest fires, to fight erosion of our natural resources, protect our wildlife.

We need tough fighters in our legislatures, on town and city councils, as well as in national government. We need vigorous reformers in our social service systems. We need to stop demanding that somebody do something and set Mars to work ourselves. We can do it by picking up a beer can from the sidewalk, by teaching children in ways that won't paralyze them from the neck up, by doing any job that comes to hand with all our hearts and with all our might.

The battle rages everywhere. We can do all the fighting we want without hurting a soul. We have the weapons to win and we can achieve any goal, however high, once we stop handling Mars as a bloody-handed lecher and set him to work as Mars Silvanus, the clearer of land and protector of herds.

Still, Mars is primarily a lover and we have to get back to

the male-female polarity in order to comprehend the full meaning of this force. We are accustomed to speak of a marriage as a give-and-take situation. Comedians add, "Yeah, he gives and she takes," and we laugh because it's supposed to be tragic. Actually, it's very simple.

We only have to remember that when Mars gives, he expects a response. If he gives his sperm, he expects a baby, or at least the gratifying reassurance that his virility could bring one into being if he so chose. If he gives protection, he expects Venus to conjure up an image of a stalwart hero whom he and she can admire together. If he gives sustenance, he expects appreciation and affection. We ought to appreciate what we do for ourselves as well as what we do for others, but it's easiest to begin by appreciating our mates.

After all, times haven't changed all that much. What's the essential difference in motivation between the banker who buys his wife a mink and the Neanderthal man who dumped a haunch of mammoth meat at the feet of his worshipping mate? If the lady doesn't happen to be in the mood for mink or mammoth at the moment, is it his fault? Why didn't she say she'd rather have diamonds or dinosaur before she sent him out to hunt? Why can't she at least show some gratitude for his efforts to make her happy? Why can't she think of *him* for a change?

She'd better. If Mars does not receive clear, conscious direction through the image-making power of Venus, he may fall under the subtle spell of another woman.

9 · Moon

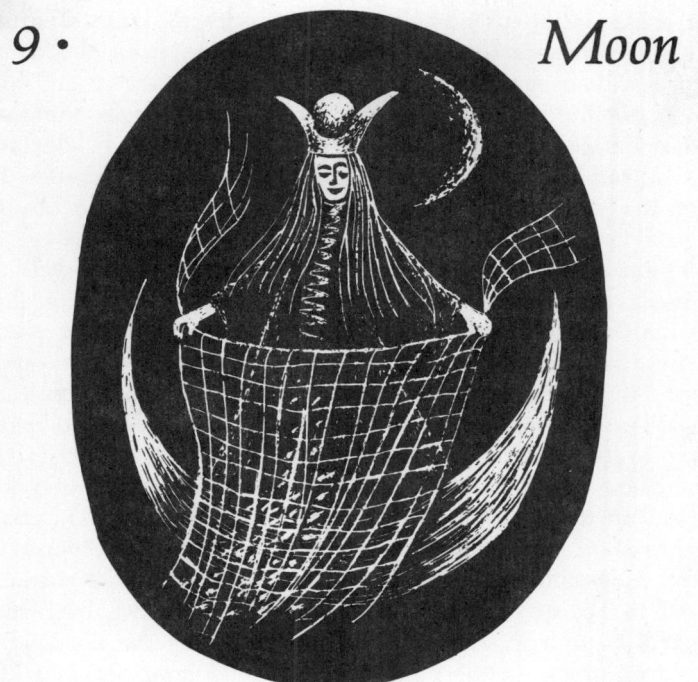

Memory, the Subconscious

COMPARED with some of the satellites in the solar system, our lone Moon appears rather impressive. Her diameter is 2,159.9 miles, over a quarter the size of Earth's. Because the Moon is so close, only 238,000 miles away, she looks as large as the Sun when seen full-face, although she is only about 1/465,000 as bright, ± 20% depending on position.

Data brought back from recent lunar explorations has shown us that our Moon is much older than had generally been thought. It now appears that she may be neither a captured asteroid nor a broken-off chunk of Earth, but a separate body which was formed at the same time from the same aggregation of materials.

No organic matter has been found in lunar rock samples, and no three-legged beings with antennae on their heads have rushed out to pelt arriving astronauts with green cheese. In fact, the Moon seems a dead, still place until we start checking the facts.

The worn and pitted surface of the satellite, as well as eroded rock samples brought back for study, indicate that bombardment by meteors and meteorite particles takes place constantly. There is strong evidence of ancient volcanic eruptions. Moonquakes occur at least once a day, as a result of lunar land tides, an especially severe one being recorded regularly every 28.4 days, when the Moon is closest to Earth. There are small oscillations in orbital motion which may be related in some way to interesting formations called Mascons, or areas of mass concentration which have been found to affect man-made satellites orbiting close to the lunar surface.

All in all, our Moon is a busier body than we ever suspected, though we still don't know everything she does. This was true of the goddess Luna, details of whose personal life are hard to pin down. She seems to have taken on as many identities at various times as her namesake does faces during the lunar month.

Luna's early identification with Selene, who was a sister of Eos the Dawn and Helios the Sun, strikes us as reasonable, although she was later identified with Artemis and Diana. She has been worshipped as the White Goddess, the Great White Cat, the Old Sow, and in divers other forms. It is easy to graft personalities on to this placid silver disk, when her own has been so elusive.

Yet the Moon is the cosmic force whose influence is usually next in importance to the Sun's in our astrological charts and in our daily perception of life. She is one of the two "Lights" of the zodiac, as of our sky.

We have not the same awe of Luna as of Sol. She cannot

blind us with her dazzle, sear us with her heat, or leave us to freeze in the dark. She just sits up there looking pretty, sometimes showing only a sliver of her crescent, sometimes peeking coyly out from behind a veil of cloud, sometimes revealing herself in full reflection of the greater light which gives her the means to cast a feeble illumination on the planet that holds her in its gravitational embrace.

The Moon would have no relevance for us without the Sun and the Earth, yet both could undoubtedly get along without her. She's something like a celestial domestic cat, in fact. We tend to wonder if our planet just keeps her for a pet. Even before our astronauts started using her for a garbage dump and a golf course, we treated her with offhand flippancy. We started rumors that she was made of green cheese, that she was the North Wind's cookie. Our popular songwriters bossed her around: Shine on, Harvest Moon; Carolina Moon, keep shining; Chrome-plated Moon over Miami, shine on my love and me. Obediently, she kept shining. What else can a moon do?

You'd be surprised.

For one thing, she can show us how astrology works. We understand that it is not the Moon herself but the gravitational pull between her and the Earth which controls the ebb and flow of tides; influences mental illness, crime, and emotional moods; affects the retention and release of moisture in human and other bodies. Knowing this, we find it less difficult to think about general concepts of cosmic forces. Noting the cyclical nature of the Moon's influences, we get a more concrete picture of the cyclicity of all being.

The Moon may be our celestial housecat, but pets do affect the families they live with. Many a household revolves around its cat! And often the Moon sign reveals more about a person than any other sign in his chart, particularly in regard to his interpersonal relationships.

Summing up what we've learned so far, we see the push-pull activities of Saturn and Jupiter keeping the wheel of life spinning. We see Mercury pointing out directions, Venus and

Mars engaged in the active, orderly creation of experience. But where is Venus getting the raw materials for her image making?

We have observed that imagination is compounded of memory and emotion. We find that emotion is generated by the interplay of masculine and feminine polarities. We can define memory as a trace left by a previously completed experience. Some memories are vivid enough to stay in our conscious minds, but most get tucked away in that dark storehouse we call the subconscious. Because impressions are constantly piling in, we easily lose the trail which leads to a particular memory. We forget.

But forgetting is not losing. Psychoanalytic methods are based on the dredging-up of memories to which access has temporarily been blocked, so we know they're down there somewhere. We have discussed what an active role forgotten memories may play in the image-making processes which determine the course of our lives without our knowing it. We knowingly use conscious memory, of course, but we tack on a great deal more to it than we realize in the process of developing a thought germ into a tangible experience.

The Moon is the librarian in charge of *memory*. It is she who takes the request for information which Mercury brings from the conscious level. She scurries back and forth among the stacks, fetching the appropriate reference materials to be elaborated and acted upon. She never makes a mistake, because she always does exactly as she is told.

Luna will travel any distance through time and space to find what you want. If your personal resources are not sufficient for your purpose, she will dip freely into the limitless ocean of the collective subconscious. It is vital to realize, however, that she will obey a veiled hint even more readily than a direct command, because this is apt to be a more accurate reflection of your real want than the wish you consciously voice.

If you insist that you want added responsibilities in your work, for instance, but your inner self whispers that you're afraid you can't handle them, Lady Moon will hear the whisper louder than the words and amiably set about cooking your goose. Since you're trying to build your ego by pretending that you feel able to cope with a bigger job, she will cooperate by arranging your failure so that it seems to be somebody else's fault. Your associates will sympathize over your unjust defeat. Your ego will have a lovely time licking its wounds and getting its fur stroked. And somewhere deep inside, that little voice will be whispering, "Whew! What a relief to be off that hook!"

The popular expression, "Don't kid yourself," is a pleonasm. You *can't* kid yourself. Mercury the trickster may lie, cheat, twist facts to create any illusion he likes at his own level of the conscious mind, but Luna is incapable of the smallest deceit. If Mercury points the way to treachery and confusion, she'll see that you get it, regardless of how loudly you shout for law and order. If you seek love and peace with hostility in your heart, she'll lead you straight to where the fighting is hottest. She's only doing her job, so don't blame her. If you're not getting what you think you want, it's because you have not made a conscious effort to analyze your real desires and set goals which coincide with them, or to change your desires to harmonize with your professed goals.

Astrologically, the sign which got you into your present situation can be an important clue to helping you move on to a more fulfilling way of life. The Moon's position in your natal chart is an indication of how your personality developed during your previous incarnation. This is why your Moon sign may reveal so much more about your character than the much-discussed Sun sign and may be especially helpful in showing you what sorts of impressions you tend to make on other people.

After all, if you have previously lived a long and full life with Cancer as a Sun sign, why should you expect to burst forth from the womb as a Leo pure and simple at your next birth? Does a youth shed every vestige of childhood on the day he turns twenty-one?

Logically, we should expect to retain subliminal memories of how we exploited our Cancerian potentialities both positively and negatively in the same way that we recall and use the experiences of our recent childhood. We may continue to dwell within this frame of reference, repeating the same acts and thoughts until they have worn deep habit patterns, dug ruts we find hard to scramble out of. Or we may seek to blend the old with the new into an increasingly rich personality structure. Either way, Luna will be happy to oblige.

Since mental ills stem from incorrect use of experience and attempts to interfere with the normal growth cycle, the Moon's position in relation to other planets, and particularly its house position, can give important insights on mental ailments. The Moon does not always mean madness—far from it—but it can help to show where the blocks lie. It also helps to clarify that much-misunderstood question of karma with respect to the unpaid debts carried over from previous lives, as we shall see later when we discuss the reading of charts.

Her ability to float at will around that limitless sea of shared memory which we call the collective unconscious gives the Moon a vital role in forming and maintaining interpersonal relationships. Seizing obediently upon every nuance of thought and feeling, she carries the threads back and forth, weaving between two souls an exquisite web of sympathy and understanding or an ugly snarl of resentments and hostilities, whatever pattern emerges from the materials we give her to work with. Remember that she cannot control what she does. She can't reason or plan. As the astronomical Moon only reflects the light which comes to her from the Sun, so the astrological Moon only reflects the light we send down from the conscious personality. She cannot lie, but she can mirror a false image.

Because we are always in transit, the problem of distinguishing what we have been from what we are trying to become leaves us wondering what we are now. And if we don't know, who does? And if we can't find some way to be at peace with ourselves, will it be surprising if we tend toward war with others? Our Sun in Leo may roar and purr and bask in the assurance that we're everybody's favorite pussycat, but if our Moon in Cancer is off in some dark corner crabbing about how our so-called friends never appreciate what we do for them, this cat's got problems. Always make sure you thoroughly understand both signs so that you can strike a workable balance between them and not be torn by conflicts of intellect and emotion.

Reconciling the past with the present is the easiest thing imaginable. All we have to do is realize how many treasures of past experience we have at our disposal, and let the Moon know exactly what we want her to do with them, now, at this precise moment in our eternal existence.

And let's remember that Luna is a lady. If we rant and scold at her, she'll just get flustered and fall to pieces. A gentle hint will accomplish more than a rough command. Talking about how desperately we want something and then making no physical effort to go after it shows her that we really meant exactly the opposite of what we said, and she'll assemble her data accordingly.

Make a conscious, definite decision as to what you want. Write it down to help you remember, but don't show it to anybody. Don't discuss it any more than you absolutely have to. Use Venus to elaborate on the details, forming the clearest possible picture in your mind. Set Mars in motion by taking some positive physical action which relates directly to your goal. Immediately, Moon will start cooperating with the other forces, bringing them whatever mindstuff they need to accomplish your purpose.

This is genuine magic. We see how the cosmic forces combine to make your wishes come true. But we still haven't solved that basic dilemma, how do you know what you want? What is the goal which the Life Force, working within you, has set for this particular step of your journey? To see our way clearly, we need a brighter light than Luna's. We need the strongest light there is.

10 · Sun Consciousness, the Ego

SINCE we are living in a solar ecology, we already know a good deal about how the Sun works. For the record, however, we should have statistics by which to compare it with other bodies. As suns go, ours apparently doesn't amount to much, being only 860,000 miles around as defined by the photosphere, that part of the surface which shows up as a solid disk in photographs. Since this mass is 1,300,000 times the size of Earth and about 750 times the combined mass of all other bodies in its system, however, to us it seems very large indeed.

We cannot look at the Sun directly without injuring our eyes; however, we can study it through heavy filters, by photography, and by Galileo's method of projecting an image through the eyepiece of a telescope onto a white card. What we see is not a solid object but a sphere of gas burning at about 6,000° C. on the surface and reaching temperatures of 20,000,000°C. at the center. The average density of the photosphere is slightly above that of water, about one quarter of Earth's density; the solar center, though still in a gaseous state, is nine times as dense as iron.

The Sun rotates on its axis in about 25 days at the equator and 34 days at the poles. Its direction of rotation is east to west, which is the same direction in which the planets orbit around the Sun. We can easily measure its rotation by the sunspots which wax and wane in intensity within eleven-year cycles, in zones between 8° and 35° north and south of the Sun's equator. These show up in a spectrohelioscope as gases whirling in an up-and-down circulatory movement, which does not surprise anybody familiar with astrological theory.

Modern atomic theorists have dispelled some of the old anxieties about whether the Sun would burn itself out and leave us to perish in the cold. No doubt our source of light and heat will lose the power to re-create itself some day, but we now have reason to believe that our Sun is both much older and much younger than early physicists surmised. It is the closest thing to immortality we can perceive in our world, though, according to ancient legend, one of the immortals almost permitted it to destroy our planet.

Phoebus Apollo was originally a humble agricultural deity in charge of exterminating mice. Being exceptionally handsome as well as strong and capable, however, he was soon given the exalted task of driving the chariot of Helios the Sun.

One evening after Apollo had brought the flaming chariot safely through its journey, a comely youth appeared at the Olympian court and introduced himself as the son of Apollo by a nymph named Clymene. Torn between guilt and pride, Apollo offered to grant the lad any boon within his power. Immediately, Phaëton demanded that he be allowed to drive Helios on his next daily round.

Apollo protested that to handle the fiery steeds took both superhuman strength and unshakable courage, but Phaëton held him to his promise. The sorrowing father turned over the reins with many warnings which his headstrong son promptly forgot.

Long before the chariot reached the zenith, Phaëton had lost control. Without guidance, the frightened horses plunged up among the stars, sending a rain of comets and meteors through the heavens. Then they plunged headlong toward Earth, scorching farmlands, setting fire to homes and trees, drying up lakes and streams.

In desperation, Mother Earth cried out to Jupiter, "Save me and my loved ones!" The ruler of the gods hurled a thunderbolt, blasting Phaëton out of existence and scaring the horses back into their proper orbit. Only by this drastic act was our solar system rescued from being destroyed to gratify the whim of a conceited boy.

As the sun-horses ran away with Phaëton, so has the Sun sign run away with astrology, and sometimes the results have been almost as disastrous. When the Sun is the center of the solar system, all is well. When it strayed out of its place, it destroyed what its energy had been given to create. If we try to interpret our individual Sun sign out of context, disregarding all the balancing forces which give it meaning and function, we send it plunging and rearing into illogic, and straighter thinkers quite justifiably shoot the astrologer down in flames.

Of course astrologers are not wrong in agreeing that the Sun sign is the focal point of any chart in the same way that the Sun is the focal point of our physical existence. It's just that we have to understand and appreciate it for what it is. Today, we are told that our Sun is probably one of the feeblest and puniest stars in the Universe. For all we know, ours may be the least of an infinitude of solar systems on whose planets live beings beside whom we Earthlings would appear less important and amiable than a swarm of cockroaches do to a housewife.

We may have come from such systems. We may be going on to such a one when our experiences here have made us strong enough to endure a brighter light. Knowing as we now do that matter is composed of nothing else than energy and order, we have no reason to doubt our ability to travel freely in time and space during our periods of immateriality. Theoretically, we ought to be able to manifest wherever Mercury directs us to go.

It is tempting to speculate on such possibilities, but the probabilities are that we shan't be going anywhere except back into the same old rut if we fail to cope effectively with the specific life which we are living now, here on Earth.

And why should we despise our Sun or ourselves? Is this golden splendor of ours less radiant than Vega or Betelgeuse merely because it happens to be smaller in diameter? Is our capacity for growth lower than any other being's because the quality of our life experience has not yet reached the level of his?

As far as we can determine, every being everywhere has the same raw materials to work with. Fundamentally, we have found no way in which we differ. Nevertheless, every one of us knows himself as an individual. We feel in our spirits, our minds, our physical bodies a sense of personal identity. Each of us knows himself to be unique and in a sense he is, since we each have selected different image-making materials and developed them in different ways.

It is this concept of selfhood, this ability to say, "I am," which astrology attributes to the Sun force. Our present Sun sign is the essential ego idea around which we are now in process of building the manifestation of this incarnation. We are not yet a Libra, a Scorpio, or whatever, any more than a child is yet a man or woman. We have set the stage for becoming that sort of adult. Everything which we have been and done until now is directing us toward that immediate goal.

Jesus Christ said, "Except ye be born again, ye cannot enter the Kingdom of Heaven." This same emphasis on rebirth keeps cropping up in religious baptism rites, in initiation ceremonies of secret societies, in cosmetic ads: "You'll feel like a new person"; "Younger than springtime"; "Skin like a baby's"; "You positively won't know yourself." Except ye be born again, the boys won't love you, the girls won't go to bed with you, doom and gloom will follow you all the days of your life, and your teeth will fall out and you'll be old. Old! Old, unless you let us con you into buying our particular brand of magic.

Be younger! Be thinner! Be blonder! Be anything except what you are. We seem to spend our lives trying to run away from ourselves and of course it's impossible. Inevitably, we become what the chain of events we set in motion is directing us to be. The road takes us where the road goes.

But who says we can't change our course? We are always adding new events to our storehouse of memory. Cosmic forces are always working within us to develop new images and put them into action. Positive and negative polarities are always seeking to balance themselves. We are always changing physically, so of course we can change our patterns of spiritual development.

The physical sun from which we receive our energy vibrations is certainly not stable. Astronomers tell us that it is nothing but a ball of gases, constantly devouring and rekindling itself, held together solely by the regenerative force of its own combustion. Photographs show that it fluctuates in size, sending a sudden flash streaming into the void, then dying back upon itself.

A human personality may flame for a while, then go into temporary eclipse. A star is always being born. Fame and obscurity are nothing but sunshine and shadow, and we can perceive each only in terms of the other. To pretend that my light is of a finer quality than yours because it may happen at the moment to be flaring wider is humbug. If I claim mine is better, I'm a liar. If you believe me, you're deluding yourself, and cheating yourself of your own right to shine.

Children are quite capable of behaving like greedy little savages but they do not generally discriminate against their peers on "I'm richer, blacker, whiter, bigger, littler, prettier," or such grounds until their elders have taught them to make these sorts of distinctions. The more ways we teach a child to feel superior, the more chances we're giving him to be miserable. Sooner or later he's bound to meet somebody in any given category who has more of whatever it is than he does.

Train a child to look for distinctions, and he'll find them. When he fails to empathize, he will begin to see other people as alien, possibly threatening. He will start to know fear, and fear will beget hostility. Anybody who does not conform to his own standards of appearance, ideas, and living habits becomes a potential foe, and he soon learns that the best defense is attack. It is this mishandling of ego which is directly, solely, and immediately responsible for every personal and interpersonal conflict we have ever faced.

Yes, you are special. Yes, you are unique, wonderful, fascinating. Yes, you are a center of light no less splendid than that which creates and sustains all being. No, you do not have to be born again as something entirely new and different. You have to die out of your silly old ideas and see yourself for what you are.

Lately there has been an epidemic of nudity. "Strip off your borrowings and let the world see the real you," sounds like a profound idea. But can we honestly believe that staring at each other's bellybuttons is going to put us in touch with Truth and Beauty? Until we can train our eyes to see beyond the warts and the pimples, through to the blazing spirit which shines alike in the clad and the unclad, nakedness of body will net us nothing but goosebumps.

Being born again means being renewed in spirit. It means forgetting all the nonsense we've learned about being different. It means being able to see the world full of light and joy and opportunities to love, as a child sees it before we teach him to blind his eyes to the wonders around him.

To become children of the Sun in action as well as in fact, we must locate the light within ourselves. This is not a matter of ascending some astral height by mysticism, but a simple exercise anybody can perform, on a day-to-day basis. We start building ourselves up, but we never, never tear anybody else down.

Here is another practical bit of white magic. Begin to regard your mind and body as close personal friends of the essential you. Get rid of the old "I, me, my, mine." Address yourself in the second person (mentally, if you're self-conscious about doing it aloud). That way, you can pay yourself little compliments without feeling conceited. You can praise yourself for a job well done, whether or not anybody else does.

Cultivating this attitude of detached friendliness toward yourself helps you see how much fun you are to be with. You begin to place a truer value on yourself as a human being. You learn how much a kind word can mean, so you start expressing kindness and generous praise toward others. You start searching out more things of which you can approve, performing more positive acts which set off chain reactions that actually do turn you into a happier, friendlier, more loving and beloved person.

Be as kind to your body as you are to your emotions. Feed it wholesome foods that taste good. Keep it trim and supple with adequate exercise. Please it with surroundings that are full of light and color and fresh air. Teach it to breathe properly. Wash it free of germs and dirt to keep it healthy. Dress it in comfortable, attractive clothing which shows it off to best advantage. A child of the Sun is not afraid to shine.

Pamper yourself with any pleasure which adds to your sense of well-being without infringing on anyone else's. Keep your hair, your teeth, every part of you glowing with loving care. Train your mouth to smile, your voice to speak with warmth and enthusiasm, your eyes to express delight in what they see. Show by every act that you're conscious of being among the shining ones. This is not selfish sensuality. You're not doing it just for yourself.

In *The Phenomenon of Man*, Teilhard de Chardin speaks of "The threefold property possessed by every consciousness: (i) of centering *everything* partially upon itself; (ii) of being able to center itself upon itself *constantly*; and (iii) of being brought *more* by this very super-centration *into association with all the other centers surrounding it*."

The more we become aware of the goodness within us, the more we learn to love ourselves as an expression of what a human being is able to become, the stronger becomes our faith in the capabilities for love and fellowship of which we become conscious in all mankind.

Each of us is climbing the path with a hand stretched above and a hand reached below. We help and are helped. We learn and we teach. By developing the potentialities of our present Sun sign into a deeper understanding and appreciation of the eternal self, we send a brighter illumination back to aid those who are struggling behind us and a stronger beam forward to light the way we have yet to go.

We cannot keep the joy of living to ourselves, any more than we can shut up a sunbeam in a box. We cannot imprison present happiness without turning it into future misery. We can only love each moment and let it go, confident that we carry the Sun within ourselves as we move on within its eternal light.

11 · Uranus Inspiration and Change

THE first of the three "invisible" planets, Uranus, is about 3.7 times bigger than Earth. Like Jupiter, it is considerably flattened at the poles. A year on Uranus equals more than 84 Earth years, but the planet rotates in slightly less than 15 hours. The most puzzling fact about this rotation is that the axis is inclined 98°, almost lying in the orbital plane. This implies a retrograde motion for which nobody so far has been able to suggest a reasonable explanation. As no other planet has an inclination of more than 29°, we immediately suspect that this planet is going to show us some astrological surprises.

Even the planet's discovery did not follow the usual pattern. On March 13, 1781, a British musician named Herschel spotted the greenish disk in a seven-inch reflecting telescope which he had made himself. At first he thought it must be a comet. When further study showed it was a planet, it was learned that various other observers had actually spotted Uranus but mistakenly catalogued it as a star. Anyway, Herschel got the credit, and we sometimes find Uranus called after his name in old almanacs. The discoverer himself wanted to call it *Georgium Sidus* after George III. It was Bode's suggestion that the new planet be called Uranus, and the appropriateness of the name caused it to stick.

Physically, Uranus must be similar to Jupiter and Saturn, although no noticeable cloud belts have been observed. We do know that the planet has five satellites, the largest of which is Titania, almost 625 miles in diameter. These revolve in steeply inclined, retrograde orbital paths in the same plane as Uranus's axis of revolution.

So even though we know little about Uranus, we can assume that whatever happens here is going to be far different from anything we've encountered so far.

The Uranus of mythology was god of the Heavens. He married Gaea, the Earth Goddess, and fathered the twelve Titans. We have already learned how Saturn rebelled against paternal authority and how Venus was supposed to have emerged as a result of his savage but spectacular act. Taken at face value, this is a pretty thin story. Symbolically, however, it makes an interesting point.

In the marriage of Heaven and Earth, we see the union of superconscious and conscious. In the severance of the father's fecundative organ, we see the end of Uranus's power to fertilize Gaea, that is, of the superconscious's direct involvement with conscious. We see the separation of spirit and matter.

The organ falls into the sea which, as we know from our discussion of the Moon, is symbolically connected with the subconscious. Obviously it has not lost its ability to function, because Venus immediately pops up from the spot where it enters the water. So we may see the legend as a whimsical but dramatic picturization of how the divine seed, the creative spark, the flash of inspiration, or whatever we choose to call it, descends directly from superconscious to subconscious, setting in motion the process of materialization which eventually manifests itself in consciousness.

In astrology it is this generative flash, this ignition point of the urge-to-become which we equate with the planet Uranus. Only once in a while, when we are especially aware of our own life processes, do we perceive inspiration as a direct experience, but it happens all the time. It is the moment when the sperm pierces the egg, when the latent idea seed is stimulated to start multiplying within the womb of Venus. It is the beginning of life-in-action.

Uranus and the other two outermost planets, Neptune and Pluto, are *higher octave* forces. They were not used by exoteric astrologers until after they had been located by astronomers (Pluto was not discovered until 1936), however, their places in the cosmic system had long been known and described.

It is rather surprising that so few, not even Reuven Shomroni who writes so interestingly and informatively on Jewish astrology, seem to have connected these three planets with the Cabalistic "Mother Letters" of the Hebrew Flame Alphabet. However, Uranus, Neptune, and Pluto have not been given a capricious scramble of attributes and hurled at random into the zodiac, as has been contended. Astrology will be working with them more intensively as time goes on, and it is most important that we develop more understanding of their functions.

Because the three higher octave planets move so slowly, they are especially influential in terms of the overall social picture. The reason we look forward to the Age of Aquarius with mounting excitement is that Uranus co-rules that sign. He makes us expect changes, thrills, adventures; sends us rushing off in unexpected directions to find the gold at the end of the rainbow.

Uranus is the higher octave of Mercury. Here, the versatile is raised to the volatile. Uranus does not merely surprise; he astonishes. Not content with showing us existing roads, he cuts a channel through the mountains where nobody thought a road could ever be made. Uranus is a blast of wind blowing us off the treadmill, the tornado that carries Dorothy to Oz.

In your natal chart, Uranus is the door to freedom. His position, his aspects to other signs and planets are clear guideposts showing you how to move upward and outward.

Sometimes the road takes unexpected twists and turns. What appears most trivial can be a springboard to great changes. Think back to some momentous turning point in your life. What actually triggered the chain of events which brought it to fruition? Was it a casual encounter with someone you'd never met before? A conversation you overheard on the subway? A minor accident? An absurd television drama? Whatever it appeared to be, that was Uranus pulling another rabbit out of the cosmic hat.

Where Mercury is the trickster, Uranus is the magician. He performs his feats of legerdemain in full view of the audience, deceiving only those who are willing to be fooled. And that includes most of us, because we do love to believe in magic. We like to think that taking a vitamin pill or a shot of penicillin will make us healthier than waging a prosaic day-to-day battle against malnutrition and unsanitary living conditions. We want to believe that turtle oil or cucumber juice or moose milk can keep us young and beautiful forever, that owning a Porsche or an ankh or a mink or a mandala will imbue us with some irresistible charisma. We like to pretend that some outside force will do the work while we sit back and enjoy the rewards. So we stick a wand in Uranus's hand and throw the black cloak of mystery over his back and hail him as the great god Mumbo Jumbo.

Right now, a surprising amount of old-fashioned nastiness is being peddled about in the guise of modern thought. Before long, we'll undoubtedly be seeing more of it. The Age of Aquarius won't be all sweetness and light and understanding. Already we've seen college girls dressing up as witches and casting murrains all over the covers of national magazines. Book clubs offer do-it-yourself guides to becoming a warlock, although nobody is quite sure what a warlock is. John Wellington Wells is opening branches in all major distribution areas. That old black magic has us in its spell, and aren't we having one hell of a time for ourselves!

Magic exists, make no mistake about that. Witchcraft can be worked, not by muttering spells but by making your victims believe in their efficacy. It is perfectly possible to acquire domination over the minds of others, to make them do your bidding. You can send out vibrations of hatred. You can commit murder by willing someone to die, and no jury will be able to convict you. But even though legal machinery for hanging or burning witches is no longer functioning, you will not escape punishment.

There is nothing in the world more powerful than an idea. Learning to concentrate on a specific goal enables us to accomplish what may look like miracles, for either good or ill. But it must be emphasized over and over again that people who do such things are *not* endowed with special powers. They are only making a stronger than average effort to harness forces available to everybody. They are not different from us except in the sense that everybody is unique. It would be unwise and unkind for us to encourage them in their delusions by paying them homage.

If you suspect someone of trying to exercise undue influence over you, by witchcraft or other means, here is an effective piece of countermagic. Place the tip of the right thumb against the end of the nose. Extend your four fingers and waggle them gently in the direction of the self-styled witch or warlock, while he's looking at you. Make no attempt to reverse the spell except by showing you refuse to accept it. That will be taken care of without your having to incur a karmic debt of revenge.

The increasing influence of Uranus on our lives is also being displayed in many more attractive ways. One may be seen in our sudden realization of the need to decontaminate our environment. As we draw closer to the Age of Aquarius, we shall, and certainly should, make increased efforts to clean up our land, water, and especially our air. Any practical student of astrology will throw himself wholeheartedly into the ecological struggle, realizing that fresh air is the life breath in the transcendental as well as the physical sense.

Uranus is specifically identified with the first Cabalistic Mother Letter, Aleph, and with the element Air. This fact may help to explain why trick breathing is so often involved in the rites of the cults we have just been discussing. Some of these practices can be extremely harmful unless they are done under the active supervision of a competent teacher, and not everyone who sets himself up as a teacher may fully understand what he's doing. It is true that correct breathing is essential for the stimulation of the physical vehicle in order to absorb and act upon higher teaching; but for most of us, special breathing exercises should be confined to the simple ones we've probably learned in gym class somewhere along the line. The thing is to perform them regularly. Here is one which can be done with benefit and without danger:

> Stand in a well-ventilated room or out in the fresh air. Slowly tense the muscles below the rib cage, expelling all the air from your lungs. Now relax the muscles gradually and allow air to flow into your lungs. Do not attempt to suck in air; just let it come. You will feel the pressure in your rib cage and in the small of your back if you're doing it properly.
>
> When the lungs are completely filled, exhale slowly by compressing the muscles again, and repeat four times. Try to perform the entire exercise without making the slightest sound.

Repeat this exercise four times a day, and oftener if you wish. You will find it especially helpful in a tense situation. If necessary in an emergency, you may call upon the power of Mercury to concentrate on breathing slowly, rhythmically, and noiselessly. You may almost have to force your muscles to perform the first contraction and expansion if you are frightened or under great pressure. However, you will find that the next breaths come with increasing ease and will have a remarkably calming and encouraging effect. You will feel refreshed, strengthened. You will be bringing the power of Uranus to bear on your situation, and a solution will be opened to you.

Note that you do not attempt to call down some mystic power from outside and bend it to your will. You use a simple method which is always available to you, putting your body to work at clearing your mind. You stop fighting against the current and start moving in the Jupiter-Saturn rhythm which is expressed microcosmically in your breathing.

It's no coincidence that the element we associate with atomic energy is called uranium; the power of the atom is the power of Uranus. We now know of two ways to release it: through fission and through fusion.

In fission the heaviest atoms are split apart. The release of energy deposits radioactive waste which is extremely difficult to cope with, and potentially lethal to all life on our planet.

In fusion the lightest atoms are fused together. Release of energy by this process does not leave radioactive waste. Therefore, we can use it to benefit mankind without setting up the possibility of destroying that which we are trying to improve.

The parallel is obvious. Black magic is powerful. You can blast your enemies right off the face of the Earth with it, once you learn the knack. This is fission. You are using "heavy" mindstuff to split yourself off from human beings made up of the same elements as yourself. By so doing, you set up both the tragedy of wanton destruction and the dreadful problem of how you're going to work off the karmic guilt you've incurred.

And the bitterest part of it all is that you will be suffering a slow and agonizing retribution for nothing. You will not have achieved your wicked purpose; you'll only have performed a conjuring trick. Elementary physics teaches us that matter cannot be destroyed. Elementary common sense makes us realize that life can't be destroyed, either. Make the bunny disappear if you're willing to take the consequences. But don't try to persuade yourself that he isn't going to pop up again and give you rabbit fever.

By fusion on the other hand, by identifying ourselves with the Life Force and recognizing our responsibility to it, we can tap the power of Uranus safely and successfully. We don't have to go all noble and self-sacrificing and insist that we want nothing for ourselves. Our wants are as valid as anybody else's. But when we deal with universal forces, we must learn to think in universal terms. We must perform as eternally living and creating member units of the universe. We are too important to waste our time and strength in petty self-seeking and self-punishment.

12 · Neptune
Reversal, Forgiveness

THE planet Neptune was discovered before it was ever spotted. Two mathematicians, LeVerrier in France and John Couch Adams in England, both calculated the hypothetical position of another planet from observed discrepancies in the position of Uranus. On the same night in 1846 when he received LeVerrier's ephemeris containing the calculations, an astronomer named Galle at the Berlin Observatory instantly recognized an eighth magnitude, starlike object as the new planet. Again, it was found that Neptune had been seen and thought to be a fixed star by previous observers.

Neptune

So far, all our telescopes have shown us of this planet is a bluish disk not much bigger than a penny. In fact, Neptune is another enormous body, slightly larger than Uranus by most recent calculations and physically similar. Since Neptune takes 164.8 Earth years to complete an orbit, we still have some time to wait before it returns to the position where Galle first spotted it. Like all the oblate outer planets, however, it has a fast rotation of only 15½ hours.

What fascinates us about Neptune is not so much the planet itself as its two satellites. Triton, the brighter one, was discovered only a few weeks after the parent body. It has a retrograde orbit inclined 40° to Neptune's orbit and 20° to the planet's equator, which astronomers find most unusual; but Triton revolves demurely in an almost circular orbit. On the other hand, Nereid, which was not spotted until 1949, is the most eccentrically orbiting satellite in the entire solar system.

So it seems we can pin down Neptune easily enough once we know how he works, but the planet itself seems to have serious problems controlling its wayward satellite children. This was also the case with his Olympian prototype.

Originally, Neptune was just a big frog in a small puddle. Starting as a god of fresh water, he became identified (around 390 B.C.) with Poseidon, who was a grandson of Uranus.

This made him one of the "big three," sharing rulership of the world with his brothers Jupiter and Pluto. To Neptune then fell power over all the waters of Earth. He could raise storms, cause dreadful shipwrecks, or send favoring winds to blow mariners safely ashore. He could undermine the land with hidden rivers, dry up ponds and streams, or strike barren rock with his trident and cause life-giving springs to gush forth. As the mood seized him, he could lash himself into a frenzy or become as gentle as a bubbling rivulet.

Neptune's amours were notorious, and he begat many children. Most were wild and cruel as the sea, yet he loved and protected them, as we learn in the story of Ulysses and the Cyclops.

Have you ever tried to paint or photograph running water? However skillful you are, the result is never quite successful. Once one tries to fix fluidity, its very nature is lost. Therefore, we may well find the character of Neptune difficult to grasp. The best way is to take hold of him as Hercules did the Old Man of the Sea, and let him go through his whole bag of tricks without losing our nerve or our grip. Then at last he may tell us what we want to know.

Neptune is the higher octave of Venus, operating more on the interpersonal than the individual scale. He works in a diffused way, concerning himself with changes on the social level as well as in our personal lives, but often we're not aware of his actions until they've happened.

We might picture Venus's activities as the grapes growing on the vine and Neptune's as the bubbles in the champagne. This would be far from a comprehensive portrait, but it would give us one clue to their relationship.

There is this heady tang to Neptune. We feel it when we walk along the beach close to breaking waves. It's a sparkle, a zest that can lift the spirit, change the mood. Neptune plays on our emotions, transforms us in a moment, as a calm gray sea flashes suddenly into swirling greens and blues and purples.

Neptune intoxicates sometimes, so we connect this influence with alcohol, gases, hallucinogens, and the experiences to which they give rise. When Housman wrote, "Malt does more than Milton can to justify God's ways to man," he was writing about Neptune and confessing that he, too, had fallen for one of the Sea God's oldest wheezes.

If you've ever been the only sober guest at a drinking party or the only nonuser in a group smoking pot, you've witnessed one of Neptune's less attractive aspects. If you were one of the participants, you've experienced it firsthand. It's Neptune who sends us high, makes us feel that we're on to something magnificent, and Neptune who keeps us from realizing that it's all a sham and the Great Thoughts we're spouting are sheer drivel.

Letting Neptune work on our minds in this way is like being in a Fun House full of distorting mirrors. We see an infinitude of images and they're all ourselves. Some are amusing, some grotesque, some flattering, some frightening. Dazzled by so many reflections, we decide some profound truth must be revealed here. But all the distortions in the world can't add up to one true picture. No serious student of astrology can delude himself for one moment into thinking that drugging his mind with any form of hallucinogen or intoxicant will lead to enlightenment.

If we are curious to enter Neptune's Hall of Mirrors, nobody is going to stop us, provided we're willing to pay the price of admission. We shall find nothing there but cheating reflections of the selves and the notions we took in. We shall take out nothing except some false impressions and a gradual realization that the experience has cost us far more than the show was worth.

If we insist on lingering, we learn to our dismay that the longer we remain, the more we have to pay. Worse, we discover that what seemed amusing at first can get most damnably dull once we're hopelessly confused by the maze of reflected images and can no longer find our way out.

Neptune is co-ruler of Pisces. Perhaps that's why mankind has spent most of the Piscean Age in a stupor. Look back over the pages of history as we know it, and what do you see: the Noblest Romans spewing wine flavored with pine pitch into their *vomitoria*; the British Stiff Upper Lip curled over a flagon of the best while His Majesty's lowlier subjects sprawled in Gin Lane, dead drunk for twopence; the American Indian defeated not by the white man's superior prowess, but by the white man's firewater; self-righteous members of the Band of Hope dosing their sore throats with patent elixirs compounded of port wine and laudanum when they'd finished shouting, "Down with the Demon Rum!"

Far too many of us have not yet learned to throw off the bad habits we contracted in an earlier and wetter age. We're still lurching around in Neptune's caves hunting for illumination in the bottom of a beer can or the glowing end of a marijuana cigarette. Nevertheless, a tremendous groundswell is gathering force as we reach the last years of this era. Drugging is becoming passé. We are beginning to use Neptune in more positive ways.

Neptune is associated with the second Mother Letter of the Cabala, Mem, and with the element Water. Water reflects. Therefore, astrology attributes to Neptune the power of *reversal*.

We have discussed the Moon as a reflective power. We have seen how moonstuff is employed to build the images which are brought into manifestation through our daily experience of life. We now have a general idea of how we build our bodies, but have we wondered what they really look like?

Of course we can't see our own faces because we're behind them. And when we look into a mirror, what we see is a reversed image. In order to get a correct visualization of ourselves, we have to stand between two mirrors and look at the reflection of the reflection. If you find this hard to follow, hold a book up to a mirror. The printing will appear backward. By reflecting this reversed image into a second mirror, however, you can make the words go the right way again.

Since the images which the Moon finds for us to use in the creative process are reflected, we have a tendency to use them wrong side up. That's why the results of our efforts so often turn out to be exactly the opposite of what we thought we were aiming toward. The reversing power of Neptune can be invaluable in helping to correct our mistakes.

We know that what our senses perceive as solid substance is in fact a temporary arrangement of moving energy particles and that by making the right sort of effort we can alter the arrangement to turn the substance into something more useful. Let's take the homely example of an ice cube. How do we make one?

We start by obtaining water from any convenient source. If we exercise discretion in choosing the source, we'll have pure water to work with, and this will enable us to use the cube in more ways than if we settle for water which may be contaminated. If we choose, we may flavor or color the water. We then pour it into a mold of suitable size and shape and freeze it. The ice may then be used to cool a drink, fill an icebag, put down somebody's back at a party, or for whatever we wish.

Soon, the ice cube loses its identity by melting. The water reemerges, only to be used again in one form or another. Perhaps we drink it, retain it for a while in our tissues, then excrete it as sweat or urine. Maybe we just dump it down the sink. Whatever happens to it, the water does not cease to exist. It may go through any number of recirculation processes. It may evaporate, be drawn up by the sun into a cloud, and be dumped back on earth as rain or snow.

We never expect to get back those same hydrogen and oxygen molecules, but that's not going to prevent our making more ice cubes. We realize that we are working not with specific units of matter but with universal forces. All we need do is have faith that by filling the ice cube tray and setting it in a freezer that's working, we shall get ice, and then perform the physical act which sets the ice-making cycle in motion at the material level.

Water's infinite capacity to dissolve other substances and take on new forms gives us a physical demonstration of Neptune as the *universal solvent*. We associate Neptune with telepathy, clairvoyance, hidden relationships, and behind-the-scenes activities. Neptune has the ability to see more than meets the eye, therefore, to understand and sympathize with the innermost feelings of others. Neptune is the ability to forgive, the image changer who washes clean the slate and gently suggests that we try again, getting the picture right-side-up this time. He is not the Healer, but he can open our minds and hearts to be healed.

Where we see this planet in our personal charts, we know there is something we need to change, some aspect of our life experience which we are viewing from the wrong angle. The house in which Neptune appears and the sign to which it is linked will indicate where the problem lies. The aspects to other planets will give us valuable information on how to cope with the problems of reversing our attitudes.

In this regard, he also teaches us where to look for beauty in our lives through the manifestation of those higher, impersonal creative urges which we call the arts. Washing at the shores of all knowledge, Neptune brings to the womb of Venus from the universal sea those treasures of greater-than-conscious understanding which can emerge as painting, music, poetry. We may perform the act of manifestation ourselves, or we may share in the artist's experience by admiring his work. Both the doing and the appreciating are essential to the completion of the work.

A work of art is an act of love. Love is not fulfilled unless it is both given and received. Neptune is both the inspiration and the expression of universal love.

Because Neptune's influence is so changeable and hard to grasp, we have made many mistakes about love during the Piscean Age. We've talked about it, written about it, sung about it, fought tournaments, and made sexy movies which were supposed to have been inspired by it. We have sat at the feet of the Masters of Life and heard their divine message, but few of us have yet managed to bring it forth in our lives. We have not yet grasped the principle that the particular must be expressed in the universal and the universal in the particular. World brotherhood is essential; but no matter how many bodies are in the bed, the act of love still has to be performed on a one-to-one basis.

We don't enjoy some abstraction called Art. We share certain expressions of the artistic idea which are made available to our senses in the forms of music, sculpture, painting, poetry. In some cases, many people may be involved in the same experience, as when an audience shares an orchestra's performance of a symphony. Still, the art experience has to come together as a unity, and we each have to relate to it personally, or it just doesn't happen.

In the same way, we cannot love an abstraction called Man. We have to love each man, each woman, as an individual expression of the will-to-be; and we have to begin by loving ourselves. Now that Uranus is influencing us to be more analytical, we may begin to understand what Neptune has been trying to teach us for so many years. Love thy neighbor as thyself; not because the Bible tells you so, but because in plain chemical, physical, and spiritual fact, thy neighbor *is* thyself.

13 · Pluto Redemption, the Master-Builder

PERHAPS the most interesting thing about Pluto is that the planet was not discovered until about forty years ago, although astronomers had been looking for it since 1905 and some astrologers had postulated its existence centuries ago. We think of Pluto as lying farther from the Sun than Neptune. This was so at the time of its discovery. Today, however, and for several decades to come, Pluto is the closer of the two, since the perihelion of its highly eccentric orbit is less than Neptune's distance from the Sun.

Pluto has an orbital revolution of 248 Earth years, and a speedy rotation period of 6 days, 9 hours, 16 minutes, 54 seconds has been established on the basis of regular variations in brightness.

As yet, we don't know how big Pluto is. Some astronomers believe it to be a smallish ex-satellite of Neptune which has somehow broken free; others think it may be larger than Earth. Pluto may even be the brightest in a series of planets lying too far out from the Sun to be picked up by any equipment we now have.

Yet astrologers give Pluto great importance in the solar ecology. Since we can't explain its function in terms of the meager astronomical data now available, let's turn to mythology.

To Pluto, third son of Cronus, fell rulership of the underworld, the House of Hades. In his Stygian kingdom he held sway over the dead, the powers of darkness, and all things under the Earth.

Pluto was known as a severe and pitiless but scrupulously fair judge. Unlike his brothers Neptune and Jupiter, he could not be influenced by flattery or sacrifices.

In spite of his stern nature, however, Pluto seems to have been capable of gentle feelings. Moved by the exquisite music of Orpheus's lyre, he would have restored the dead Eurydice to her grieving husband, had not their human emotions caused them to attempt a reunion before they had returned to the sunlight. Enraptured by sight of young Proserpine, he carried her off to be his wife, hoping that the girl's fresh loveliness would relieve the gloom and loneliness of his dark domain. However, she grieved so deeply that he agreed to let her return to her mother for part of every year.

In this strange mating we find a clue to Pluto's astrological meaning; Proserpine was Springtime, and her mother was Ceres, goddess of agriculture. Pluto's carrying the maiden underground symbolizes the planting of crops, the start of the growth cycle, which takes place in total darkness. It may be recalled that the number of months Proserpine had to stay underground was determined by her having swallowed some pomegranate seeds. The pomegranate is a symbol of the female principle, the ability to bring forth young.

So we see in Pluto not merely the stern old undertaker but the god of rebirth. He is the inexorable governor of the cycle of lives and deaths from which no bribe, no entreaty can set us free but who always gives us another chance to redeem ourselves—if we don't foul it up, like Eurydice, by demanding too much too soon. In his union with Proserpine we recognize what the poets have been trying to tell us since the beginning of time: if winter comes, can spring be far behind?

Although the planet Pluto was not discovered by modern astronomers until 1930, esoteric astrologers had long ago identified his influence with the element Fire and with Shin, the third Mother Letter of the Cabala. This is the higher force of Mars, operating at the level of *universal desire, universal action,* and *reason.* Pluto is superconscious activity, the generative force which brings into manifestation the inspirations which have been sparked by Uranus and gathered together through Neptune.

Pluto is the violence of an atomic explosion, the fierce surge-to-become which impels a tiny green plant to force its way up through solid rock into the light. Pluto is the reformer, the revolutionary, the purger by fire. When misunderstood and misused, Pluto is ruthless, savage, lethal; the gangster with the machine gun, the mugger, the slasher, the murderer.

And Pluto is the Redeemer, the Master-builder. This force is responsible for the dramatic innovations in technology and medicine which have been coming faster and faster since the official discovery of the planet showed us that mankind now has the mental capacity to use the force. It has created a climate for the discovery of how vitamins, minerals, nutritional and environmental factors can help us to build bodies able to do better work and more congenial surroundings for them to grow in. It is making us think more intelligently about problems of social welfare, showing us the horrible truth about war. Pluto is exploding old concepts, tearing our most cherished shibboleths to pieces, knocking down barriers set up by ignorance and illusion so that more useful structures can be erected on their ruins.

From this dark god's domain comes our wealth. Under the Earth lie precious stones, veins of gold, silver, copper, iron, tin, rare elements and minerals which are needed to make our bodies, our dwellings, our implements, every tangible thing we use, wear, live with and by. Our economic structures are based on Pluto's treasures; our governments are set up partly to distribute but mainly to protect it.

Many bitter lessons concerned with property have taught us that Pluto is in fact both just and ruthless. We have seen what happens when one person or one nation takes more than a fair share of Earth's good things at the expense of others. Does this mean, however, that we ought to forgo the enjoyments of wealth for fear of running into trouble with the god of the Underworld?

By no means. Rigid self-denial is as ridiculous a misuse of wealth as is wanton sensuality. Making a cult of not having is in no way more laudable than devoting one's life to gathering possessions, because it still makes materialism the basis of morality. To balance the Pluto force correctly is to accept joyfully and thankfully whatever legitimate pleasures and comforts come our way. Want and gloom are no part of the cosmic plan. The Life Force's workings show us that we are to use what comes and pass it on, confident that more will come when we need it. "He who kisses a joy as it flies lives in Eternity's sunrise," said Blake, and we become more convinced with experience that Blake knew a great deal about both joy and eternity.

Do we have the right to demand that somebody share his wealth with us simply because he has managed to accumulate more than we have? This is a difficult question. Theoretically, the decision as to whether to share or keep should be up to the holder of the goods, since it is he and not we who will have to endure Pluto's sentence of punishment if he has in fact grabbed more than he deserves at our expense.

Being human, though, we can get fed up with waiting

around, cold and hungry, while he sits warm and well fed in his stately home, refusing to make a decision in our behalf. This is the sort of situation that starts riots and sometimes wars. Physical struggle usually does not lead to a satisfactory solution. We have learned that it is more apt to result in the victors' switching what's left of the wealth over to their side, causing further imbalance and setting the stage for another battle.

One interesting example of Pluto's workings may be seen at the present time in some phases of the Labor movement. Unionization of industry has been widespread during the past century. The movement began for the valid reason that employers had refused to give workers a fair share of the profits. It seemed only just that those who earned the money should receive a sufficient wage to keep themselves and their families adequately fed, clothed, and housed. The unions were organized by desperate men and women who envisioned a world where there would be enough for all. They were founded in a welter of broken heads and the struggle was a fine and noble thing. But what of the victory?

It's hard to recall that we in the Affluent Society are the grandchildren of Joe Hill. In any event, nobody can accuse us of ancestor worship. Once we got the bit in our teeth, too many of us were ready enough to forget the austere ideals of Labor's early leaders. We adopted the clothes, the customs, the two-cars-in-every-garage standards of the bosses. We not only condoned but fought to maintain featherbedding and slacking. Picayune quarrels over who was going to do what for how long at what rate divided the brotherhoods into bickering factions. We started demanding higher and higher wages for less and less work.

We dreamed of milking the sacred cow of capitalism for all she was worth, then blamed Big Business for catching us up in a wage-price spiral that led to recession. We lost sight of the concept of overall good and concentrated on taking all we could get, just as the bosses had done when they were in control.

We proved that all men are indeed created equal, and now our children despise us for not being better. And their kids will condemn them in turn for battening on what they profess to reject. And so it will go until we learn to stop feeding our little egos on other people's mistakes and recognize the contribution which each generation has made in building the Great Pyramid and learn to share what belongs to all of us.

You see, we keep coming back to this delusion of separate entities. We insist on thinking that other people are somehow different from ourselves. Even though we admit that we all have exactly the same raw materials to work with and the same powers to set the process of manifestation in motion, we manage to persuade ourselves that somewhere out yonder lie resources which we don't possess.

We stubbornly keep on endowing material objects with some mystical quality of permanence which we have to confess does not exist in our own bodies. We surround ourselves with antiques, both physical and ideological, because we don't dare hope that what lies ahead of us will be better than what went before.

We learn in elementary school that money is only a medium of exchange having no intrinsic value. But how often do we slave for it, steal for it, lie for it, hoard it by denying ourselves comforts, or squander it to purchase toys falsely labelled "status" or "pleasure?" Even those who affect to disdain it may condescend to panhandle from lowlier souls who are willing to perform honest toil for honest wages.

We prattle, "Money is power," but in fact money has no power at all unless an entire society is willing to believe in its worth. Not the dollar bill or the pound sterling but the general acceptance of an idea which that note represents will enable us to exchange it for food or whatever satisfies our need of the moment.

Furthermore, this willingness to accept money in return for goods is of no value to us unless we carry out the physical act of buying and selling. Therefore, the real power of wealth lies solely in the *act of exchange*.

Each act of exchange, whether or not it involves tangible wealth, requires a decision and brings about a transformation. And who is to say which is trivial and which is important? In the most seemingly casual acts of our everyday lives, Uranus is providing the spark and Pluto is exercising his surging power to drive us onward to greater changes. Pluto the Builder is always working underground to alter and improve the foundations of our life experiences.

It is vital to realize that we *have* the power of transformation, and that we are using it all the time. We can profit by systems of training which aim at stimulating this power *only* after we have developed physical and mental structures which are strong enough to handle more intense energy charges. In spiritual as well as material situations, Pluto can be ruthless with those who try to take more than they can use. It is not in some occult, ethereal state of being, but in this body, this life, this time, this world that Pluto is making his treasures available to us and judging how we use them.

Where Pluto appears in your natal chart, you have a sacrifice to make. In order that a more satisfying personality structure can be built, some outworn idea, some faded keepsake from the past will have to be got rid of.

This is true on the general social scale as well as in one's personal life. Because Pluto moves so slowly through each sign of the zodiac, entire generations are born under the same influence. Here we may see an explanation of the so-called generation gap and get some valuable insights about our elders and juniors as well as ourselves and our contemporaries. Parents born under the fussily protective influence of Pluto in Cancer may be less disconcerted when their Leo-born offspring develop into a pride of shaggy-maned young lions and lionesses, lolling about in the sun and roaring, "We want it *now!*" like true kings of beasts. They can console themselves with thinking what a jolt the lions will be in for when they find out what a set of dedicated whisker-washers their own Virgo-born cubs are going to be.

Adjusting to such divergences of personality is not easy, but there's no sense in our asking for pity. Pluto has none to give.

His riches are ours for the taking, but he leaves it to us to make an honest effort to employ them wisely and to take our medicine if we fail.

The best advice an older astrologer can give a novice—and we are all novices in terms of what we have yet to learn—is that which astrologers and alchemists have been giving their apprentices down through the ages. Learn. Dare. Be silent.

Keep your thoughts and emotions under control. Do not give way to anger or frustration. Do not lose faith in the ultimate goodness of life. Waste no time in complaining about what you might have been or what ought to be. The power to achieve what you want is at your disposal. You can use it safely as long as you act in accordance with the cosmic laws. Set yourself a positive, practical, constructive goal and get to work. Now.

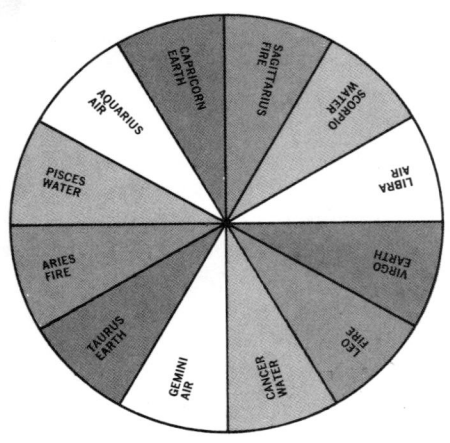

THE ELEMENTS

14 · Introduction to the Signs

Now that we're well acquainted with the fascinating family of planets, we shall have less difficulty in understanding the signs of the zodiac which they control. Before we discuss the individual signs in detail, though, we ought to know a few things which they have in common.

To begin with, each sign is either *masculine* or *feminine*. This categorization has nothing whatever to do with the sex of the person born under that Sun sign. It means that this sign is primarily involved in what ancient alchemists called the Red Work of the Sun or the White Work of the Moon. As we might expect from our previous discussion, the red work is associated with the male energy principle of projecting, giving, initiating, doing. The white work is that of receiving,

Introduction to the Signs

gestating, creating, producing, which we associate with the female principle of energy.

Masculine signs are therefore identified with the alchemical elements Fire and Air. Feminine signs identify with Water and Earth. We have already learned something about the elements when we studied the higher planets Uranus, Neptune, and Pluto.

Fire is the archetypal world, the Father of the Trinity. It relates to rhythm, daring, originality, the urge to initiate, to overthrow, and rebuild. Fire may symbolize warmth, geniality, or raging destruction, but we should not be apt to picture it as dull and quiet. Nor are those persons born under the Fire signs Aries, Leo, and Sagittarius likely to be mousy types.

Water is the creative world, the Mother of the Trinity, expressing itself subtly in thoughts, feelings, desires, assimilation, and dissolution. Like the ocean with its flashing waves, its powerful undercurrents, its tides, its alternating depths and shoals, its teeming and often mysterious life, the water signs appear changeable and moody. Yet the ocean never alters its basic nature. It absorbs oxygen, washes away earth and stone, quenches fire. Water always seeks its own level. In their own inscrutable ways, Cancer, Scorpio, and Pisces are the most individualistic, the most stubbornly persistent of all the signs.

Air is the formative world, the Son of the Trinity, expressing itself in essentialization, imagination, emotion, action. Like the winds which roam where they will, air signs love freedom, space, changes. They hate to be tied down. They want to take off and fly to new scenes, higher places, when the whim takes them. They can blow hot or cold, be a gentle zephyr or a rushing gale. They're great fun but sometimes difficult to cope with. Gemini, Libra, and Aquarius are Air signs.

Earth is the physical world, the kingdom which brings all the elements into balance and practical use. Manifestation and consolidation are its functions. Earth signs Taurus, Virgo, and Capricorn like to keep their feet on the ground even though they may be climbing higher all the while. They want to touch, to taste, to smell, to hear, to see what this world has to offer. They appear to be the most solid of citizens. But let's pick up a clod of earth and study it carefully. It's not such a stodgy lump at that. We can crumble it to bits. We can dissolve it in water or bake it in the fire. On close inspection we find that it's not one homogeneous element but a conglomeration of many different organic and mineral compounds. We can easily alter it to serve our purposes; tilling it to be friable and porous for growing food or flowers; or molding it into clay from which we can fashion a statue, a sidewalk brick, or a delicate porcelain figurine. We shall soon learn that Taurus, Virgo, and Capricorn aren't the mud-encrusted peasants we may have been led to think they were.

When you start to analyze a chart, always study the elements first. Write them down in a column:

Fire:
Water:
Air:
Earth:

Beside each element, put the number of planets in the chart which fall in that cateogry (e.g., Fire, 3; Water, 1; Air, 4; Earth, 2). This will immediately tell you something about the subject. You will be able to see whether the masculine and feminine polarities are well balanced, if the subject is apt to be more of a giver or a taker, whether he or she will be likely to take the active or the passive approach to a situation or a problem.

These polarities are particularly interesting when we compare the charts of present or prospective partners. Here's where we often find the answer to that age-old question, "What does he see in her, or she in him?"

What he or she sees may be exactly what he or she lacks to make up a workable balance of male and female elements. Many of those pseudorelationships which totter along for years without seeming to make any sense have in fact strong undercurrents of mutual need. The tragedy is that a bit of simple arithmetic could have shown what each partner lacked and helped them both to find balanced relationships with more congenial partners.

A preponderance of signs in one or two elements does present problems which would not exist in a more even distribution, but it should by no means be taken to indicate a "bad" chart. There may be strong influences which compensate for the apparent imbalance.

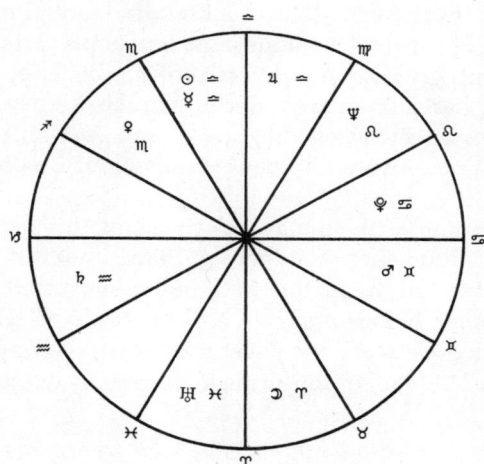

Suppose, for instance, the subject has a Libra Sun and not a single planet in an Earth sign. We start thinking, "He's probably great fun at a party, but I'd hate to be in business with him. He's too indecisive. He'd never be able to make a decision and stick to it."

But then we notice his Ascendant is Capricorn, a strong Earth sign. Furthermore, he has Saturn in Aquarius falling in the first house. Since Saturn is a ruler of both Capricorn and Aquarius and is exalted in Libra, we see that he's already "pinned down." In fact, he may be too firmly anchored and need to be pried loose!

If he has literally no settling influences in his chart, the subject still isn't licked. He could always marry a beautiful, bossy Virgo and live happily henpecked ever after. Should he be attracted by a Gemini who is equally weak in Earth signs, though, he'd better kiss her goodbye fast (which is about the only way one *can* kiss that sort of Gemini) and find a more stable mate.

It is not necessary or even advisable to make a big thing of balancing partners' signs on a strict one-for-one basis. That flighty Gemini might be thoroughly miserable with a mate so loaded with Earth signs that he's literally bogged in the mire. Such a man probably wouldn't find her unpredictable whims anything but grounds for divorce. She'd be happier with a Pisces who has just enough Earth signs in his chart to keep them both from flying off into space, and enough romance in his soul to be captivated by her ever-changing airs and graces.

When dealing with human relationships, it's never safe to make snap judgments or adhere to hard and fast rules. We should analyze all the factors both individually and in relation to one another before we give a "Yes" or "No." Even if the prognosis doesn't seem too favorable, there's always the possibility of a "Maybe, if you want it enough to work at making a go of it."

THE DECANATES

The zodiac is based on a circle of 360 degrees with each sign's house occupying one-twelfth of the circle, or thirty degrees. Each house is further divided into three segments of ten degrees each. These are known as the *decanates* and are sub-ruled by the planets which rule the succeeding signs associated with the same elements.

For example, Aries is the first Fire sign and is ruled by Mars. The second Fire sign is Leo, ruled by the Sun. The third is Sagittarius, ruled by Jupiter. This means that each sign in your chart has not only the fundamental influence of its nature but also a modifying influence imparted by the ruler of its decanate.

Introduction to the Signs

Suppose your Sun sign is 6° Aries. You then fall within the first decanate, which is both ruled and subruled by Mars. The Martian characteristics which we associate with Aries would then tend to be especially marked in your personality. If your Sun were 16° Aries, or any degree between ten and twenty, you would fall within the second decanate, subruled by the Sun, and your fiery Aries nature would be modified by sunny Leo. Over twenty degrees, you would be within the third decanate and feel the influence of proud Jupiter. Any aspect between your Sun sign and the ruling planet of its decanate thus takes on added strength.

It's very easy to work out the decanates of all the signs in a chart by means of the diagrams shown here. Begin at the

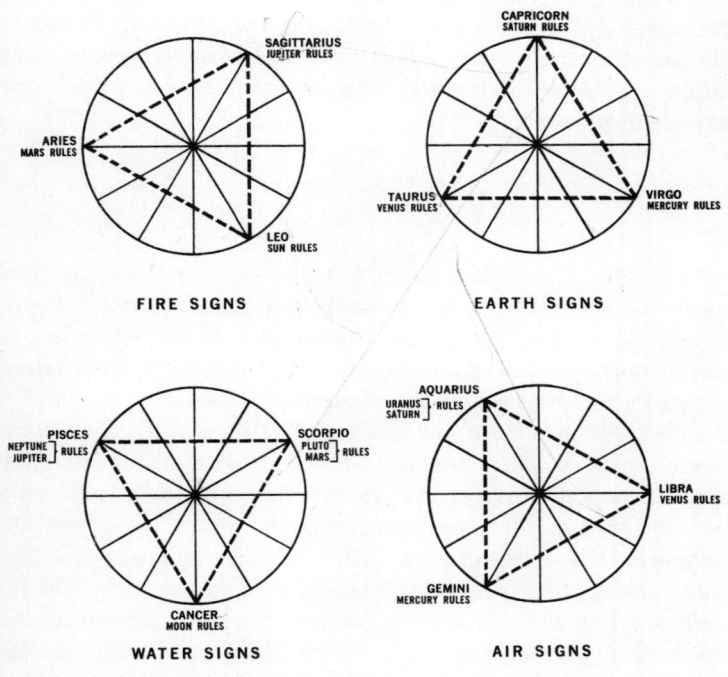

THE DECANATES

given sign and move counterclockwise, counting ten degrees between each two points.

We often hear people say, "I was born on the cusp," meaning that the natal sign was exactly at the junction of two houses or two decanates of the same house. If this is the case, we take the characteristics imparted by both sides into consideration. However, a few minutes' work with an ephemeris will usually enable us to determine the precise degree and place the planet definitely on one side or the other.

Working out the decanates of both our planets and our houses can be great fun and extremely illuminating. We've described natal charts as road maps for lives. If you look at a large-scale travel map, you'll find small inserts which show in more elaborate detail how to find your way through the intricate traffic patterns of particular cities. In the same way, the decanates are charts-within-charts. They can help us to locate the less obvious byways, the twists and turns which lead us safely and joyfully through the life experiences which we have laid out for ourselves.

THE TRIPLICITIES

In looking for balances and imbalances in a chart, we also study the *triplicities*, the Cardinal, Fixed, and Mutable signs. Again, we start by tabulating the number of signs we find in each category; and again, we find out some more fascinating things by this bit of simple arithmetic.

Cardinal signs are Aries, Cancer, Libra, and Capricorn. These are involved with *will*. Their power is mental. They tend to exhibit the Martian characteristics of the person who lives by action, who goes after what he wants. Patience and forbearance are not always their outstanding characteristics.

A subject with many Cardinal signs in his chart would always see two sides to every question: his side and the wrong side. He might have a tendency to play Big Daddy or Big Momma, to domineer, even to bully. How he handled his dominant personality would of course depend on his general level of development, on his understanding of cosmic law, his empathy with fellow beings. He could be a kindly teacher, a wise statesman, or a ruthless dictator, but he would almost certainly be in some position where he would command leadership.

Conversely, a subject with few or no Cardinal signs would be content to stay in the background. He might be glad to let others dominate him. He might be physically lacking in the old get-up-and-go. Caspar Milquetoast the "Timid Soul" and Sherlock Holmes's phlegmatic brother Mycroft are two extremely different characters who would no doubt have had one thing in common: their deficiency in Cardinal signs.

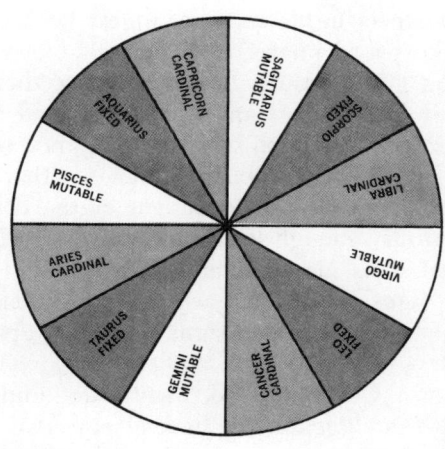

THE TRIPLICITIES

When you see a Cardinal Sun in a chart, pay special attention to the sign of the Ascendant, to any planets which appear in the first house, and to any aspects they make with other planets. Here's a person who likes to keep his goods right out in the shop window, where they can be seen and admired and put to good use.

Fixed signs are Taurus, Leo, Scorpio, and Aquarius. They are associated with *wisdom* and vital power. We see the force of Saturn in their ability to hang on to their individuality, to stick to what they believe is right.

Where you see a preponderance of Fixed signs, don't bother starting an argument. Go find some more amiable and yielding audience, such as a Missouri mule. These characters will never give an inch. Right or wrong, they'll hold their course like Jim Bludsoe of the Prairie Belle, until they've reached the goal they've set their sights on. They may not like it much once they've got there, but you're not apt to catch them admitting they were wrong.

One who is lacking in Fixed signs will be just the opposite, ready to start anything but unable to finish it unless he has a strong Saturn aspect in his chart, or unless he finds a partner who's able to keep a firm hand on the reins.

A Fixed Sun gives a much truer picture of the personality than any other Sun sign. "I am what I am. And if you don't like what I am, the hell with you." He may not say it, unless he was born under Scorpio, but you can bet that's what he's thinking. This is the most independent of the triplicities, although it's contrary enough to seem the most hidebound in its ways. Cardinal signs may appear more dashingly flamboyant and Mutable signs the most ready to experiment with new ideas, but it's among the Fixed signs that we're apt to find the true extremists.

Mutable signs, Gemini, Virgo, Sagittarius, and Pisces are concerned with *intelligence,* the neutral power of Mercury to choose impartially and unemotionally among various courses of action. They are versatile, clever, good actors, boon companions, able to catch the spirit of the moment and adapt themselves to it.

An excess of Mutable signs with nothing to anchor them down indicates the person who can always see so many alternatives that he finds it hard to concentrate on any one thing for long. Here is where we spot the laughing charmers who flit from job, from school, from lover, from home, from wife, from husband, from whatever is here to whatever over there seems more attractive. For them, the grass is always greener in someone else's yard.

These are seldom people of strong passions, although they can throw themselves with such wild enthusiasm into the role of the moment that they can make us think they mean it. Mercury's skill as a trickster is especially apparent here. Such persons don't have the follow-through to make a success of crime on the grand scale, but they are past masters of deceit because they are constantly kidding themselves along with everybody else.

With no Mutable signs, however, a personality would be unbearably drab. We need the sparkle of Mercury to brighten our wits, sharpen our awareness of the delights which lie all around us.

Because it is never quite sure of its identity, a Mutable Sun tends to rely heavily on the Moon in its chart to help define its personality characteristics. The Moon is always a key factor in any chart, but here any Sun-Moon aspect is an invaluable clue to netting the Mutable social butterfly.

THE SYMBOLS

Astrology has a simple shorthand which we'll find it convenient to learn in order to understand an ephemeris or read a chart which has been set up by another astrologer. Each planet and each sign has a symbol. If you copy them over a few times, you'll find they'll stick in your memory. You will note that those for the planets are based on just four basic symbols:

The Sun	☉	the giving masculine principle
The Moon	☽	the receiving feminine principle
The Cross	+	of matter
The Arrow	↗	of direction

As well as being associated with the cosmic forces we have already discussed, the planets, shown with their symbols below, each have physical and psychological attributions, as follows:

Planet		Physical Region	Psychological Function
☉	Sun	Cardiac ganglion	Will
☽	Moon	Pituitary gland	Subconsciousness
☿	Mercury	Pineal gland	Self-consciousness
♀	Venus	Thyroid, parathyroid	Emotion
♂	Mars	Prostatic ganglion	Action
♃	Jupiter	Solar plexus	Expansion, optimism
♄	Saturn	Sacral plexus	Contraction, pessimism
♅	Uranus	Higher function of pineal	Originality
♆	Neptune	Higher function of pituitary	Perception, compassion
♇	Pluto	Higher function of prostatic	Divine desire

The symbols for the signs of the zodiac are abbreviations of the pictograms with which everyone is familiar. In the curving ♈ of Aries, we see the horns of the Ram. The symbol for Taurus is clearly a simplified Bull's head. The waving line of Leo is the lashing tail of the Lion. Just for fun, see how many other resemblances you can pick out from the following table:

Sign		Physical Region	Psychological Function
♈	Aries	Head	Reason, sight
♉	Taurus	Throat	Intuition
♊	Gemini	Chest	Discrimination
♋	Cancer	Stomach	Ingestion, speech
♌	Leo	Heart, spinal cord	Digestion
♍	Virgo	Upper intestine	Assimilation
♎	Libra	Kidneys	Elimination
♏	Scorpio	Generative organs	Dissolution
♐	Sagittarius	Hips, sacral region	Equilibrium, trials
♑	Capricorn	Knees	Observation, illusion
♒	Aquarius	Ankles	Reformation
♓	Pisces	Feet	Organization

Notice that no fewer than seven of these pictograms carry a

suggestion of duality. These are Aries, Taurus, Gemini, Cancer, Libra, Aquarius, and Pisces. This twoness immediately suggests an ability to turn the other cheek, to change, to adapt, to explore both the positive and negative aspects of an experience.

Depending on the context, duality in a sign can mean many things. Generally speaking, it could indicate a certain ambivalence of approach. Values need not be sharply clearcut. The subject would be able to discern the grays as well as the blacks and the whites, to make allowances, to appreciate subtleties of meaning, to see alternate possibilities relating to the sign's area of activity. Good manners, tact, flexibility, poise, diplomacy, willingness to share, to communicate, to empathize would be positive traits. Hypocrisy, fickleness, indecision, deceit, nosiness, gossiping might be some negative aspects.

Two signs suggest unity, oneness. These are Leo and Sagittarius. Here we might expect the native to be preoccupied with his personal self-expression, and this is apt to be the case with both these signs. Neither is likely to be troubled by doubts as to who is the center of his particular universe. The big difference is that Leo, a Fixed sign ruled by the Sun, tends to see himself as the center around whom the world revolves. Sagittarius, a Mutable sign ruled by Jupiter, is more interested in drawing others into his rapidly whirling orbit. He wants to be noticed not so much for what he is as for what he does.

The injunction, "Be yourself," is wasted on either of these two signs. They couldn't be anything else if they wanted, and it would never occur to them to try. Honesty, self-confidence, and a desire to make friends with many people are among their more appealing traits. Tactlessness, selfishness, and a tendency to expect too much of others could be negative characteristics.

There are two triple signs, Virgo and Scorpio. These two do not merely accept life and try to adjust themselves to it. They are the multipliers, the creators, the builders, the naggers, the pests who want to take the world apart and make it over.

Mutable Virgo may be softened by a dual influence in its Moon, but a Scorpio is a Scorpio is a Scorpio.

One sign fits into none of these categories. Capricorn is called the Sign of Mystery. It starts out double and winds up single. Meditate on this.

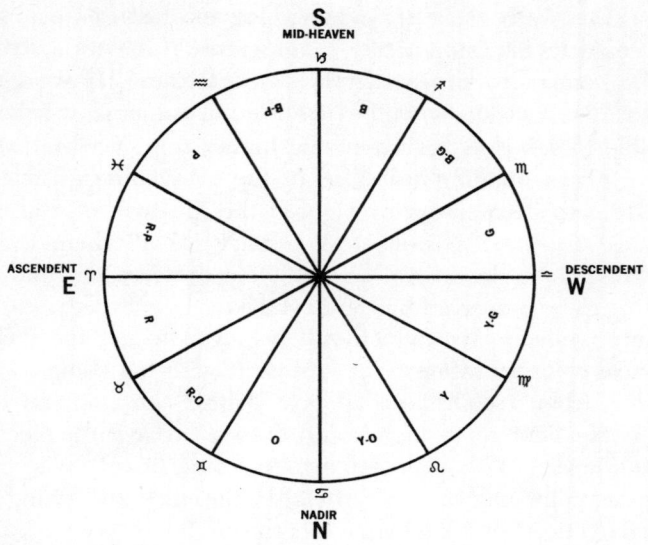

15 · Colors

EACH planet and each sign of the zodiac is associated with a specific color. The zodiac is the rainbow, the same range of hues we get when we break down a colorless beam of light by means of a transparent glass prism.

If we could color all twelve houses of a chart with absolutely pure pigments, then spin the chart rapidly, we should see only white. The faster we spun, the more dazzling would the white appear. If the rate of vibration were sufficiently increased, we should see nothing but light, the substance of which both chart and pigments (as well as the spinner) are made.

The chart would not cease to exist as a separate unit of

matter simply because it was spinning too fast for us to see. We could take a "stop-action" photograph of it with a stroboscopic camera to prove that it was still there. If we could speed up our vision as well as we can our cameras, we should be able to see it as plainly at the higher rate of vibration as when it was standing still. One of the many things astrology can do is to sharpen our eyesight at the spiritual, mental, and physical levels of existence. We shan't see all there is, but we'll be able to detect a great deal more of what surrounds us, waiting to be perceived by those who have eyes to see.

Here is an exercise which will help you to get the feel of zodiacal color vibrations. You can do it with the compass and crayons from a child's pencil box. Adjust the compass to a radius of about three inches and draw a circle on a piece of white paper. Without changing the adjustment, place the compass point anywhere on the circumference and swing the pencil to make a mark where it hits the circle.

Place the point on that mark and measure off another segment in the same way as before. Continue marking until you have divided the circle into six equal segments, each equal to the radius. (You've probably learned how to do this ages ago in geometry class.) Draw lines across the circle through the center to connect opposite marks, so that you form six pie-shaped wedges. Now, draw lines across cutting each segment in half so that you have twelve pieces of pie instead of six. You can measure with a ruler or adjust the compass to half the previous radius and mark from already determined points.

On the circumference, mark the point where each line joins with one of the symbols of the zodiac (see diagram on page 133). Start with Aries at the left-hand side. This corresponds to the direction East and is the *Ascendant*. Label it so. Note that Cancer is at the lowest point, the North, called the *Nadir*. Libra at center right is the West, the *Descendent*. Capricorn is at the top of the chart, the South, which we refer to as the *Midheaven*.

Now, use crayons, paints, or magic markers to color each segment in order as follows:

Aries—Red
Taurus—Red-orange
Gemini—Orange
Cancer—Yellow-orange
Leo—Yellow
Virgo—Yellow-green
Libra—Green
Scorpio—Blue-green
Sagittarius—Blue
Capricorn—Blue-purple
Aquarius—Purple
Pisces—Red-purple

As you fill in each segment, try to experience the sensations of the cycle of growth. Associate yourself with the seasons of the year. Think what the colors mean in terms of the life experience: red, the color of blood, of maleness, of the impetus to penetrate and fertilize; red-orange, the color of fire, the quickening of the seed. Move into the golden hues of summer, the greens of the harvest. Feel the chill as blue heralds the approach of winter. Gradually let the heat of red come creeping back, back, back to start a new experience of the will-to-become.

Colors associated with the planets give us more information at the sensory level. Mars, of course, is red. Venus, his Olympian other-half, is his opposite on the color wheel, the lush green of growing plants. Jupiter is splendid royal purple. Saturn is black or a deep indigo blue. Mercury, as we should expect, is bright yellow. The Sun blazes in hottest orange; the Moon drapes herself modestly in retiring blue.

Two of the higher octave planets are pastel in tint: Uranus, the delicate straw yellow of a slanting sunbeam; and Neptune, the clear light blue of fresh water on a summer's day. But Pluto is the smoldering dark red of a volcanic fire ready to erupt.

On another piece of paper, draw ten little circles. The easiest way is to trace around a small coin. Color each circle in the shade which represents one of the planets. Cut them out and keep them in a small box or envelope.

As we go on to study the signs, keep your chart in front of you. As soon as you learn what are the ruling and exalted planets for each sign, place the appropriate colored discs in that segment of the chart. This apparently childish exercise will prove an effective visual aid in making it clear what goes on inside each house and how they all work together. We're going to discover later on how helpful this simple equipment can be in chart interpretation.

Understanding color relationships in terms of zodiacal affinities can reward us in many ways. Psychologists have already established the fact that responses to different color vibrations have deep and far-reaching effects on human behavior. Our likes and dislikes in the shades we choose to wear and live with depend not on whim or fashion so much as on specific personality traits. Anybody who knows even a little about astrological color theory can easily "read character" in his associates and himself by observing these preferences. More importantly, we can bypass the lengthy processes of questioning and testing on which psychology relies for its results and go straight into practical applications of hue and tint to alleviate tension and promote a feeling of well-being.

Psychiatrists tell us, for instance, that mentally disturbed patients prefer bright emerald green, but this doesn't necessarily mean that we should paint our hospitals this color. Astrology associates green with Libra, the sign of balance, and Venus, the planet of imagination. We have learned that Venus has a violently negative side, so we may well hesitate to surround an already unbalanced person with even more of the Venus influence. If the patient must have green, we can temper it with accents of other colors or soften it by the addition of white.

Yellow is a wonderful color to have in an office, study, or library because of its association with Mercury and mentation, but we might think twice about using it in a conjugally shared bedroom, where it's not the intellect we wish to stimulate. The crimson plush in Madame Fifi's House of Joy proved Madame a shrewder psychologist than many a modern interior decorator.

Consider your own color preferences, relating them to what you now know about the planets and the signs. Even if you do not yet have a copy of your natal chart, you will doubtless be able to make some interesting surmises about what it's going to reveal. Subjects frequently show an overall tendency to prefer shades which relate to the predominant element in their natures. Earth people adore warm browns, tawny rusts, sienna, ochre, umber, the muddy, sombre tones of raw earths and minerals. Air people will have none of these. They like pale blues, pinks, yellows; iridescent fabrics; soap-bubble prints that could vanish in a puff. Water people love mysterious blues, greens, purples; moiré textures; swirling patterns that are never quite what they seem to be. Fire people crave dramatic reds, orange, spectacular black-and-white; colors that flame; contrasts that startle.

Reasonably enough, the colors in our range of preference are apt to be also those in which we look and feel our best. This doesn't mean we have to stick with them, however. In some cases, it might be better if we didn't. An Earth boy trying to make an impression on a girl who's all Air and Water had better not show up for their date looking like the Man with a Hoe, no matter how dearly he loves his old brown sweater and mud-encrusted corduroys.

More seriously, an Earth person wishing to develop the more spiritual side of his nature might stimulate himself by livening up that beloved brown sweater with a pale yellow shirt. His conscious choice of this shade will bring the power of Uranus to bear on his mind. Each glimpse of it during the day will serve as another gentle reminder to Lady Moon that he'd like to have subconsciousness bring an exciting change into his life. Or he might use Neptune's pale blue to dissolve his landlocked consciousness and float him clear of the bog so that he can start to build a more well-rounded personality.

An Air person, on the other hand, may find that Earth tones have the settling effect he needs. It would be silly to promise that a pair of brown shoes can help you to get both feet on the ground. However, wearing those shoes in conscious awareness of what their brownness represents and avoiding the flighty influence of your beloved pastels for the time being could be the psychological boost which will start you putting your affairs under more practical control.

A word of caution here: color reactions can be much more violent than you realize. While their possibilities for aiding you to change your image are virtually limitless, you won't accomplish any worthwhile objective unless you first decide exactly what you want to do and how best to go about it. Then do it *gradually*.

There's no sense in painting everything you own bright red just because you feel the urge to build a fire under yourself (figuratively speaking, of course). Such oversaturation of a color you've probably always avoided would be more apt to send you flying for relief to the nearest spot of green. It's much better to introduce one small red object which stands out in vivid contrast to everything else in your room. This may be a vase, a pillow, a lampshade, a candle, or a single flower. Choose whatever pleases you and will attract your attention without pounding you over the head and arousing your antagonism.

As time goes on, you'll begin to want more of this cheerful stimulation. Almost without realizing it, you'll replace drab old possessions and drab old habit patterns with more exciting ones. Because you've let it happen easily and naturally instead of trying to cram it down your throat in one great lump, the change will be real and lasting.

We shan't be talking specifically about color, but as we go on to discuss the twelve houses of the zodiac you will gain many insights about how color can help you cope with situations relating to the self, the home, career, studies, marriage, health, with every phase of material, mental, and spiritual existence. In this kaleidoscopic world, we are constantly exposed to color, so we may as well use it consciously to focus the forces at our command toward building a more satisfactory life experience.

A NOTE ON THE ZODIAC

Astronomically and astrologically, the zodiac (from a Greek word meaning "little animal") is a zone of the heavens within which lie the orbits of our Sun, Moon, and major planets. It is bounded by two imagined circumferences about 18° apart, equidistant from the ecliptic, the great circle which is the apparent orbit of the Sun.

This band exists, of course, only in the same sense that Earth's equator exists, that is, purely as a measuring device. It is divided into twelve equal sections, each 30° in extent, counting from the position of the Sun at the vernal equinox. Each division is identified by one sign: Aries, Taurus, Gemini, Cancer, Leo, Virgo, Libra, Scorpio, Sagittarius, Capricorn, Aquarius, and Pisces, respectively.

When these were accurately measured and recorded by the great astronomer Hipparchus (*fl.* 146–127 B.C.), the astrological signs as we know them corresponded closely with the astronomical constellations which bear the same names. Hipparchus also discovered, however, that the equinoxes move westward at a rate of more than one degree per century. Because of this precession, a discrepancy now exists amounting to the breadth of a whole sign, so that the space originally allotted to Aries has been gradually traversed by the constellation Pisces; thus, each sign has moved up one space and will continue to move into a second space from its "home base," and so on for as long as the celestial clock continues to run.

This astronomical disparity suggests many possibilities for research, but it does not seem relevant to the concept of astrology which is being explored in this text and generally throughout the Western world at this time. Dane Rudhyar explains the zodiac as the magnetic field through which the various cosmic forces are brought to bear in specific ways on our planet and its inhabitants.

There is nothing difficult about this idea. Anybody can use any sort of prism to break down invisible light rays into the colors of the spectrum. We can experiment with these colors on ourselves and our associates and have already produced significant evidence of their widely varying effects. We can therefore postulate that the invisible but omnipresent cosmic forces can be broken down and channeled in somewhat the same way as light waves, since we know that fundamentally they *are* light.

Moreover, we know that the spectrum always breaks down in the same order. In addition to the tints we see, we have detected higher vibrations which are invisible to the naked eye but can be put to work for us if we can devise the right sort of equipment to channel them. We know that the experiment works no matter where or how we try it. We can thus regard the spectrum's arrangement as a *constant,* unaffected by time, place, or condition. A child who has not the faintest notion of color theory can rattle off the colors of the rainbow in their proper order and be right every time, because *that's the way it always happens.*

Thus, even though we may not know precisely what the zodiac *is,* we can use it in astrological research because ages of experiment and experience have shown us a great deal about what it *does.* We are able to perceive our association with the zodiac as a relationship between microcosm and macrocosm. We have learned that the system works in basically the same way for everybody. We can rely on our natal charts to be accurate life maps because we've learned that *they work,* provided we learn how to read them, and don't expect them to perform functions not properly theirs. What they do is to give us a better understanding of ourselves and show us the directions we can move in most effectively to fulfill our duties in the solar ecology.

Since we are dealing with constants, we may omit any consideration of the ever-moving constellations. Astrologers generally agree that it is best to consider the houses solely in terms of the interior stars, or planets. If we can understand how these work in their various departments, we shall have all the practical information we need to put astrology to work for us.

16 · Aries

First Fire Sign, Cardinal, Masculine, Dual
Mars Rules, Sun Exalted
Color: Red; Symbol: The Ram

ARIES is the sign of the Ram. What some of us don't know is that this is also the sign of the King. Of old, the king said, "Let it be done," and it was done. His will was law, until some usurper managed to topple him from the throne and reign in his stead. Both the imperiousness and the precariousness of the kingly nature and position can be discerned in this first and fieriest House.

Before we analyze His Majesty, however, it will be helpful to take a quick survey of our astrological kingdom. Here is a capsule description of what each house stands for:

1. Aries—Your personality; how you see yourself; your general approach to life.
2. Taurus—Wealth, or anything of special value to you.
3. Gemini—Knowledge, learning what to do with your assets; education in self-expression; travel, both physical and mental.
4. Cancer—The home, domestic concerns; the foundation of your life.
5. Leo—Children, talents, speculation, creativity; realization of the individual ego.
6. Virgo—Health, both physical and spiritual; service.
7. Libra—Love and marriage; partnerships; interpersonal adjustments.
8. Scorpio—Physical regeneration or decline; birth and death; practical use of occult forces; sex.
9. Sagittarius—Ideology, philosophy, religion, higher education.
10. Capricorn—Vocation, material ambitions, public position, influence of employers and superiors.
11. Aquarius—Hopes, fears, wishes, spiritual aspirations; friends and social life.
12. Pisces—Inhibiting factors; private and secret matters; involvement with organizations, institutions, hospitals, prisons, mental illness.

We shall learn much more about each house as we progress through the zodiac, but now we must go back and start from the beginning. This is what Aries is best at. The house Aries rules on your own natal chart indicates the frame of reference from which you begin any important activity.

For example, if you have Aries rising, that is, in its own house, you are most apt to start for the pure joy of doing your thing. You'd think, "I want to do this because I want to," if you stopped to think at all. However, you would probably plunge ahead without stopping to weigh the probable consequences too carefully.

With Aries ruling the second house, however, you'd think first, "How much is this going to cost me? Can I afford it, in terms of money, prestige, or whatever I value most? Will it add to my wealth, tangible or intangible?"

Aries on the third house would lead you to wonder, "What can I learn from this experience? Will it be more fun than something else?" You might then decide to learn what you could about the project before you committed yourself and might get so engrossed in the finding out that you'd never get around to the doing.

Ruling the fourth house, Aries might make you a nomad, always thinking you'd operate more effectively from a different location, or a demon housekeeper, making your home the focus of your energies and the springboard for all your activities.

And so on around the wheel. Fifth-house Aries could be a compulsive gambler, a creative artist with unbounded faith in his talent, an uninhibited parent who produces child after child without considering how he's going to keep them fed and clothed. A sixth-house Ram might become a hypochondriac who moans, "Will this effort be too much for me?" or a healer whose approach is, "Will this service be of genuine aid to somebody?"

Aries at the seventh house would begin by looking about for a partner to share the fun, but this wouldn't necessarily make him or her the perfect husband or wife. He'd usually be a zealous co-worker, a scrappy teammate, happiest where the scrum is thickest, great fun in a crowd, and always glad to see a new face. Like Papageno, he'd be true forever—provided somebody more exciting didn't come along.

Governing the eighth house, Aries may do some strange things, for this is the residence of the occult, the mysterious phenomena involved with life and death. Aries here is fully aware that in order to build anew, he must first destroy existing structures. His first step in any program may be to kick over an old applecart or stamp on somebody's toes. What he does may not make any sense to others, but he'll forge ahead because something inside him is saying, "Go on. Do what must be done no matter how they hiss and boo. If they set up barricades, knock them over and keep going." This is hardly a comfortable position for Aries, but it can be an exhilarating one.

At the ninth house, Aries should be happiest of all. Here he can live in harmony with Jupiter, hitching an endless stream of wagons to the stars. Here he can turn his bounding energies to the study of abstract subjects, evolving new ideas for the betterment of himself and his world. Should they not bring material rewards, he can dwell at ease in his cloud castle, busy at spinning ever more beautiful fantasies.

No such wool-gathering will be tolerated by tenth-house Aries. He knows Life is Real, Life is Earnest, and even a king has to buckle down to business if he wants to remain on his throne. This Ram plans ahead and makes every move count in his steady progress toward his goal, which is to be Top Man. In such a position, Aries must take care not to let his drives turn him into a self-seeking tyrant. He may have a tendency to make unreasonable demands on his employees and his family. All this Mars-Sun-Saturn influence is apt to give him a temper like a tinderbox, and it's going to blaze up often because nothing will ever happen fast enough to suit him. Color him green; he needs plenty of Venus's tenderizing action to balance the double Mars.

Ruling the eleventh house, Aries might induce one to become a great reformer or the neighborhood busybody. The tendency here would be to get involved in some form of social activity. The eternal clubwoman, the indefatigable party-giver and -goer, the public relations director, the politician who loves to get out and kiss babies might be types we'd meet in Aquarius's house. This gregarious person could be a great success as head of the entertainment committee and a failure in some plodding behind-the-scenes job. Nor would he be apt to stick at anything long, unless it presented constant change and new challenges.

The twelfth house is another spot where Aries could feel both comfortable and useful. Pisces is the house of organization, so Mars here would have a suitable environment in which to marshal his force for the wealth-gathering activity which rising Taurus is about to demand of him. This is also the house of karma, so Aries ruling here could indicate a willingness to wipe the slate clean of old debts and start a new cycle on a higher level of awareness. In this position, Aries will have to make sure that his motives and methods are honorable and based on reason.

Of course this is oversimplification, but it should give you some idea of the many different things Aries can mean in the houses. It should also be emphasized that Aries *ruling* a house is quite a different influence from Aries linked with one of the ten planets *within* a house. The house is the environment we have created for ourselves by the forces we have previously set in motion, therefore it is an indicator of the outside influences which will be brought to bear on us in this life. What goes on inside it is the activity which we are in the process of performing with relation to that particular section of the magnetic field.

In other words, we build our houses and we live in them. Our lives are conditioned by the environmental conditions we have set up, but we do have a great deal of flexibility when it comes to making repairs and alterations. We have freedom to decide which of many available choices to follow in decorating and maintaining it. We decide whether the house will be lively or peaceful, neat or untidy, fun-filled or dull, bright or drab, folksy or formal. We can fill it with laughter or tears, music or the dissonance of quarreling.

Some of us are perfect housekeepers; some are hopelessly inefficient; most are somewhere in between. We try to keep the living room tidy, but the rest of the place usually seems to get cluttered up again as fast as we think we've got it put to rights. We try to tackle the whole job alone and find it's just too much to cope with, while those wonderfully capable servants of ours wander around messing things up for lack of proper direction. Once we understand how Aries functions, we know where and how to begin managing our households so that the life cycle will run on more smoothly and happily.

Astrological Aries is equated with *seeing*. Consciously or subconsciously, we start any new course of action by saying, "I'll look into it." We examine its possibilities from our personal vantage point, as has already been mentioned. We also look into ourselves, to determine what resources we can bring to the project, what will have to come from someone else, and what we expect to get out of it. Therefore, Aries must be involved both with physical sight and the inner power of visualization.

Our eyes are marvelous cameras, which instantly record and transfer to the storehouse of memory any scene we focus them on. And what wretched photographers we are! How seldom do we use our equipment up to its full potentiality. How little we see of what we look at.

"We see what we want to see" is an old saw that still has teeth in it. We have a knack of looking straight past whatever we don't feel able to handle, until the visual evidence piles up so high we can't avoid it any longer.

Every so often, we read some newspaper story which seems incredible. One which comes to mind concerned a mother who kept her son shut up in a basement room for several years in order to keep him from being drafted. We asked ourselves, "How could such things happen in this day and age?" Then we read another "Prisoner in Own Home" story and another and another, until the angle got stale and the newspapers stopped printing them. Some of these were gruesome enough for any gothic novel, but none happened in lonely mansions in the middle of nowhere. They took place for years on end in crowded cities, in those suburbs where everybody is supposed to know everybody else's business, but nobody saw a thing wrong until somebody happened to open his eyes one degree wider.

Doctors are familiar with this phenomenon. "Just now, I examined a patient suffering from an ailment I'd never seen before. And I know from experience that I'll have another case exactly like it before the day is over."

We might ask cynically, "How many such cases had actually passed through that doctor's hands before he at last made an accurate diagnosis?" but we should be doing the medical profession an injustice. Some sort of chain reaction seems to take place in such instances, as though one afflicted person suddenly realized that his ailment could be treated in a certain way by a certain doctor, and others operating on the same wavelength because of their similar problem had picked up the message.

Whether such occurrences link clairvoyance with Aries is a subject for further research, but we certainly have plenty of material to speculate on. Why, to cite an instance directly related to the first house's ruling planet, did Deimos and Phobos remain so long undiscovered? Mars, as the nearest planet to Earth, had been scrutinized by astronomers for centuries. Granted, its satellites are not the easiest to spot and until the latter part of the eighteenth century telescopes were not very good. Still, Swift had described them with remarkable accuracy in Gulliver's voyage to the Island of Laputa as far back as 1726, and astronomers had long suspected their existence.

Whatever the reason, they were not officially discovered until Asaph Hall spotted them in August 1877, with a twenty-six-inch reflector made by Alvan Clark & Sons, who observed them at almost the same time—as did the Harvard Observatory in Cambridge, Massachusetts. Now that we know they exist, we have been able to spot them with far less powerful telescopes than Hall's.

And so it is with many discoveries. Any good miler, it seems, can break the four-minute mark since 1954, when Roger Bannister in Great Britain and John Landy in Finland within seven weeks of each other exploded the long-held myth of its being physically impossible. We begin to see a broken record not as an isolated achievement but a shared experience of pushing back the barriers.

Neil Armstrong's first words on reaching the Moon's surface were, "That's one small step for man, one giant step for mankind." His feet made the physical move, but his being able to make it was both the culmination and the beginning of an endeavor shared by all the civilizations that had gone before and all that will come after. Not every action is invested with so much drama, but in precisely that same sense, every least thing we do is both an end and a beginning in which our entire solar ecology is involved.

Innumerable instances of parallel discovery could be cited,

but what they all seem to boil down to is that any intensely concentrated effort of seeing tends to stir up not only the personal but the collective subconscious. Therefore, each interested person stands a better chance having the necessary mindstuff brought quickly to consciousness and used to fulfill his purpose.

Again, we see what we want to see. We may not take in the entire picture at first glance, but if we keep our attention concentrated on what we want to see, the details will gradually emerge. Aries's problem is that he's always in such a rush. It's easier to take a quick glance, select what strikes our fancy immediately, and ignore the rest. The effect can be much like what's going to happen if we stroll down a garden path admiring the roses and forgetting to look out for poison ivy, wasps' nests, muddy spots, and other unattractive details. If we learned to pay attention to the total picture, we could enjoy its beauties while avoiding the painful slips, bumps, and stings.

Most of our so-called bad luck is the result of not having made the effort to spy out perfectly obvious pitfalls. The extent of the misfortune depends on how fast we're traveling. Bumping into a tree when you're out for a stroll is embarrassing, probably rather painful, but seldom serious in its consequences. Hitting that same tree in a car going sixty miles an hour could be fatal. Yet we have to put on speed if we expect to get anywhere, so we can see how helpful it is to have Aries show us where to start off on the right foot.

Astrologers are always pointing out how Aries loves to be up and doing. Persons in whom this influence is strong do tend to find it absolute torture to sit still, unless they're with lively companions or watching a football game. The father who sent his son down to the corner saloon to find out whether a fight was going on, "'Cause if there is, Pop wants to be in it," is a lovely example of the primitive Arian.

Ruled by Mars, this sign loves the battle for its own sake. It approaches life with the eagerness of the child who hasn't yet learned to dread the fire. We find something childlike in any Arian personality, even at an advanced age. His zest for adventure never dies, unless he becomes a burnt-out case, consumed by his inner fires.

In the life cycle, Aries is beginning-to-become. Here we see the Sun exalted, warming the soil, quickening the seed into growth, the person-that-is-to-be held up as a constant, shining goal. We see Mars's force driving toward the light of self-realization.

If Aries appears preoccupied with his personal problems and interests, we have to realize that here is not the calculated selfishness of the adult but the naïve egocentricity of the child. He is exploring his potentialities, testing his powers to find out what they can do. He uses other people as sounding boards, as an infant uses its mother's breast because it's the most convenient way to get nourishment.

Fidelity is not the Ram's strongest point. It's not that he means to be fickle when he suddenly bounds away to pastures new; simply that he's learned all he can absorb here and he must find another teacher. Aries is a sensitive creature (after all, what's more tender than a baby's skin?), but it may not occur to him that others have feelings, too. Mama's little darling can't understand why she won't let him nurse any more now that he's cut those sharp little teeth. Instead of trying to see her point of view, he's more apt to go into screaming fits. Her only hope of quieting him down and keeping him from hating her forever is to get him interested in using his new equipment.

This is not to say that all Arians are egotistical monsters. Remember that this is only one of twelve houses, and any number of mellowing influences may be brought to bear on it. However, much unhappiness can be averted here by bearing in mind that while children can be charming and stimulating companions, they have limited attention spans. The partner of a predominantly Arian person must be prepared for sudden switches of interest. Either stand aside to avoid the stampede or gallop along and enjoy the fun, but don't try to involve him or her in any long-range plans. The mere idea of being committed makes Aries feel trapped, and being trapped is scary.

We have been given such a dynamic portrait of Aries as

Tarzan of the Apes that we forget how large a part fear plays in the growth process. How much derring-do is prompted by a need to prove we're not chicken-hearted? We should remember that Aries does not simply come out of the Everywhere into the Here, but evolves as another manifestation of an endless life cycle, bearing with him subliminal memories of the tragic failures, the silly mistakes, the terrifying punishments as well as the joys and the triumphs which have happened to him in past incarnations.

He's got to get out there and grow because that's what he's being born for, but how does he know what sort of mess he'll land in this time? His great comfort lies in the knowledge that this is a new opportunity, and that another beginning can always be made if he fluffs it this time. This is why Arian personalities tend to handle their difficulties not by working doggedly toward some sort of solution, good or bad, but by chucking it up and trying something else.

Often this is the right answer. An Arian quarterback would know better than to keep calling the same play after it's failed more than once. An Arian inventor would cast about for a fresh slant on his idea instead of plodding along down a blind alley. Any profession or occupation which calls for boldness in trying different angles of approach can provide a productive outlet for the Arian personality.

We can all use the Arian influence in our charts to keep from getting bogged down, or to unstick ourselves. A practical way is to relate the specific problem confronting us to Aries's position. Suppose, for instance, you are dissatisfied with your present job but aren't sure how to change for the better. Where is Aries in your natal chart? At the first house? Maybe your disgruntlement isn't really with your job but with yourself. Are you the person you'd like to be? Start a course of self-improvement study. Change your hairdo. Buy an outfit you'd never dream of wearing, and wear it. Break an old habit. Do something to wake yourself up, and the act will give you a new slant on that job. You may find it has advantages you hadn't noticed before. Perhaps you can use it as a springboard to a better position instead of just quitting. Resist that impulse to bolt until you're sure it's not yourself instead of the job you're trying to run away from.

If Aries rules your second house, appraise the job in terms of its value. Are you dissatisfied solely because it doesn't pay well enough? What do you want more money for? Do you actually require a higher income, or could you learn to manage better on what you get? Is it your scale of values that's wrong? Are you trying to buy status symbols? If you honestly feel you must earn more, does this position offer possibilities for advancement? If so, what must you do to get promoted?

Having already learned something about what each house stands for, we needn't go all through them again. You see, it's just a matter of asking yourself the questions which your personal frame of reference suggests and taking the time to observe your own reactions to them.

Any planets in Aries will give you an even surer indication of how to proceed, as well as of the difficulties you may encounter or the mistakes you'd be most apt to make. Bear in mind that any of the forces can work in either a positive or a negative way. Jupiter in Aries cries, "Damn the torpedoes! Full speed ahead." A headlong plunge into dangerous waters is a thrilling way to achieve a spectacular victory. To be sure, you also run the risk of being blown sky-high, but that's part of the fun, isn't it? If you'd rather make the voyage safely, however, let this sign in your chart remind you that you're always tempted to take on more than you can handle. Make Aries use those marvelous eyes of his to observe the warning signs along the road before you set out on the Quest Perilous, or bet your week's pay on a pair of treys. On the higher level, Jupiter in Aries gives a breadth of vision which may set the astronomer scanning the skies for new galaxies or give the reformer fresh insights on social welfare problems. Whether grand or grandiose, this combination will enable you to look beyond the picayune and commonplace.

Saturn in Aries might be called by some astrologers a "bad sign," as indicating a tendency to ailments of the head or eyes.

This leaden planet could also dampen the Arian fire, making it more than usually difficult for the subject to get started on a project. In this case, however, such an anchor might be an advantage rather than a handicap. Saturn would cause Aries to look before he leapt, and make him more tenacious about sticking with a job and carrying it through. It's doubtful if this combination would sweeten the disposition, since Aries tends to flare up quickly and Saturn's holding influence could turn a spark of anger into a lasting grudge. If your chart shows this aspect, you would be wiser to employ Saturn as a rein to check that quick temper, rather than to blow up and give him a chance to dig in his toes and turn sullen.

Mercury in Aries is a versatile sign indeed. His agility in finding new paths to explore combines with Aries's readiness to try anything, producing more quick changes than the Cat in the Hat. This subject could start off like a racing driver, seeing the most favorable opening and making a beeline for it before his opponents noticed it was there. His problem would be that he could *always* see new openings. He might be there and gone before he'd taken the time to look around and observe what opportunities lay in front of his nose. His need is to find a way to put on the brakes long enough to extract the most good from each experience he encounters.

Venus in Aries, on the other hand, doesn't quite know what to do with herself. She's apt to behave like a shy young thing out on her first date with a lusty youth four years her senior. She doesn't know how to handle all that bursting masculinity, and she's often afraid of it. She realizes she isn't ready for intense heterosexual relationships and is apt to avoid them unless she has strong help from other aspects within the chart or can overcome her fears with outside counseling. Don't be surprised if you find this aspect in the chart of a perennial bachelor, or of someone involved in a relationship where there is no strong emotional tie. One conjecture is that it indicates a person who has taken vows of celibacy in a previous incarnation or has changed over to the opposite sex in this incarnation and is just beginning to learn how to handle this polarity.

Longfellow paints a sweetly pretty picture of Venus in Aries:

> *Maiden with the dark brown eyes*
> *In whose orbs a shadow lies . . .*
> *Standing with reluctant feet*
> *Where the brook and river meet. . . .*

Mozart's pert little peasant girl Zerlina gets the point across more melodiously as she warbles, *"Vorrei e non vorrei"* (I want to and I don't want to) to Don Giovanni's urgent, "Let's go!" Zerlina makes out all right in the end, though not with the amorous Don.

We purposely introduce Don Juan at this point because he gives us such a swashbuckling image of Mars in Aries. Not everybody with this combination has the same hobby, we hasten to state. Whatever the interest, however, it will no doubt be pursued as zealously as Leporello's unpredictable boss collected names for his list.

Let's not underestimate the Don's character. Whatever we think of his intrigues, we must admit that he showed fearlessness, resourcefulness, and determination in carrying them out. He stuck to his principles, such as they were, even when the awful statue of the murdered Commendatore commanded him to repent or be damned. Had he been capable of the least spark of genuine compassion, he might have been in fact the admirable person his victims were fooled into thinking he was.

Don Juan's complete selfishness in gratifying his own desires was his undoing, and this is the pitfall which Mars in Aries always has to look out for. He's moving so fast that it may not occur to him how his actions are affecting others. His ruthlessness is not prompted by malice or a desire to hurt so much as by a blind compulsion to get what he wants. Like a racehorse in blinkers, he can see nothing except the winning line toward which he's galloping. If the other horses haven't sense enough to get out of his way, that's their tough luck.

But people aren't horses and it's no fun galloping alone, especially when you at last open your eyes and see, like Don

Giovanni, that you've run straight to Hell. Aries gives you the power to see inside, outside, and all around you. Take off the blinkers and watch where you're going.

The Moon in Aries is particularly interesting. Since she operates at the subconscious level, it's more difficult to see what she's getting you into. Like poltergeists, some children seem to generate chaos. They walk into a room and all the pictures fall off the walls. "I didn't do anything," they wail, and often as not they didn't. Yet somehow it's always when they're around that the cat jumps for the canary or the baby grabs the tablecloth and tugs.

The young maid Edith in Noel Coward's play *Blithe Spirit* gives us an accurate, amusing, and frightening picture of what these innocent diffusers of the Arian vibration can be like. Edith is a rusher-about. She does everything at the run, unable to slow down even when her mistress begs her to do so. Accident-prone, she falls and bangs her head, and we recall that Aries rules the head. While incapacitated from this injury, she diverts that tremendous Martian drive to mediumship, without realizing what she's doing. She materializes Elvira, throws Charles Condomine's household into chaos, then causes the death of Ruth. Only under hypnosis is she able to confess to Madame Arcati that she has been the agent, because her conscious self knows nothing of what's been going on.

Of course this combination does not always bring disaster. Sometimes it brings the most amazing good fortune. Fairy godmothers appear from nowhere to turn pumpkins into golden chariots. A prince on a white charger gallops up in the nick of time. The heroine is snatched from the railroad track, the mortgage is burned, Horatio Alger's benevolent millionaire turns up with a pocketful of gilt-edged bonds for a wedding present, and they all live happily ever after.

What happens is that Aries is always generating impulses at the subconscious level, casting invisible bread on uncharted waters. What comes back depends on the sorts of hostile or benevolent vibrations sent out. Little Mary Sunshine finds that Love Conquers All because she has borne with her misfortunes gaily and courageously. Once astrological analysis has shown us what we're doing here, we can use Mercury to send messages down to the subconscious which will set up desirable results.

The Sun in Aries hardly seems to require exposition. The exaltation of Heaven's blazing orb in the first fire sign is too dazzling to overlook. We naturally expect anybody born under this influence to exemplify Flaming Youth, to be the Jazzbaby dancing the eternal Charleston across the pale parabola of joy. Any astrology book will tell you here's a real red-hot mama (or papa) full of the old get-up-and-go, and every time an Aries-born gets up and goes, they chuckle, "That's Aries for you!"

Often these subjects take off like rockets without warning. A wife who's always professed to be blissfully married picks up the baby and heads for the wide open spaces, leaving her bewildered husband wondering what it's all about. Your best friend the Ram suddenly has no time for you. Old Faithful, whom everybody in the office relied on, goes off to join the Foreign Legion, taking the combination to the safe with him.

This can be hard to take, but we have to consider that the motivation of the first house is the urge to realize the self. When a baby is born, the first thing that must be done is to sever the umbilical cord, or it won't survive. In the same way Aries must keep cutting the apron strings, breaking loose from each stage of development so that he can go on to the next.

It is during the first few years of life that a child does most of its growing. The changes from babyhood to childhood and from childhood to adolescence are rapid and dramatic. Because we see in them this promise of growth, we are able to find babies adorable. Viewed dispassionately, they would appear hideously disproportionate creatures, with enormous heads and tiny bodies. Their personal habits are abominable. They are thoroughly and completely selfish, shrieking in anger and frustration whenever their wants go unsatisfied. On the other hand, when a baby is happy, it's completely so: delighted with the simplest plaything, overjoyed at finding it can get its toe into its mouth, gurgling with joy at the wonder of being alive and sentient. In this tiny, pulsating form we see a living proof of our faith that out of darkness comes light, out of death comes new life. We experience the fact of incarnation.

So we love our babies and tolerate their squalling and wetting and upspitting and allow them to make slaves of us because we know they won't be like this forever. We were babies ourselves, so we realize that growing up is a painful process. We sympathize with the infant who has yet to go through the long process of testing and trying, of falling and being hurt, of having to face the humiliating fact that he's not the only pebble on the beach.

Knowing what we do, we may make a shrewd guess that when Aries makes a bolt out the door, he may be running scared. He could be seeking escape from the pressures of growing up which bear on him more immediately than on any of the other Sun signs. While he has tremendous potentiality for doing, he will require plenty of help and understanding if he's to stick with the job of developing into a well-balanced adult. No matter how many years he's been on this planet, the approach that works best will be to kiss him when he stumbles, tell him to look where he's going next time, and encourage him to try again. He will. Aries is always ready to try again. He mustn't waste too much time on new beginnings, though, or he'll never find out what's farther on up the road.

The biggest problem with having the Sun in Aries is that you're always in your own light. You can find it extremely difficult to detach yourself from your immediate problems or pleasures and take a long, objective look at what you're actually doing to yourself and those close to you. Hence, more than any other sign, the Aries-born can benefit from good advice. He ought never to hesitate to ask assistance from parents, teachers, anybody older and hopefully wiser. Of course he must examine any such advice carefully before acting on it. No matter if he's still a kid at heart, he has to assume responsibility for his life, like everybody else. The object is to get other slants on the problem, in order to see all around it and achieve a more comprehensive solution.

It should be noted that since Aries rules the head and induces that involvement with self which, too intensely pursued, may lead to neurotic problems, any really unhappy and confused Arian would be especially apt to benefit from psychotherapy or psychiatry. By getting some help in focusing his ability to look within, he might achieve good results after even a few consultations.

Remember that Aries is a *dual* sign. The Ram works better in association with other people, even though he doesn't want them leading him around by the nose. If he feels pressure building up, he would be wiser not to try going it alone. A helping hand is sure to be extended somewhere, so let him use that high-powered vision to look for it. He need not worry about being a clinging vine. He'll let go fast enough once he finds himself on firmer ground.

Aries's relationships to the three higher planets is of more academic than immediate interest to most of us. These are all now in other signs, have been for some time, and will be for years to come. Only those born between March 31, 1927, and March 27, 1935, will find some of them—Uranus—in their natal charts associated with Aries.

Think of some things which happened when Uranus was in Aries: the Labour Government of Ramsay MacDonald which altered political philosophy both in Britain and abroad; the craze for gambling on the stock market which triggered the crash of November, 1929, and the Depression Years in the United States; the overthrow of a conservative Republican government and the election of Franklin D. Roosevelt, the daring innovator who sent the Blue Eagle soaring to undreamed-of heights of social reform; the rise of Hitler and the Nazi Party which sowed the seeds of World War II; the transformation of a pennywise, tradition-oriented society into a nation of nomads living on the installment plan.

We saw what we wanted and made a grab for it. Anything new and different appealed to us, and we have seen this tendency affect the whole way of life of those born under this influence. The period following World War II, when the Uranus-in-Aries babies grew up, could be called the "Gimme Generation." We'd buy anything from propellor beanies to pink refrigerators. Planned obsolescence became a tenet of our economy, and the planners took pride in their abilities to make products that would collapse after a few years' use. Who wants old stuff, anyway? Throw it out! Buy new! Never mind if it's less efficient than what you had before, as long as it's shiny and colorful and different from last year's model.

We must not overlook the positive side of this influence. Aries in Uranus also enabled people born under its influence to envision and commence dramatic advances in medicine, in technology, in every field of human endeavor. It showed us opportunity where none had been thought to exist. We saw ways to perform what couldn't be done, to break unbreakable records, to climb the unscalable mountain, dream the impossible dream and make it come true. It will be up to those who come after to finish what Aries has started here, to unscramble the good from the worthless and weave it into the ever-richer pattern of this civilization.

As we entered the twentieth century, both Neptune and Pluto were in Gemini, and neither will have returned to Aries until years after we have begun the twenty-first. By that time, we shall know a great deal more about astrology than we do now, so we may as well reserve any speculation on what to expect from these influences.

Whatever its position or associations in a chart, the method of dealing with Aries is basically the same. You will recall that in discussing Mars we learned the importance of setting our affairs in order. By tackling your personal problems at the logical starting point *for you*, you are putting the cosmic forces to work without wasted time and effort. You may seek advice from those best-qualified to give it from your special frame of reference, but the work will be done by you.

Physical action is vital, in the literal sense of the word. We must do in order to be. However, we must bear in mind that physically we live entirely in the past. Nothing under the Sun is new, no matter what the advertisements say. The very light in which we live has taken time to travel through space. The action we perceive as happening this moment has already occurred by the time the eyes have transferred it to the brain. What we do in response to what we see will have to be formulated in thought before the mind can telegraph appropriate messages to the muscles: in other words, we must see with the *inner eye* before we can relate to what we see with the *outer eye*. Therefore, Aries means primarily inner sight, and this is what really determines our beginnings.

17 · Taurus

First Earth Sign, Fixed, Feminine, Dual
Venus Rules, Moon Exalted
Color: Red-Orange; Symbol: The Bull

As the sign of the Bull, Taurus immediately brings to mind green pastures, manure-smelling barns, huge animals ponderously obeying the urge to copulate and reproduce their kind. We identify the bull with brute strength, ferocity in attack and tend to see him as the embodiment of male animal sexuality, hence we may get a jolt to learn that Taurus is a feminine sign.

This is our first experience with polarities in the houses. As we progress, we shall learn that masculine always alternates with feminine, active with passive, giving with receiving. We abandon preconceived opinions about the signs and open our minds to the message of the life cycle. It is in Taurus that we first come to grips with the earthy side of existence. If Aries is the whisker-frisking tomcat who pounces over the garden wall and scatters his sperm where he will, Taurus is the betrayed tabby who gets stuck with bearing the kittens. Though the Venus-Moon combination may suggest a dreamy romantic, this pussycat is more apt than not to get reality thrust upon her.

In fact, Venus's rulership ought to give us an immediate clue that Taurus will be concerned with the work of gestation. In plants, the growth process begins underground. In animals, it also begins in the dark, as the fetus stirs toward manifestation within the womb. Seed development takes place wholly on a subconscious level at this stage, implicitly obeying the rhythm of the life cycle, as the Moon must always obey.

We know how long it will take from the time of planting for our lettuce seeds to germinate. Knowing the date of impregnation, we can calculate to the day when a calf, a kitten, or a human baby will be born. The waiting period varies with the species, but the progress of the conception-to-birth for that species will always proceed in the same manner over the same period of time. The seed may fail to germinate or abort somewhere along the line, but to achieve a normal birth, the infant will just have to wait until its time is come. We can see, therefore, why the obedient Moon is exalted over Venus, the power of gestation, in this house.

Because this attunement to the primal rhythms is so easily recognized, astrologers sometimes develop Millet-inspired pictures of gum-booted Taureans spending their lives knee-deep in the reeking barnyard, contentedly shovelling up the muck. What's wrong with that? "Keep your feet on the ground" is a maxim which has been preached at us all our lives, so keeping our feet *in* the ground ought to give us an even closer contact with reality, oughtn't it? This would account for the religious fervor with which our most urbanized youths and maidens chant the Anglo-Saxon term for bovine excrement, no doubt.

It is interesting to ponder on how strongly this Manure Mystique or Cult of the Bull has pervaded our mythos. It doesn't take a Bulfinch to recognize how the legend of the Minotaur came out of the function of Taurus. Boys and girls are "devoured" and turned into adults by the inevitable process of growing up, unless they are "devoured" by death while still young. The bullfight may be regarded as an outgrowth of the same idea.

A strange perversion of the Myth of the Bull was the practice of haruspicy, or prophecy by inspecting the entrails of sacrificed animals. There is a sound astrological basis for this weird superstition that "The Bull can tell us something if he will."

Taurus is associated with the sense of *hearing*. The practice of rewarding a victorious toreador with the bull's ear may be a carry-over from a time when the sacrificial rite was performed in full awareness of its inner significance. Our familiar expression, "Lend me your ear" may once have had a less abstract meaning than it does now, for all we know. In any event, it suggests a sense of sharing which we don't get in Aries. Who ever says, "Lend me your eyes?" Seeing is something we do alone, but hearing implies conversation, an exchange of sounds to convey thought and evoke sympathetic response.

There are, of course, two kinds of hearing: that which is performed through the external orifices on which we hang our earrings; and inner hearing, or *intuition*, which comes as a "still, small voice from *somewhere*." Perhaps we actually hear it, perhaps we only get a hunch. Something tells us. However it works, we know it when it comes, and experience may have taught us that this whatever-it-is can be a more reliable guide than what we regard as logic.

People who are most conscious of natural rhythms are the best receivers of the inner voice. Women's intuition is proverbial, and astrology shows us why. To begin with, Taurus is a feminine sign, and hearing is a passive activity; that is, sound is received within the ear. Think of how an ear works as contrasted with how the eye works. The eye is constantly in motion, whereas the ear doesn't move at all. The eye is convex —outwardly rounded—while the ear is shaped surprisingly like the female vagina, and we've learned that we ought not to overlook clues we find in such physical resemblances.

Furthermore, a girl who has reached puberty gets a regular monthly reminder of the biological effects of lunar rhythms on the physical structure. Her menstrual period shows that she is now capable of bringing forth new manifestations of human life. Short of surgery, the only way she can interrupt the menses is to get pregnant. However intensely she may want that baby, she must passively accept Nature's time plan for its birth.

Hence most girls are intimately involved with the Moon-Venus vibration for thirty or more years at a stretch. How well they use Taurus's function of inner hearing in daily life depends much on environment and upbringing. A woman's contemporaries may be amused, impressed, contemptuous, or frightened by the accuracy of her intuitions. They could bring her honor or get her burnt at the stake. She may regard her allegedly mystical powers as a sacred trust, to be used in the service of humanity. She may exploit them for money or notoriety. She may deny them to the point where they become totally blocked from consciousness. Or, as is most often the case, she may be so busy talking that she forgets to listen.

Over and over it must be emphasized that there is nothing "occult" or "psychic" about being able to listen with the inner ear. The power does not have to be purchased by allegiance to any cult. It does not come from observance of elaborate ritual or sacrifice. The skill can be sharpened by practice, but basically it's purely a matter of recognizing that the power is as natural as physical hearing and giving it a chance to work, by sitting still and paying attention.

Intuition is by no means an ability that women possess and men don't, of course. It is feminine only in the sense that it involves passive receptivity to the influx of mindstuff which the Moon is constantly washing up on the shores of subconsciousness.

We all know how the ocean tide's ebb and flow can carry

flotsam thousands of miles, then cast it up wherever wind and currents have caused it to drift. We like to prowl along the beach picking these things up, wondering where they came from and whether they're worth keeping. Some of us lug home armloads of treasures every time, while others never find a thing.

Telepathy, clairvoyance, clairaudience, psychometry, and other methods of picking up information without using the usual sensory communications channels, all seem linked to this process of psychic beachcombing. Certain groups such as the Australian aborigines and the Scottish highlanders have spectacular abilities to pick messages out of the air. We talk about how glorious it must be to have such gifts and read books on improving your psychic powers; but if they're all that marvelous, why don't we cling to them when we have them? As babies, we had no great trouble making our mothers understand what we wanted before we could talk. As parents, we feel rapport with our own babies. Animal lovers empathize with their pets. Yet instead of developing this magical gift to its fullest extent, we install a telephone. Why?

One reason may be that we have found telepathic communication too limiting. To receive, we have to empty our minds and let somebody else's image-making power reflect on the screen of consciousness. This means temporarily suspending the process of imagination by which we develop into more skillful and intelligent human beings. The most effective senders and receivers seem to be those who operate in an established social framework where mentation usually takes place on more or less the same wavelength. For example, Mrs. Alexandra David-Neel, the first Western lama in Tibet, claimed that the quietness of that land, the absence of crowds and of the busyness of more economically developed areas, created an untroubled ether favorable to telepathic communication; but the factors of cultural isolation and racial homogeneity were also present.

Fairy tales start, "Once upon a time." As primitive Earthlings, we were certainly closer to the Taurean rhythms than we are now. We had no tremendously complicated accumulation of mindstuff to muffle the messages of the inner ear. We were in an ideal position to listen and learn. The difficulty was that we had so few hooks on which to hang our new-found knowledge.

In its Cabalistic context, Taurus signifies a nail or hook, an implement which secures, pins down, holds something in its correct relationship to other things. Knowledge is of no use to us until we nail it into the structure of culture, until we perceive it, lay hold of it thoroughly, and claim it for our own. Visually, we perceive by means of contrast. Mentally, we perceive by comparing, relating, or opposing a new idea to existing ideas. We can take in only as many concepts as we can associate with our life experience.

In the primitive state, we have little time for philosophy. We see our world in terms of things to eat or wear, things to enjoy or fear: plants, wild beasts, flints, fire, water, wind, sun, rain, fellow tribesmen and women. Faced with an abstract idea, we anthropomorphize it into something we can see, hear, taste, smell, or touch. Coveting an enemy's courage, we eat the enemy's heart. Sensing the existence of controlling and regulating forces, we try to locate them in air, fire, water, earth—elements we are permitted to use but must handle with respect lest they turn hostile and destroy us. We invent gods in the shapes of animals. Wearing their skins, horns, teeth, claws, or whatever, we perform ceremonies which relieve us of our anxieties by giving us a chance to work off accumulated tension. In short, we bring the world of spirit down to earth. We turn a general idea into a specific symbol, the abstract into the material, just as the Life Force turns the concept of growth into a bumblebee, a daisy, a rabbit, or a human child.

Roughly speaking, this is what Taurus does in our lives. Subjects born with the Bull as a Sun sign are traditionally expected to be no-nonsense types. They go for the sturdy and substantial in their homes, their clothes, their politics. They believe in keeping a well-stocked larder.

Wherever Taurus appears in your chart, you will find this urge to pin down, to collect, to make manifest. Look around your home and you'll probably be both amused and surprised to realize how graphically the objects you've assembled represent your special orientation to this Venus-Moon vibration. We do love to gather together those things which particularly stand for our urge-to-become.

This concern with life is one of Taurus's more charming attributes. Unless there are strongly negative aspects, we should never expect to find a Taurean "half in love with easeful death." On the contrary, these subjects are apt to be on the very firing lines of the battle against sickness. As doctors and nurses, they seem to carry healing in their hands. Blood, urine, vomit, the results of bodily malfunction which cause many stomachs to churn, have no horrors for them. This is life, and they accept it.

The village wise woman, ministering to her neighbors with herbs and potions, is an atavistic Taurean figure, combining primitive anthropomorphism with that innate knowledge of how to make whole which comes from attunement to the upswinging life cycle. Witchcraft has always been popular with the spiritually undeveloped, and it keeps being rediscovered when we are getting ready to do some more growing but feel frightened, having to face what we don't yet understand.

Just now, we seem to be as susceptible to its charms as when we were fresh out of the trees. Let us not mistake it for anything more than what it is, and let us not forget its stultifying effect on the mind. Jesus enjoined us, "Unless ye become as little children, ye cannot enter the Kingdom of Heaven." We may not know precisely what is meant by this statement, but we do know that to become as children does not mean to act childish.

Taurus is still a child in terms of the life cycle. The Bull delights in toys, jewels, luxurious fabrics, imposing mansions, elaborate furnishings, rich furs from the animals to whom it feels so akin, yet so superior. Children demand plenty of nourishing food, but they'll eat junk if we don't discipline them. The main thing is to satisfy the need for frequent, tangible gratification. After all, Taurus is eating for two, to use the pregnant's woman's frequent justification for constant stuffing.

Both the Moon and Venus are *users*. These are the only two forces which actually depend on a supply of memory experience to keep up the process of manufacturing what we call realities.

We may not stuff ourselves on haunches of beef and mince pies, as the typical Taurean is supposed to do. We may not be avid in our pursuit of the dollar. Yet gluttony does almost always manifest itself somewhere in our personalities. We're almost certain to collect more of something than we really need or can use, and we've already mentioned how this tendency shows up in our charts.

Don Juan the arch-Arian, for instance, would have had Taurus ruling its own house. He was wealthy, and he spent his money on his personal comforts. He was sybaritic, fond of music, even hiring an orchestra to serenade him while he feasted alone. He collected sensual experiences, carefully keeping a list of names of the ladies he had seduced. According to Leporello, he carried out some of his amours merely to get a few more names on his list. We begin to wonder whether he was really interested in making love or in the statistics of sexual encounter. At any rate, he needed some tangible record of his stolen moments. We see this same concern with tangibility wherever Taurus is influential.

Taurus ruling the first house would give quite different traits. This subject would look long and carefully before he leapt. He mightn't leap at all, unless he could see a substantial reward for his effort waiting on the other side. Here, the fieriness of Aries could act on the ascending Earth sign the way fire hardens clay into bricks or pottery.

Taurus rising may act even more like the typical Taurean than this Sun sign in some other house. This subject may plod along at a slow, steady pace, squirreling away a portion of his wages every week, taking a stitch in time, knowing which side his bread is buttered on, and calmly aware that the race is not always to the swift. His thought processes might be slow, but details would be painstakingly worked out. He could be an accurate bookkeeper, a reliable clerk.

Such a solid citizen would naturally be distinguished by the serenity of his disposition. Astrologers have often painted such charming pictures of a zodiacal Ferdinand placidly sniffing the flowers under his dear, familiar cork tree. We recognize this admirable trait in our own Taurean-inspired characteristics. We recall some of the famous Taurus-born Ferdinands of history: Queen Victoria, Ulysses S. Grant, Nicolai Lenin, Harry Truman . . . oh, dear! This doesn't seem to be working out quite the way we've been led to expect.

Consider again the ruling and exalted planets working here, unbridled emotion and subconscious accumulation. Remember what we learned about Venus Victrix, the goddess of victory, determined as Queen Victoria to assert her authority regardless of how much the victory cost. "Walk wide o' the Widow at Windsor, For 'alf o' Creation she owns. We 'ave bought 'er the same with the sword an' the flame, An' we've salted it down with our bones. Poor beggars! It's blue with our bones." Think about it. Think about the inexorable will to grow which can choke a garden in weeds and defeat its purpose of providing food, unless we keep weeding and pruning. If you still don't get the full picture, go stand in front of a raging bull.

Taurus may not know what he wants, because his motivations are subconscious, but he knows he does want. And whatever it may be, it's his and he's going to have it. Cross him in his purpose and he'll bellow. He'll paw the earth, toss you, gore you, trample you to jelly without compunction, not because he has anything against you personally but just because you're in his way.

Aquarian Franklin D. Roosevelt could interest himself in the theoretical possibilities of atomic energy as a weapon, but we wonder if he could ever have brought himself to order its use. For Taurean Harry Truman, the decision was hateful but inevitable. This was the quickest way to end what would otherwise be a longer and bloodier conflict. Therefore, let it be done.

At the time, some of us thought he had brought Armageddon upon us, but obviously he hadn't. He was performing essentially the same act as a farmer putting poison down a woodchuck hole. The simile offends and shocks us, but the parallel is clear. The farmer may love all animals and detest the thought of putting such appealing little creatures to death. He may recognize their right to coexist with him as examples of the handiwork of the Life Force. Nevertheless he kills them because experience has taught him that if he doesn't prevent their eating his crops, he may not have enough food for his own family. His job is to get on with the business of living. We can't call him insensitive or heartless for doing what he conceives as his duty. If we're all that torn with pity for the woodchucks, those of us who are more intellectually endowed ought to show him a more humane way of handling his problem, instead of inventing stronger poisons.

Harry S. Truman's life gives us a superb illustration of the Taurean vibration working through a beautiful spirit. It will be years before we appreciate his greatness, but that's our problem, not his. He has explained to us over and over again who he is, what he stands for, what he intended to do as President, what he did, and why he did it.

As a beginner in politics, Mr. Truman did not hesitate to work with the unsavory Pendergast machine. This was the tool he found ready to hand when it was time to go to work. He knew that having to clean out the pigsty doesn't make a man a dirty swine. Later, when he could have scraped the mud off his boots and played the fine gentleman, he refused to turn his back on his old cronies. The ex-haberdasher's election to the vice presidency was supposed to be the political joke of the century, but Roosevelt was already a dying man then and a great many voters must have realized Truman would probably have to serve out that historic fourth term. When it happened, he said, "I felt like the moon, the stars, and all the planets had fallen on me," but he didn't say, "I can't handle the job."

He performed the most horrifying task any President has ever faced and never pretended that he didn't know exactly what he was doing. Announcing the dropping of the first atomic bomb, he said, "It is a harnessing of the basic power of the universe. The force from which the sun draws its power has been loosed against those who brought war to the Far East."

Having ended the war, he came back for reelection in the hope of winning the peace. Faced with predictions of overwhelming defeat, he took his wife and daughter out to grub victory from the nation's fields and furrows. His inaugural address on January 20, 1949, is Taurus at its most majestic. Listen to this:

> We must embark on a bold new program for making the benefits of our scientific advances and industrial progress available for the growth and improvement of under-developed areas. More than half the people of the world are living in conditions approaching misery. Their food is inadequate. They are the victims of disease. Their economic life is primitive and stagnant. Their poverty is a handicap and a threat both to them and to more prosperous areas.

A hostile Congress balked him time after time, but he refused to stop trying to be a good farmer. He kept a sign on his desk that said, "The buck stops here," and it did. His bullheaded refusal to dodge responsibility scared the pants off us. We rushed to elect a kindly father-figurehead who did nothing to upset our delicate sensibilities.

Harry went back to pass the time of day with his old neighbors at home and tend his own garden. In later years, stung by unjust criticism of his term in office, he went on national television to explain once more precisely what he had done and what were his motives. Then he hung out the "Do not disturb" sign and went back to minding his own business.

In *Backstairs at the White House* we meet Harry going down to the kitchen hand-in-hand with his adored Bess to see what was cooking for supper, washing his socks by hand because he thinks this is a distasteful task no man should ask anyone else to do for him, threatening to punch a music critic for making nasty remarks about Margaret's singing. We remember his delight in playing "The Missouri Waltz" on the White House piano, his early morning walks, his twinkly eyeglasses, his puckish grin. He was no romantic like Tom Sawyer, but he did have much in common with that other practical-minded Missourian, Huckleberry Finn.

From him we get a feeling of the Taurean nature—which applies wherever this influence shows up in a chart—as forthright, earthy, stubborn, physically tough, and, like Aries, essentially young though not infantile. We see a strong urge to make things real. We see the child's appreciation of watching the growth process. We see his delight when he gets his own way, his explosive temper which he doesn't. Even in such a highly developed character as Mr. Truman's, we find an element of boyish devilment which no amount of trouble could ever dampen.

Some Taureans are like animals, quickly reaching the peak of their intelligence and strength, then continuing for the rest of their lives on more or less the same level, sticking to the ideas, the habits, the occupations of their youth. The question in this second house always seems to be, "Where do I stop?" At what point does a conservative become a stick-in-the-mud? When do material desires begin to throw mental and spiritual values out of perspective?

Wanting the good things of life is not wrong. Everything around us shows that the whole pattern and purpose of the solar ecology is to convert desire into satisfaction, idea into object. Any want is a result of a sense of lack, a need to fill an empty space, to complete ourselves. The problem is to decide why we want what we want. What are we really asking for when we fasten all our earthly hopes on pink wall-to-wall carpeting or a stereo cassette? Taurus can make things grow, but he can't always distinguish the wheat from the tares. Luckily, however, we have a special department to handle this matter.

18 · Gemini

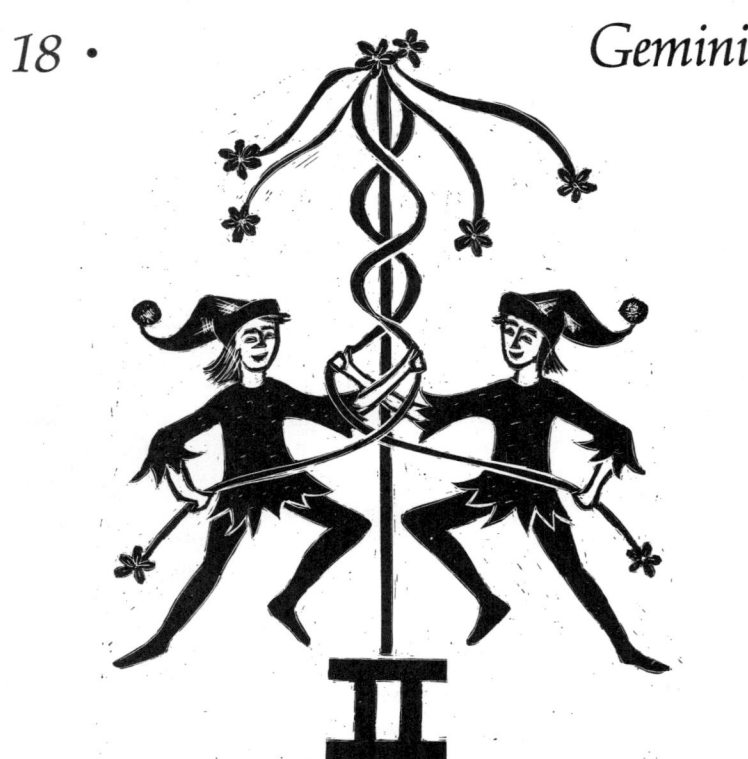

First Air Sign, Mutable, Masculine, Dual
Mercury Rules, No Planet Exalted
Color: Orange; Symbol: The Twins

WE have already learned that the third house is concerned with *education in self-expression*. Now we see Mercury as the lone planetary influence and realize that intellect rather than emotion is going to be emphasized here.

Gemini

We've met Mercury as the patron of travelers, the finder of roads, the seeker and explorer. It is natural to find him here, since the logical next step for the child who has begun to grow up physically is to realize himself mentally. Who am I? What can I do? How do I relate to my solar environment? What is this great, wide, wonderful Earth all about, and what's in it for me? Mercury is yellow, remember, and yellow is, indeed, curious.

To Gemini, astrology attributes *discrimination*. Here we use the concentrated power of Mercury to sort out, relate, contrast and compare, put into categories. The Cabala calls this sign Zain, the sword, since it is essentially divisive in nature. As we cut a child's food into pieces small enough for him to cope with, Gemini chops up the indigestible chunks of knowledge Taurus accumulates and picks out the bits which appeal to his individual mind.

It should be borne in mind that division can lead to unification. A botanist, for instance, may dissect an exquisite flower not to destroy its beauty but to place it in its proper category. His aim is to clarify understanding of his subject, hence to unify knowledge. He may be intending to apply the knowledge to some specific task in horticulture, pharmacology, or other related field, or he may simply want to know more about how flowers work. In any event, he's doing it for a reason, even though others may think he's being cruel to destroy something that smells so sweet and looks so pretty.

Gemini can be cruel, no doubt about that. Contrary to popular sentiment, small children often behave abominably to the furry animals they're supposed to adore. It's never safe to trust a tiny child with a pet, because he hasn't yet learned to handle this two-edged sword of discrimination. He's eager to try out his new skills of squeezing, pulling, poking, mauling; and this wiggly, squealing object presents a far more interesting laboratory than his stuffed bunny. It won't occur to him that what's fun for Baby may be death to the pet.

Grownups in whom the Gemini vibration is strong can be equally ruthless, although they will probably have developed more subtle methods of torture. Starting malicious rumors is an entertaining way to study social psychology. Playing one friend or lover against another for material advantage or just for kicks can be tremendously exciting sport, provided one has no intense emotions with which to reflect the sufferings of those played upon. If we don't feel much we don't get hurt much. Therefore, Gemini is reputed to skim through life like Pippa passing, always light-hearted, sparkling, laughing, recording only the sunny hours.

The Bible, which is, among other things, a rich astrological casebook, gives us a demonstration of Gemini in action in the allegory of King Solomon and the two mothers. These women brought a baby before the king, each claiming it as her own. To settle the dispute, Solomon suggested that he cut the child in two equal parts and give each woman half.

One agreed that this was a reasonable solution. However, as the king drew his sword, the other woman pleaded, "Give *her* the child and in no wise slay it." Her concern showed the great judge who was the rightful mother, and he handed over the baby to the woman who had begged for its life.

The first woman may well have been born under the sign of the Twins. Her willingness to make a fair and equitable distribution of the baby ought to appear entirely laudable to anybody who reasons without emotion, or so it would seem from the many similar stories we read in our history books and hear from certain social reformers. The roars of approval which greeted Mr. Chamberlain on his return from Munich in 1939 were set off by a typically Geminian stroke of diplomacy.

Where Gemini appears in our charts, we must guard against not only a superficial intellect but also the kind of detachment which results in unconscious cruelty. As Portia told Shylock, mercy must season justice in order for the Earthly mind to reflect the cosmic truth. This is something we have to keep constantly in mind at this particular stage of our development, if we are not to turn into robots.

After science fiction created the cyborg, computer technologists set about making the man-machine a reality. We are intrigued by the idea of a robot that could perform the most intricate mental exercises with none of the complications resulting from emotions which distract us meat-people. Amazing things have already been done with computers, and a race of cyborgs could come into being any day now. Can you imagine anything more horrible than a creature which thinks but does not feel?

It appears that in terms of the solar ecology this civilization must be very young, only some 35,000 years in duration, as far as we have been able to determine. We have progressed through the Arian stage of hunting, exploration, and similar individual activity; and the Taurean stage, where we developed agriculture and religion and expanded Aries's hand-to-hand conflict into world war, to suit Taurus's more grandiose ideals. Now we're being clever. We invent all sorts of gadgets nobody needs, because we've learned how. We convert priceless natural resources into plastic bubble-bath bottles shaped like Dracula and Frankenstein's monster, which couldn't be more appropriate.

You see, Gemini is a crook. He'll steal a forest to make pulp paper for funny books. It never occurs to him that some day we might need those trees for a nobler purpose than Batman. Comparison of convicted criminals' birth dates has turned up almost twice as many swindlers, forgers, confidence men, and counterfeiters born with the Sun in Gemini than in any other single Sun sign. This is not to say that all people born with this influence are dishonest—there may be balancing influences to keep them straight—but it's amazing what twisters the Twins can be. Even Geminians who take pride in being scrupulous about money may do things like returning merchandise they have worn or damaged and demanding that the store return their money. They may borrow other people's possessions and forget to return them. At a higher professional level, they may scorn such practices but not stick at a spot of deft plagiarism or adroit stabbing-in-the-back to further their careers.

The disturbing part is that they don't realize they're doing anything out of line. If the wrongness of the act is pointed out, they will produce all sorts of logical justifications. "You can't mix business with sentiment," they'll tell you scornfully. "One must be objective. We can't let personal considerations interfere with the overall good." They're probably more clever than we are, so they can easily make us feel cheap and inferior. We go off with a flea in our ear, but hours later that flea whispers, *"Whose* overall good?"

Mercury is not concerned with making judgments or fixing responsibilities. His job is to investigate ways and means. "Can this job be done? If so, how?" These questions occupy his attention so completely that he fails to ask the necessary third, "Should it be done?" Mercury the patron of thieves and pickpockets is, alas, more apt to muse, "Can I get away with it?"

Right now, we are considerably perturbed over youthful thievery. What we forget is that children have traditionally been thieves. We've brought them up on stories of how Grandpop raided Farmer Brown's orchard and risked a shotgun load of rock salt in the seat of his knickerbockers. We've persuaded them it was all jolly fun, no harm done. We never explain how the farmer felt about seeing the brittle limbs of his carefully tended trees snapped off, the fruit which was to have paid for his summer's toil lying bruised and trampled on the ground. Is it less criminal to steal an apple than an automobile? Does the monetary value of the goods determine the rightness or wrongness of the act?

We are certainly right to take a firm stand on thievery: it is a silly, stupid, irresponsible thing to do. Each antisocial act, however petty, holds us back in our struggle to become, as individuals and as a civilization, something more than we are now showing ourselves to be. Each failure to discriminate, each decision that "Little Me wants this" as opposed to "Grown-up Me is able to get along without such toys" is going to have to be corrected before we can take the next step up.

This is not middle-class morality but simple arithmetic. If you subtract, you wind up with a loss. To get back on the plus side, you have to restore what you took away. The heavier your liabilities, the harder you have to work to turn them into assets. Nobody need worry about forgetting this simple rule. We'll be reminded when the time comes to pay the bill.

The reason Gemini tends to be so much more a taker than a giver is that he usually doesn't know what he wants. A tot will pull out toy after toy, scatter them all over the house, then run whining to his mother that he has nothing to do. He hasn't yet learned to handle the desire nature of Venus. A somewhat more mature child can choose one specific plaything and use it to stimulate his imagination. By multiplying images, a boy or girl can become for the moment a fireman, a cowboy, a nurse, a mother, a painter, a musician, whatever the object suggests.

But Gemini isn't ready to become that deeply involved. Seeing so many choices, he hesitates to commit himself. By fixing on one thing, he's afraid he might miss something better. This is why his emotional involvements so often skim the surface, even when he is old enough to be classed as an adult. The Twins are apt to take their pleasure at what we call the social level. Parties, visits, theater, movies, any kind of amusement in which he is not called upon to make a solid commitment can provide intriguing morsels to tempt his insatiable but finicky appetite for knowledge. He loves new places, new scenes, new faces, new anything, as long as it doesn't make too many demands on his time or attention.

We can see, then, why astrologers tell us that having Venus in the third house* is an exceptionally fortunate aspect. Connecting the ability to choose with the ability to want gives this subject unusual ability to put what he learns to practical use. Instead of the perennial student, he becomes the practical achiever, the Rikki-Tikki-Tavi who goes and finds out, then settles down with the lady mongoose of his dreams to produce litter after litter of healthy, happy, busy little mongooses who delight their mother's heart by their beauty and charm then go forth to spread their father's zest for knowledge and help to slay the cobras of ignorance.

If you are not blessed with this delightful aspect, don't

---

* A *house* is one of the twelve 30° segments of the zodiacal circle. Each house is identified by a sign.

despair. You have both Gemini and Venus somewhere in your chart, and Mercury will always help you to find a connecting link between them, if you put him to work.

Since Gemini is concerned with distinctions, this is a good place to clear up any misunderstanding you may have about the houses. In reading a chart, the house at the position of the Ascendant is *always* the first house, always concerned with the subject's personality, and so on around the wheel. Aries always exerts an influence there, because it is Aries as the beginner of the life cycle which determines the activity of the first house. Your *personal* Aries may rule any of the twelve houses or may be intercepted and rule none. On whatever house it appears, it will modify the function of that particular house in helping to determine the subject's basic character and general approach to life. If planets are joined to Aries or appear in a house ruled by Aries, they will influence the subject to act in Arian ways.

As we shall see, this opens up a number of possibilities for Venus-Mercury relationships. You might have Gemini ruling the second or seventh house where Venus is the universal ruler, or the twelfth, where Venus is universally exalted. Your chart might show Venus in Gemini, or falling in the Gemini-ruled house. There are many other possibilities, which will be discussed later. In each case, the emphasis would be somewhat different.

From what we've seen of Taurus, for instance, we can picture how Gemini would behave as ruler of the second house. This subject might combine wit and versatility with imagination to gather the tangible wealth in which Taurus delights. He could be a fine craftsman, a shrewd and farseeing investor, an imaginative and attractive confidence man, or a number of other things, depending on how he handles the vibration; but material gain of one sort or another would almost certainly be his goal.

Venus in Gemini would be likely to act out a variety of roles, according to the fancy of the moment. He or she would often be in love with somebody or other, but more often with two at a time. "How happy I'd be with either, were t'other young charmer away!" is his cry. "I gotta love for Angela, I love Carlotta, too. I no can marry both o' dem, So what I gonna do?" He'll need strong reinforcements or a very determined partner to make up his mind.

Perhaps it's because Gemini needs Venus to warm him up that so many weddings take place during his yearly reign, in late May and early June. Somehow, we sentimentally picture the Heavenly Twins as a boy and girl, but if you'll study the old astrological treatises, you'll find they're both boys or (rarely) both girls. Hence the interplay of active and passive, positive and negative, the masculine-feminine polarity is lacking.

In what we are pleased to call the lower animals, masculinity and femininity are taken for granted. Differences in sex are signalled by obvious physical characteristics: the lion's mane, the peacock's tail, the tomcat's hyperactive scent gland, the female baboon's reddening backside. When the estrus cycle rolls around, everybody knows who's who. They do what comes naturally, then go away and concentrate on something else.

Not so *Homo sapiens*. Once he's got beyond the infant stage of the growth cycle, he starts asking, "Who am I? Where did I come from? How did I get here? What am I supposed to be doing?" This can be terrifying. His natural impulse is to find someone or something to cling to. The easiest person to identify with is someone as like himself as possible. Having a twin, or a twin soul, is ineffably comforting. In the partner we see a reflection of ourselves, a living laboratory in which to test the process of becoming. Here is a behavior pattern to emulate, a mind which will exchange ideas with us, help to sort out the avalanche of information that is threatening to engulf us. Our twin probably won't stand for doing all the listening and giving while we talk and take, so we must learn to *reciprocate*, which is a function of the third house.

We see, then, that in Gemini we are beginning to discover the concept of love. We are not yet loving because we haven't yet realized our own ego idea to the point where we feel confident about balancing it against the opposing polarity.

We're still taking inventory of the materials which we gathered in Taurus. We don't know what others want from us, we're not sure we have it to give, and we mightn't want to part with whatever it is when we do find out, so we're playing it cool. Our earliest attachments outside the family circle are usually to children of our own age and sex, because these are the least demanding and, at this stage, the most enlightening.

Some subjects may continue to be satisfied with these identical-twin relationships through one or more life cycles. Strictly speaking, a homosexual relationship is *any* reciprocal feeling between two persons of the same sex. We are in error, according to the psychiatrists, when we use the word to refer exclusively to those associations in which physical sex play is practiced.

If you examine the shorthand symbol for Gemini, you will note that it consists of two vertical lines joined at top and bottom by horizontals, but not connected in the center. This suggests union at the levels of superconscious and subconscious, but not on the material plane. Anyone who enjoys the blessing of a close friendship immediately understands what this means.

> I can tell you anything, because you understand me. You don't laugh at my aspirations; you respect my mentality. At the high level of mind and spirit we communicate freely, yet we can be together for hours and not have to talk at all. When we're apart, a subconscious tie exists between us. I just know when things are going well or ill with you. Something tells me if you need a letter, a phone call, a visit, a word of cheer, comfort, encouragement from me. Still, we each have a separate life with a different mate, other friends, other interests. We neither need nor wish to share our physical existence on a day-to-day basis.

These are among our most beautiful, most satisfying, and often most lasting experiences. To have a real twin soul, a comrade who dispassionately evaluates you and accepts you for what you are is to know genuine love, even if the two of you never even so much as clasp hands in greeting or parting.

Then why has society so frequently and vehemently condemned homosexuality? Why, when Ganymede Gemini flounces into the barroom in his sister's evening dress, does burly Tom Taurus slam down his pint and rise in his wrath to tear Ganymede apart? Well, Tom may be a dumb ox and uncouth in his manners, but he's loyal to old Ma Nature; and Ma says it ain't fitten' because it don't get you nowhere.

It has been argued that any love is better than no love, and this is a statement hard to refute. If friendship is the best we're capable of at this stage in our development, then by all means let us be friends. If we find that we can give and receive sexual stimulation in no other way than by fondling genitalia similar to our own, we may reason that at least this is a form of sharing, therefore a step up from the selfish practice of masturbation. Either is preferable to letting unsatisfied sex drives turn us into seething neurotics. Both are now recognized as being natural phases in a child's sexual development, but who wants to stay a child forever?

At the moment, homosexuality seems to be back in fashion. This is something that happens from time to time. The usual excuse is that it's a way of controlling population growth. It is on a par with binding girls' feet to develop muscles which make them more cushiony bedmates, or inserting wooden disks in their lips so that men from other tribes won't want to steal such hideous women. Having accepted such practices out of what appears as expedience, those involved always try to convince themselves that the resultant deformity is beautiful. Eventually, they have to face the fact that there is no beauty in trying to hold back or interfere with the course of Nature.

Steering the growth process toward improving itself in accordance with the cosmic laws is something else again. Darwin demonstrated that natural selection constantly goes on; Teilhard de Chardin gave us a breathtaking description of man's evolution. Nevertheless, it is an alchemical truth that nature unaided always fails. Everything in the solar ecology teaches us that it is not only our impulse but our duty as thinking, feeling, believing men and women to take an active part in improving the quality of creation. We may reject some of the Piscean mores, but we cannot afford to refuse the responsibility of growing up and learning how to love. Only through the power of love shall we be able to fulfill ourselves as citizens of the Sun.

We now know that vague sentimental yearnings are not enough. Mercury gives us intelligence to discriminate between what is and is not genuinely lovable in ourselves and in the objects of our affections. We can apply our mental powers toward understanding more about how love works and what it is intended to achieve. By so doing, we avoid being led astray by blind emotion and those false concepts which have resulted from our past failures to read the label before quaffing the magic potion. Once we know the mechanics of forming genuinely happy relationships, we find that love is not disillusion and heartbreak, but never-ending delight.

19 · Cancer

First Water Sign, Cardinal, Feminine, Dual
Moon Rules, Jupiter Exalted
Color: Yellow-Orange; Symbol: The Crab

WHAT do we know about the crab? It wears its skeleton outside and is soft in the middle. In order to become larger, it has to shed this protective covering and grow a whole new shell. It seems to have no sense of direction and usually walks sideways with an odd, scrabbling movement. Crabs are so stubborn about holding on to what they've grasped that their powerful pincers sometimes get pulled off. If this happens, they grow new claws. Crabs live in and around shallow water, are easy to catch but hard to keep, unless you handle them just right. Some are edible; others not. Altogether, these spidery crustaceans are perplexing, contradictory creatures.

Strange indeed must be the goings-on in a house which adopts the Crab as its symbol.

Cancer is the Latin name for Crab. Lately, some astrologers have begun to drop the term because of its unpleasant medical associations, preferring to call fourth-house natives Moon Children. This strikes us as artsy-craftsy and not very accurate. It may tend to emphasize mistaken notions about Cancerians' being completely dominated by the Moon. We sometimes forget that Jupiter is exalted here, possibly because a Moon-Jupiter relationship can be hard to explain, much less cope with.

Cancer is a tough one, no doubt about that. Not by accident have expressions like "crabbed," "crabby," "old crab" scuttled into our vocabulary. The Oxford Dictionary gives one particularly delightful definition of "crabbed": "perversely intricate; hard to make sense of; difficult to decipher." Nevertheless, each of us has Cancer somewhere in his chart, even if it's only as an intercepted sign, so it behooves us to make the effort. Let's sneak up on that crab and pick her up carefully from behind so her pincers won't nip us and take a good look at this mysterious little creature.

To begin with, we note that Cancer is a lady crab, a feminine sign, passive, receptive, a taker rather than a giver. This makes sense. Here are two great pincers ready to clutch and retain whatever goes swimming by. Since she follows Gemini, we assume she has been schooled in distinguishing what will serve her needs from what won't. She's not a stupid crab, you see. At least she needn't be, unless she's too obstinate to take advantage of the educational opportunities in the bright orange schoolhouse next door.

In Taurus, we saw the Moon exalted over Venus, the multiplying power of imagination dominated by the subconscious. In the fourth house, however, subconsciousness lies under Jupiter, the power of acceptance and expansion, of getting on with it. Cancer may not know where she's going, but she knows she's got to go. So she putters about, now frontward, now backward, now sideways, nibbling at bits and pieces of the life experience she finds in her path, not for the fun of tasting them like Gemini, but because she knows she needs to absorb nourishment enough to strengthen her shell.

In the crab's shell we observe the primary function of Cancer. The Cabalistic meaning of this sign is "A field enclosed by a fence." In order to achieve anything at the self-conscious level, we have to stake out a field of endeavor and confine our efforts toward expansion within this area. Where Cancer appears in our charts, the process of defining our life work begins. Having found our strength in Aries, learned the basic skills in Taurus, tested our abilities in Gemini, we're ready to begin cultivating our gardens.

Aries is associated with vision, Taurus with hearing, Gemini with smelling (since the nose is a most powerful organ for detecting differences between people, animals, and objects of all sorts). Cancer is related to the faculty of *speech*.

We have learned that in order to get anything done, we must furnish Mars with accurate directions. This involves expressing our desires in precise statements, verbalized or formulated mentally. Each statement involves setting a limit, drawing a boundary around an idea. We mean this, not that. We're referring to him, not to her. We want the black one, not the white one.

In order to form intelligent definitions, we have to know what we mean by both this and that, him and her, black and white. We have to realize that what we mean by these terms may not be what somebody else means. Since we are not working just for ourselves, we must communicate, and we can't do that until we are able to discern differences and concurrences between what we mean and what others mean. It's easy to understand, therefore, why Cancer relies on the Moon to form those subconscious connections which we call empathy. The more connections are formed, the easier it will be to shed that confining shell and grow into a bigger and finer crab.

At the practical level, dealing with meaning involves using a highly developed system of sound codes which we call language. Our handling of the problems we face can be greatly facilitated by learning correct habits of speech. If we concentrate on saying what we mean, we cure ourselves of sloppy thinking. We then communicate our thoughts to others without running the risk of being misunderstood. We begin to appreciate the power of words.

Since time began, occult practices, the evocation of forces which can be discerned only by their results, have been built around sound. The tribal war cry whose very utterance struck terror into the enemies' hearts, the magical incantation, the repetition of prayers and hymns, country music, soul music—each cult, whether religious or secular, has a distinctive "group noise" which *holds it together*.

Even babies understand the magic of sound. The first time we set up a howl and get our diapers changed, we find out that making the right noise can produce a desired result. Nations spend millions of our hard-earned dollars in developing the fine art of propaganda. Modern communications media such as newspapers, radio, and television have altered the structure of our civilization.

We are told that the medium is the message, but this is not true. In the beginning was the Word. The question is, do we allow ourselves to be controlled by words, or do we ourselves control their immense power?

Think of the riches we dissipate every day, the endless stream of words we pour out over the telephone, over cups of coffee and at cocktail parties in meaningless chatter to which our hearers don't even bother to listen. What if we were to expend even a fraction of that wasted energy in studying how to choose and employ words in combinations of genuine power and meaning, words which could convey thoughts of love and joy, words which could lead our hearers to meditate great acts and inspire them with confidence to carry out their dreams, and by so doing strengthen our own characters? What if we were to stop using words out of context, quit applying the same tired adjectives and expletives to everything from a Kleenex to a catastrophe?

Much of the time, we haven't the remotest idea what we're really saying. Take the popular noun "pig," for instance. The dictionary defines it as "a sow or boar of the genus *Suidae*, comprising bristle-bearing, non-ruminant hoofed mammals." Because pigs like to eat a great deal and roll around in the mud, we used to call greedy, dirty children "little pigs." Gradually, we started applying the term to overweight, unattractive persons of sensual habits, which still made sense. In recent years, some of us have started referring to policemen as pigs. Now, what are a pig's less superficial characteristics?

In *Animal Farm*, George Orwell astonished his readers by placing the pig in authority over the other animals because of its superior intelligence. Breeders assert that, given the opportunity, pigs are fastidious creatures and that they wallow in the mud for the same reason women give themselves mudpack facials, to soothe their delicate skin. People who raise pigs seem to grow remarkably fond of them on a pure, platonic level. The love of a man for his pig is beautifully exemplified by P. G. Wodehouse in the characters of Lord Emsworth and the Empress of Blandings.

A boar is the most virile of lovers, a sow the most devoted of mothers. Pigs do not bite, claw, or say naughty words. They live quiet, peaceful lives, do useful service as scavengers and garbage disposal units, then yield up their blameless ghosts and donate their bodies to be made into pork chops, ham hocks, fatback, and chitterlings, which are quite properly referred to as "soul food." We consume these to renew our strength and energy, so that we can rush out and shriek, "Off the pigs" at persons who may qualify on the basis of neat habits, superior intelligence, and willingness to lay down their lives in the service of mankind but are not members of the genus *Suidae* and therefore not entitled to be called pigs, however flattering this supposedly derogatory epithet may be.

When we allow ourselves to fall into these sorts of verbal traps, we not only proclaim our ignorance but also drive another picket into the stockade which surrounds our personalities and keeps us both from knowing our neighbors and becoming the type of neighbor whom others would wish to know better. If we content ourselves with parroting catch phrases, we are generally letting somebody else's mistake adversely influence our character-building process. A wise crab takes the trouble to find out whether this is something she really wants, instead of seizing any bait offered and being drawn into the net.

We are all fenced in by preconceived ideas, bad habits, blindly accepted customs. The important thing to remember about any fence, however high or low, is that it has both an inside and an outside. We may not be able to get through it by hurling ourselves at the palings, but we can leap over it by using the power of Jupiter which is exalted in Cancer. No matter how thick a wall of ignorance and prejudice we've allowed to grow up by accepting whatever nonsense has been foisted off on us, we can always pole-vault to the other side. We start by making a strong resolution to free ourselves, and we express that resolution in *words*. Having formulated a specific goal, we start organizing our activities toward that goal. An important part of the work is learning the vocabulary we'll need in our new position.

Bernard Shaw's play *Pygmalion*, which became the popular musical *My Fair Lady* was written specifically for the purpose of illustrating how what we *are* is conditioned by what we *say*. The transformation of Eliza Doolittle from a guttersnipe into a fine lady was accomplished not by washing her face and changing her clothes, but by teaching her to select and pronounce words in a manner which would cause her hearers to place her at a social level commensurate with the sounds she produced.

Learning what kinds of noises a lady makes, Eliza absorbed the suggestions of refinement which they conveyed. Every syllable carried a reminder to her subconscious mind, "You are in the process of becoming a lady." Accordingly, the Moon force brought appropriate mindstuff to consciousness for practical use. Her gestures, her facial expressions, her manners of sitting, walking, eating, drinking became those of a gentlewoman. Rising in her own esteem, Eliza grew to respect her mental abilities. She learned to reason instead of to react. At last she was able to see herself as a free spirit, and to choose her own destiny. She had leaped over the fence.

In the show, Professor Higgins and Colonel Pickering do a little duet congratulating each other on their achievement. To the audience, it's perfectly clear that all the credit goes to Eliza herself. She was the one who made the resolution to better her lot. She was the one who sought out Professor Higgins and made the decision to accept his unorthodox teaching methods. All he could do was set an example. She was the one who had to incorporate what he showed her into her personality structure.

While we're on the subject, Professor Higgins gives us a splendid example of the Cancer-controlled subject. He is slovenly in his personal habits but extremely critical and ready to blame others for his own shortcomings. He deliberately obscures his correspondence by writing in a shorthand of his own invention which nobody else can read but also encloses a translation lest he not make himself understood, thus doubling his work and exasperating the recipient to no purpose. He's a dreadful nagger. When Eliza declares her intention of marrying Freddie, he gives way to a spiteful display of jealousy. He is completely self-centered yet is willing to expend any amount of time and effort on Eliza so long as she concedes his absolute authority. If she had failed to carry off her public appearance brilliantly, he would have heaped abuse on her; when she succeeds, he gives her not one word of praise and tries to claim all the credit for himself.

Doesn't all this remind you of the jokes about Jewish mothers? Now do you see why astrology associates the fourth house with motherhood? Still, we love Higgins, and we love dear old Mom—in spite of her overbearing ways, she makes good chicken soup. She represents protection, security, a willingness to take care of us and help us grow up.

There used to be a superstition that baby bears are born completely shapeless and are licked into the shape of cubs by their mothers' tongues. It is true that a mother animal's first act after parturition is to lick her baby clean. The stimulation of the mother's lapping helps the newborn creature to start breathing normally. Human mothers trying to make an obstreperous child "shape up" still exclaim, "I'll give you a licking!"

However we use our tongues on our children, the principle is much the same. Cancer feels herself obliged to nag and scold, because her job is to lick Gemini's accumulation of information into shape, to enclose the sorted-out mindstuff in a solid shell so that it can be recognized and put to use.

This is not always a pleasant task. Even though a punishing mother admonishes her wailing offspring, "You'll thank me for this some day," she knows perfectly well he'll do no such thing. He'll go off with some dizzy blonde and leave his poor old gray-haired mother alone to moon over his baby shoes and that one lock of baby hair she can't bear to part with because Cancer, under that hard crust, is soft, sweet, and spineless as a bowl of milk pudding. Rebounding from Gemini's cold intellectualism, she fairly wallows in sentiment.

Again, let's consider that lovable old crab, Professor Higgins. When Shaw wrote *Pygmalion*, he had every intention of allowing Eliza to marry Freddie. The original book of the play winds up with a detailed explanation of how right Eliza was in declaring, "I wouldn't marry you if you asked me," because she realized that to Higgins she would always be the puppet of his creation, that they could never establish a relationship on equal terms, and a lot of other tosh which shows how much Shaw knew about women. He thought the two young people would settle down as greengrocers and florists, with Eliza leading not only Freddie but also Higgins and Pickering around by their noses forever after.

No doubt this sounded logical, and it might have worked if Shaw had not made the mistake of creating two real, live human beings in whom Cancer's influence is strongly demonstrated. Eliza might well have been born under Taurus, with Cancer rising. She and Higgins could no more have let each other go than a crab would relinquish a particularly delectable morsel of dead fish. Shaw's ending was rejected: Leslie

Howard married Wendy Hiller. Rex Harrison married all those other ladies and we left the theater feeling that Life Can Be Beautiful and we'd got our money's worth.

To Shaw, it was natural that a man should allow himself to be taken care of by dominating women, or so we assume from the fact that he himself did it all his life. To most of us, however, the idea is repugnant, whether or not we submit to the actuality. In the light of astrological interpretation, the reason is obvious. The masculine principle is the active aggressor; the feminine, the passive receiver. In an Eliza-Freddie match, the principle would not have operated effectively. Eliza is extremely feminine and not really all that dominating. Freddie is just plain spineless. There would not have been enough active thrust to the relationship to keep Jupiter turning smoothly. The pair of them would have been a drag on the Life Force.

On the other hand, Eliza and Higgins are a fair match for each other. Essentially the more tough-minded, she can keep his boorishness in check without impeding his intellectual activities. She can lick him into shape as a reasonable human being without devouring him.

This is the problem Cancer always faces. How can she perform her function of shell building without squeezing the meat inside into a formless pulp? How can she rear the brainchild into a mature action without either compressing it into a rubber stamp of ideas she has coped with before or causing it to shoot out of her sphere of influence as a grape does when we pop its skin? She's so big, and it's so small. She's a Cardinal sign. The temptation to impose her will is enormous.

"You're going to do what I say because I'm going to make you obey me," is such an effective way of quelling infant rebellion and keeping her charge out of what she believes to be harm's way that even the most Montessori-minded parent can't resist using it at times. Nor is this always the wrong approach. At least it shows the child he's not being left to shift for himself. The Cancerian lover exclaims, "You're mine, all mine, body and soul," and the beloved murmurs, "Yes, darling," even when intelligence insists, "I'm nothing of the sort!" because it's so delightful to feel warm and protected and to belong to somebody.

Cancer is another dual sign. Part of its function is to make us feel that we belong. In our charts, it gives hints as to how we are likely to direct our efforts to "join the group" by accepting responsibility, by defining our aims in words that will turn on the Jupiter-Saturn vibration and start the process of bringing them into being on the physical level. We begin to direct our willpower *otherward*.

Accepting responsibility, however, does not always mean that we are responsible, and being able to exert our will power over persons who seem to have less of it than we do does not necessarily make us any better or wiser than they. While those who are temporarily under our protection may cause us to lecture, nag, scold, and even punish, we have to be extremely careful not to squeeze too hard, not to expect too much, be jealous, overprotective, or show resentment if they don't show appreciation of our efforts.

To make use of will power, we now know, is to take a personal hand in the direction of Cosmic forces which are *equally* available to us all. "Your will" is no stronger than "my will" because in fact only *one* will exists. We do not control will. We can control our personal attitudes and actions if we try, but we must do it within the context of the forces by which we operate. We cannot practice self-control effectively until we know what the self is. We shan't have the confidence to let our thoughts expand freely, so that we can become liberated human beings instead of identical dolls from the old Cancerian mold, until we develop an awareness of what identity means. And how do we find that out? The Crab isn't going to tell us. We shall have to ask a Lion.

20 · Leo

Second Fire Sign, Fixed, Masculine, Single
Sun Rules, Neptune Exalted
Color: Yellow; Symbol: The Lion

The Sun whose rays are all ablaze with every-living glory
Does not deny his majesty. He scorns to tell a story.
He don't exclaim, 'I blush for shame, so kindly be indulgent,'
But fierce and bold in fiery gold he glories all effulgent.
I mean to rule the earth as he the sky.
We really know our worth, the Sun and I.

THERE was no false modesty about Yum-Yum. She was the prettiest girl in Japan and she jilted the Lord High Executioner to marry the son of the Mikado and, presumably, lived happily ever after. The King of Beasts and his sinuous consort are experts at getting what they want.

Leo is the youth in his pride, the thirteen-year-old who stands up at his Bar Mitzvah and squeaks, "Today I am a man," and sometimes means it. Mahbub Ali bragged to Kim that by the age of fourteen he had shot his man and begot his man. Why not? Killing and copulation are the raw materials of the life cycle. It's reasonable that the young apprentices should get the job of preparing them for the more delicate refining processes.

Astrologically, the first thing we notice about Leo is that this is not a dual sign. Each of the previous four houses has been associated in some way with the concept of working in harness. Each has been involved with something else, not a *ding an sich*. Now along comes Popeye the Sailorman shouting, "I yam what I yam an' that's what I yam," felling anybody who gets in his way with one swing of his mighty fist. He attributes his strength to eating plenty of fresh, green spinach. Surely we don't have to belabor the symbolism of that!

Popeye shows another facet of the Leo-inspired personality. Only the fiercest determination to convert geese into swans could make a sailor choose a girl as homely as Olive Oyl for his sweetheart. But this is the sort of thing at which Leo shines. Look at the lights in the fifth house: Sun ruling, Neptune exalted. Leo loves to brighten the corner, and he has the ability to do it by means of psychedelic lighting, if he so desires.

Astrology has been so carried away by the sunlit splendor of Leo that we sometimes fail to notice the indirect lighting in the upper story. Neptune is the higher power of Venus. Since Venus is Imagination, Neptune must be imagination on the grand scale.

A President's widow trudges alone behind the caisson bearing his casket and we sigh, "How queenly!" To her, born with the Sun in Leo, this is the natural and normal way to behave. When the widow marries the head of a shipping empire, we wonder at her choice, but what else could she do? Kings are in short supply these days. As the girl in the old movie *The Cabinet of Dr. Caligari* explained, "We who are of noble birth are not free to follow the dictates of our own hearts."

Through the transforming power of Neptune, Leo makes the best of what's available. He is so good at pretending to be what he wishes he were that he frequently gets away with it. Sir Walter Scott, also born with the Sun in Leo, created an Age of Chivalry out of scraps of old armor and fragments of old ballads. But fantasies spun on paper are not enough for Leo. The Sun will soon burn away those Neptunian mists. Leo wants to build his tower of genuine ivory and move into it with all the goods and chattels he shows such aptitude for collecting. Nor is the Lion as lazy about making his dreams come true as he's often accused of being. Scott worked prodigiously at rewriting history in the light of his heroic fancy, shoveling hidden treasures by the cartload out of the peat bogs and rubbing them up with his pen so that thousands upon thousands of his worshippers could revel in their glitter. If some of his jewels turned out later to be paste and pinchbeck, that wasn't his fault. The Sun shines alike on the just and the unjust, the fine and the phony. Scott's job was to illuminate, not to judge; he did give us a grand show for our money, though he spent all his own and more beside in the process.

In every discussion of Leonian personality traits, money seems to pop up. Gold is the metal of the Sun. The "bright golden guineas," being miniature reflections of Sol's benign face and having some of his power to bestow material blessings on their possessors, are clearly intended for Leo's use. And how he can use them! Here is where Neptune's influence asserts itself again, because where Leo reigns, money certainly does tend to flow like water.

A catty biographer describes the President's lady as constantly overspending on clothes and adornments, even trying to use the power of Neptune to transform jewels from a sword of state into an ornament for herself, on the no doubt reasonable grounds that nobody would ever know the difference. Indubitably, the gems would have shone more brightly on a beautiful woman than on an ugly old weapon, and she owed it to her position to make a good appearance. Leonian logic is often hard to refute, especially since we adore our pet lions and want them to be happy.

Scott's biographers have had a hard time explaining how the writer could be meticulous over household bills, yet never demand an accounting from the publishing house he milked of nonexistent profits in order to build a majestic estate and entertain like royalty. How do we reconcile greatness of character with business practices which remind us that the Highlanders he revered lived mostly on sheep they stole from less picturesque Lowlanders?

It's very simple. The king can do no wrong. He's sure he's acting from the noblest motives, and who are we to doubt him? Youngsters will skate over thin ice regardless of "Danger" signs, confident in the strength and agility they've just found out they possess. The Sun sets tonight fully confident that it will rise tomorrow, because it has the power to do so, and nobody can take that power away. Reaching the fifth house, we learn that we have the ability to become what we want to be. We start to value ourselves as independent beings.

Note that there is no evidence of sharing in this. Sharing implies equality of right, and Leo does not acknowledge equality. He may bestow, graciously and kindly. He may display warm solicitude for those who place themselves under his protection. Much as he loves the good things of life, he will often deny himself in order to gratify their wants. *Noblesse oblige.* His Majesty will take care of his subjects, so long as they acknowledge his sovereignty.

Now we understand why astrologers call the fifth house the House of Children. Paternalism is the essence of the Leonian vibration. In our charts, the sign ruling this house and any planets found therein give strong indications about how we relate to human children as well as our brain-children. Opposing signs and planets will tell something about our fathers, and about the influences which will be brought to bear on our talents and aptitudes.

People in whom the Leo vibration is strong will be good father-figures, regardless of their sex or whether they themselves have children. Instinctively, young people will turn to them for counsel, for friendship, for just a smile and a pat on the head. Such contacts inspire the hero worship which is the beginning of altruistic love.

When we studied the Sun, we learned that all love begins with self-love. In Leo, we can see how the process works. By the strength of his self-approval, the Lion creates a sort of magnetic field which apparently exerts much the same gravitational pull on less positive natures as the Sun does on the Moon. Why should other people not love him, when he is so lovable? And since they're kind enough to show their affection, it's the least he can do to shed the light of his countenance upon them and be gracious unto them.

As the planets revolve around the Sun, as the lion snoozes while his wives are out catching a zebra for his supper, so is Leo most in tune with life while he's sitting quietly in the midst of his admirers. And so is the beginning of love to be found at the still center of being. And where love is, there God is also.

Astrologers give Leo rulership over the heart. Poets ascribe this function to Eros, the god of love. Whatever we call it, we know how it works. If we wish to be loved, we start by making ourselves lovable, and letting others know we're here. We let our light shine among men, and if we're not sure how best to do so, we study our charts to ascertain where our most appealing traits may be put on view.

But we can't expect a masculine fire sign to be content playing the role of the flame that attracts the moths. The astral Lion may be an ardent wooer, and we mustn't be surprised if we find that he still believes in the *droit du seigneur* A lion's loyalty is to his pride, a chief's to his clan, a king's to his country. A father can love his children without having to clutch them forever to his bosom. Knowing that he commands their respect, that he has taught them as much as he can of what they need to know, he can let them go forth to become kings and queens in their own right.

Fidelity in the individual sense may not seem very necessary to a Leonian personality. It will be enough for him to know that he's kindled the fire of love in another heart. He's not likely to sit around forever after, toasting his toes at the same old hearthside, although he'll be glad to pop in occasionally just to make sure his photograph is still in the place of honor on the mantelpiece, his silken cushion and his saucer of cream waiting for him, and a full cast of adorers primed to play their parts in the heartwarming melodrama, *The Hero's Return*.

Nobody will enjoy the reunion more than Leo. He'll let the babies pull his whiskers, the lovely maidens twine roses in his mane, the older ladies ply him with goodies. He'll flex his mighty talons for the edification of the youths, share a knowing wink and a convivial glass with the gaffers, electrify his audience with noble tales of the hunt. Then he'll drop into a contented catnap while everybody sits around admiring the sheen of his coat and the dignity of his countenance and whispering about how overjoyed they are to find he's still their own lovable old pussycat. Then he'll considerately go away so that they can have the fun of staging the pageant over again at a later date.

This is not Leo's sole reason for withdrawing. He has a genuine need to get off by himself occasionally. Since he's such a sociable animal as a rule, this sudden craving for solitude may puzzle and distress his admirers. Realizing what the fifth house means, however, we can sympathize. No doubt we feel the same urge to insist on a degree of privacy in that segment of our lives which the lion influences.

We have to keep testing our ability to stand alone; and the stronger the Leo vibration, the more testing we do. Tom Sawyer had to lick every new boy in town, just to prove he could. Many societies have formalized rituals in which a youth goes off to find himself. Even if this does not take place at a specific age and within a specific frame of reference, the need is usually recognized. American Indian boys who must remain isolated from the tribe until their dreams have revealed the names by which they will thenceforth be known are acting out the principle of the fifth house. So are little girls who run away to Hollywood to become movie stars.

Puberty rites take many forms, but all have the object of marking a formal separation of child from adult. How desperately we need such rites is being pointed out to us in the turmoil which young people are going through at this time.

Fifty years ago, we didn't have this much trouble telling the men from the boys. When Willie got his first pair of long trousers, he wasn't a kid any more. When Susie let down her skirt hems and pinned up her hair, she became a young lady, eligible to be "sparked." Arbitrary as these divisions were, everybody knew who was which by the simple act of seeing how they were dressed.

Once the immediate needs of conserving bodily warmth and protecting the skin have been served, we use clothing mainly as a signalling device. When stylists talk about the language of fashion, they mean something definite and meaningful. This is the true Esperanto, and learning to speak it is part of Leo's initiation. Clothes play a far more important part than some of us realize in developing individual personality as well as a culture.

Parents who rush children into adult clothing may be making serious mistakes. It's one thing for a little girl to put on Mommy's dress and shoes and clomp around the house playing grownup. It's quite another for her to be shoved into a miniature copy of a B-girl's go-go costume and told that she looks cute. She doesn't look cute. She looks ridiculous and Mommy had better reexamine her own values. No wonder the children of the Affluent Society have been rushing to the thrift shops and decking themselves out in ancient velvet. Somehow, they feel, they must restore the dignity that was stripped from them by making them wear training pants with "Sock it to me" printed on the seats.

During the past few years, the kids born with Pluto in Leo

have been giving us a fashion show, turning out all the old stage properties and parading around disguised as pioneers, Indians both Asiatic and American, gypsies, peasants, downtrodden members of the working classes (one of Leo's wilder fantasies!), and whatnot. They have moved up through Davy Crockett, William Morris, Texas Guinan, George Raft, to what may be termed "the Ann Sheridan era." It's all jolly fun and we rather hope they'll keep the pageant going a while longer.

However, the handwriting is on the wall. Pluto in Virgo, of whom more anon, is already beginning to prune the beards, encase the unhygienically flowing tresses in snoods, nets, and headbands, and protect the bare feet with Dr. Scholl's scientifically designed arch support sandals. This is progress, so how can we knock it? Secretly, though, some of us may come to wish Virgo didn't have to be such a cosmic party pooper.

The recurrence of fashion influences ought not to surprise us, though it usually does. We're so used to working within the illusory framework of single, apparently unconnected lifetimes that we forget how long it takes the Life Force to get things done. We even forget how time-consuming our bodily functions are. We gulp down a tunafish sandwich and say we've eaten, when all we've done is swallow. The overall process of eating, by which the food will be transformed into various body-building components and absorbed into the physical structure or excreted as being of no immediate value to the body will go on for hours. Had we the opportunity and the patience, we might watch each bite of that sandwich go through a fascinating series of adventures. We might become as absorbed as the tunafish and resolve to devote ourselves henceforth to the exploration of the alimentary canal, the glorification of its wonders, and the better regulation of its functions.

Astrology ascribes to Leo the physiological process of digesting what Cancer has ingested. We see this idea carried out at the mental level in Leo's love of history.

History is the commonly shared memory of human experience. It is the sea from which the Moon must draw when our individual pool of stored experience fails to yield materials needed to effect a desired materialization. Merely tossing great globs of happenstance into the memory pool could hardly aid human progress, any more than swallowing indigestible objects contributes to physical growth. Each experience has to be mulled over, discussed from various angles, broken down into components for more detailed study. Its motivations must be determined, its outcomes realized. Before we can fully assimilate any event into our store of wisdom, we must learn all the lessons it has to teach.

Collecting what he calls antiques and others call junk, prizing what his forefathers discarded simply because it belongs to an era that has passed, singing old songs, reading old books, reexploring old ideas, dressing up in old clothes, and replaying old roles in the comedy of life, Leo is merely trying to put his young self into a position where he can better understand some event which he has not yet thoroughly digested. He's using visual, audible, tangible teaching aids in the manner approved by modern educators.

Each of us has Leo in one room of his temporal dwelling. This is the one that tends to get cluttered up with outmoded junk, but we ought not to be too hasty with the new broom. Before we discard anything we find there, we'd better hold it up to the light of a new day and examine it most carefully. We must remember that Neptune has been reigning here, and that his trick mirrors have a way of turning things around so that what they reflect may be totally different from what actually exists. That attic may hold priceless treasures disguised as worthless trash—or vice versa.

Whatever we find, we ourselves have put there. Nobody else has the key, as has been pointed out before. This being the case, it occurs to us that we can put Leo's digestive powers to effective use in building our spiritual as well as our physical dwellings, and that we can use precisely the same approaches.

We know, for instance, that a baby needs calcium to make teeth, so we feed it milk, which gives calcium in the most easily digestible form. We shan't expect to see a full set of uppers and lowers sprouting from the infant's gums after a bottle or two. We're familiar with the human life cycle, so we realize we'll have to keep pumping in milk for months before the slow, painful teething process begins. It's a tedious and often messy job, but we do it faithfully because we know that if the child doesn't get his quota of calcium, he'll be plagued with bad teeth for the rest of his life.

This is, of course, only one of many reasons why we try to feed babies properly, and why we should all practice intelligent eating habits throughout our lives. We may not make the effort, but we admit we'd be healthier people if we did. In the same way, we can build human happiness by watching the quality of what we store in our memory pools. The more selective we are in refusing to clutter up our minds with depressing trash, the more happiness we can take out.

By using the Sun's radiance to search out the precious jewel Shakespeare tells us adversity wears in his forehead, we can use Neptune's transforming power to turn what looks like misfortune into a valuable teaching experience. Triumphing over ills, we begin to feel our strength, to rule our lives like real kings. This life experience will be recorded on our permanent scroll as a victory and will provide memory-stuff which we'll later find valuable in gaining ever greater victories of the spirit. Cancer will build us not another ugly shell but a suit of shining armor, in which we shall proudly take our honored place in the ongoing procession. We'll be fully alive, and we'll know it.

21 · Virgo

Second Earth Sign, Mutable, Feminine, Triple
Mercury Rules, Mercury Exalted
Color: Yellow-Green; Symbol: The Virgin

CONTRARY to popular belief, Virgo does not mean "virgin," nor does the sixth house confer a prediliction to celibacy on persons born under its influence. The name is derived from the Latin *virginis*, which is correctly translated as "maiden" or "girl." Old engravings show Virgo as a busty wench holding an ear of grain. The constellation Virgo was attributed to goddesses of the harvest: Isis in Egypt, Demeter in Greece, Ceres in Rome.

The mistake in translating is natural enough, both from the sound of the word and partly because the ancient astrological symbol for Virgo was supposed to represent the girdle of Hymen, god of marriage, whose name was later given to the membrane which partially covers the opening of the vagina. The state of that membrane on the wedding night has been a matter for deep concern in some societies, but we need not explore tribal taboos to extract the obvious inference.

Virgo, we note, is an Earth sign. In order to reap a harvest, we first have to break the earth and sow the seed. To achieve any practical manifestation of the growth principle, whether it be a book, a child, or a turnip, we have to work at three levels.

First, we have to have faith that the growth principle exists and that we can set it in motion by performing the acts of motivation in their correct order. Whether or not we realize it, this faith connects us with a power outside ourselves. We invoke the aid of the Life Force—or God, if you prefer—not necessarily by prayers or rituals but by making a conscious determination that we are going to attempt to make something happen.

This decision is a signal to our subconsciousness. Obediently, she sets our muscles to work at performing whatever acts the mind directs.

Halfway through the zodiac, we thus find ourselves working with the superconscious level, as represented by our faith in the principle of growth; consciousness, as represented by our decision to plant; and subconsciousness, as represented by our bodies' performance of the acts of planting under the control of the conscious mind, whose directions are determined by a need to operate within the laws of the growth cycle. Now we understand why Virgo is a triple sign.

Triplicity is also revealed in the planting process. A force from above the Earth breaks its visible crust, drops the seed into the furrow, covers it up, and *trusts*. The seed has been told what to do in its previous growth cycle. All it has to do is obey.

Note how Mercury operates here. Strictly speaking, there's

not a blessed thing he can do about the growing process except to apply it to a practical purpose. He can't govern the weather, but he can choose a favorable time of year to plant. He can't make a seed, he can't make soil, but he can select seeds which are likely to do well in the type of soil he has to work with. He can improve the soil by adding fertilizer. He can't make rain, but he can convey water from some existing source. Once the seed has sprouted, he can appoint Mars Silvanus watchdog to keep the young plant free of insects and weeds. He can't make a plant grow and bear fruit, but he can help it to fulfill its innate capability by using intelligence to bring about the conditions under which it can best flourish.

Here we are employing the Mercury force not to enrich the personality as in Gemini, but to relate the totality of our being to our environment. Having found ourselves to be individuals in control of our separate destinies, we now begin to act also as units in the solar ecology.

Well, of course this is terribly exciting and Virgo's first impulse is to tell everybody how to do it. This is another of those chatty feminine signs, but the subject matter is new. Where Cancer wanted to complain about her wounded sensibilities, Virgo prefers to talk about *you*. She'd love to take you apart, find out what makes you tick, then put you back together with improvements of her own devising.

Negative sixth house vibrations can lead to gossiping and nagging. Constructively, they favor teaching, lecturing on and off the platform, and textbook writing. Communication, or transferral of information which has been accumulated in the various phases of the life experience already gone through, is carried on here. Virgo is concerned with *assimilating* this information into the structure of mind, body, and spirit. Naturally, therefore, she is extremely interested in how the structure works. As has been explained, this is the house of health, both physical and mental.

Virgo's preoccupation with health is a far cry from Taurus's nursing ability. In the second house, we found the wise woman, the natural-born nurse or doctor who seemed to imbibe his ability to restore the natural bodily rhythms from the Earth to which he is so closely attuned. Where Taurus is Old Doc Brown with his shabby satchel and his bottle of paregoric, Virgo is the surgeon with the scalpel, the researcher with the microscope, the public health nurse who is interested not so much in making you feel better as in making you become better. Taurus does what comes naturally. Virgo is aware that Nature unaided always fails and is not bashful about straightening the old girl out.

With Pluto in Virgo during the past decade 'or so, we have made dramatic advances in the field of public health and started trends which children born under this influence will carry forth. One of the things we've done is to rethink some of our basic attitudes about clothing. We are not talking here about Leo's sartorial play-acting, but about more important achievements such as the invention of panty hose to replace the stockings-and-girdle combination which held the female abdomen in thrall during the Pluto-in-Cancer era. This has been a death blow to the corset industry, and Virgo is dancing on its grave. No matter what the advertising copywriters say, a girdle of well-tuned muscles is a far more effective and healthful support for the organs than a Saturn-inspired web of elastic. The television commercials based on the theme, "My girdle is killing me!" are an interesting example of how the Life Force is continually making us tell the truth even when we mean to prevaricate.

Women's liberation hasn't progressed quite so far in this area as some of us like to think, however. We still do some remarkably silly things, like subjecting ourselves to the discomfort of going without brassières, while encasing our feet and legs in unbearably hot, tight, vinyl plastic boots. We still wear chastity belts. An amusing bit of research recently turned up the fact that a sexy-looking young model in the briefest of "hot pants" was wearing panty hose, a panty girdle, and underpants. Those four layers of tight-fitting nylon stretch-knit constituted a far more effective barrier to amorous dalliance than Grandma's petticoats and pantalettes, which, by the way, were open at the crotch. Perhaps we're going to encounter more virginity in Virgo than we expect!

Virgo

Virgo has a way of telling you things for your own good which can be absolutely maddening. No doubt this is why so many spiteful things have been said about strongly Virgo-influenced subjects. Whereas Leo will avoid hurting your feelings if he can manage it without too much effort, Virgo will sometimes refuse to admit you have any feelings to hurt. She's likely to come up with theories that sensitivities are the result of faulty brain patterns and whatnot and assure you that your moods can be corrected surgically once the doctors have learned where to plunge the knife, but that you could do it yourself by an effort of will if you'd only pull yourself together and try harder.

Self-discipline is a big thing with Virgo. Any powerful Virgo influence—Sun, Moon, Ascendant, or a combination of planets in Virgo—can make the subject a real tiger for work, and wherever this house appears in your chart you'll find it easiest to buckle down to business. Whereas Leo is concerned with becoming himself, Virgo is focused on doing something with the realized self. In the Cabala, this sign is exemplified by the letter Yod, which means "hand." Astrologers often say that this Sun sign imparts deftness in hand skills. We can go farther and say that craftsmanship will probably be marked in any strong Virgoan subject. What form skills take would depend on where the sign shows up on the chart, and how well they are developed depends, as always, on the will of the subject to develop them.

This "hand" image is extremely important in astrology. Here for the first time, the zodiac gets away from animal imagery. So far, all the attributes we have been discussing could apply in some measure to either man or beast. Any living creature can and must be born, beget its kind, grow to maturity, find food, and be able to discriminate between what is wholesome and digestible to its system and what is not. Any animal can preen and strut and flex its muscles and assert its right to a place in the sun. Many mammals have extremities which look surprisingly like human hands: the incredibly dainty mole, the raccoon, the koala, the panda, the bear. But only the primates have thumbs. Only those of us who have learned to walk on our hind legs can truly perform the act of manufacturing, or *making by hand.*

Touch the tip of your thumb lightly against the tip of your forefinger. What do you see? A shape roughly like an egg. What is an egg? Matter in the process of becoming.

To be sure, the cleverest hands cannot make an egg. But think of all the things we can do with eggs. We are the only animals on this planet who can fry, bake, poach, boil, or scramble our eggs instead of having to suck them raw out of the shell. What has this fact to do with the solar ecology? What has anything to do with anything? This is what Virgo, with those two Mercury vibrations, wants to find out.

We may argue that eggs are full of cholesterol and we shouldn't eat them because they'll harden our arteries, which they won't. We may say it's mean to take them away from the poor hens who've worked so hard to lay them. We may argue that eggs grow up to be chickens and a chicken is a living creature and it's wicked to deprive living creatures of life so we should abstain from eggs and live on raw carrots and wheat germ.

Well, O Wise Virgin, what is a wheat germ but an egg? What's a carrot? Isn't it a living creature, too? If we accept, as it seems we must, the concept that everything is made of the same One Thing, then why isn't a carrot entitled to its season in the sun even as you and I? We might wait till the carrots die and eat them rotten, but we'd probably starve to death in the process. Then we'd be killing other living creatures and would have failed in our responsibility to care for the Temple of Life which is the human body.

Virgo does tend to go in for food fads. Right now we are seeing the influence of Pluto in Virgo in the proliferation of natural food stores, macrobiotic restaurants, organically grown vegetables, newspaper stories about how this, or that, or the other staple food is lethal to the human system. A good deal of this is pretentious nonsense. Some is valid, and a needed antidote to the elaborately decorated garbage which has done so much to weaken the backbone of the nation.

Now that Pluto has entered Libra, we may hope for a better balance between sound nutrition and attractive presentation. In any event, our nutritional climate is certain to change drastically under the influence of the generation now coming to adulthood. While accepting the basic soundness of what they will try to do for us, we must be on guard to separate the wheat from the chaff, and this won't apply only to our breakfast cereals.

This chapter is being written and no doubt being read by a person who has been reared on a reasonably adequate and balanced diet. Only by external evidence, therefore, can we form conclusions about what happens when we are malnourished. Britons watching *Mayflower II* being built must have wondered how the Plimoth Companie could have survived being crammed into such a tiny space, but when she was sailed to Plymouth, Massachusetts, and the life-sized waxwork figures put in place, the mystery was solved. Even the redoubtable Captain Myles Standish stood less than five feet tall. Tourists are amused or let down to learn that the oft-heralded "Mary, Queen of Scots, slept here" boudoir seems like a child's room, and that Good Queen Bess's sumptuous gowns would hardly fit a modern nine-year-old.

Our eyes tell us that the human race is getting taller. Nutritionists explain that we grow more now because we ingest more adequate growth materials. If we doubt their words, we can easily prove their theories by giving or withholding fertilizer in our gardens, or by visiting economically deprived countries.

One of the salutary effects of Virgo's strong influence lately has been the emphasis the communications media have been placing on human deprivation. We have seen videotapes of people starving in Biafra, in Pakistan, in Appalachia. We have been told what a horrifying spectacle this is and, to do ourselves justice, we have been horrified. This reaction in itself is a far greater step forward than we perhaps realize. It's only been within recent years that starvation has had any news value.

In the good old days, which Leo so artistically romanticizes, going to bed with a full stomach was a luxury the vast majority of humans seldom got to enjoy. Pease porridge hot, pease porridge cold, pease porridge in the pot nine days old was what most of us lived on, when we could get it. Choosing from a wide assortment of viands was unheard-of, except among the rich. We ate whatever was around and gave thanks to God, because our undernourished wits couldn't collect the Mercury force intelligently enough to find us better fare.

Just think how long it must have taken *Homo sapiens*, even after he became sapient, to realize that instead of killing a wild cow and eating her meat once, he could domesticate her and have milk to drink day after day; that instead of always having to hunt for wild grasses, he could plant the seeds and harvest a crop large enough to tide him over the winter months when no seeds would be available; that instead of gorging himself sick on a fresh kill and having to waste what got too rotten before he could eat it up, he could dry or salt the surplus and keep it for leaner times. Think what ages must have passed before he got it all together, keeping animals which could pull his plow so that he could plant more grain, give their milk, then at last be slaughtered for meat. Think what cycles of crossbreeding, hybridizing, sowing, hoeing, mowing, reaping; what agonizing battles with Nature red in fang and claw; what an infinitude of patient endeavor mankind has endured so that we can step up to a lunch counter and order a meal from which both the flavor and that nutriment have been painstakingly removed. No wonder Virgo nags and scolds.

A remarkable television series called *Star Trek* has shown Americans scenes of interstellar travel which we shall probably see materialize some day, even as Jules Verne's nuclear submarine and so many other science fiction creations have become realities. We have seen films of United States soldiers soaring across the rice paddies of Vietnam by means of flying belts similar to the ones Buck Rogers and his friends wore in the comic strips of the '30s. Buck's trusty disintegrator ray gun was no doubt some variation of the now familiar laser beam. Buck's creator made only one mistake. He placed his hero in the twenty-fifth century, seriously underestimating the time it would take for his fantasies to become facts.

The rapidity with which we are advancing technologically is posing serious problems for us humans. We have already been faced with tragic evidence that the human body as it now exists is inadequate to perform the functions which will be required of it if we continue to stretch out into space and to probe the depths of mind and spirit. Three cosmonauts die and the world weeps, but what of all the other deaths caused by unbearable stress? Mental and physical breakdowns are as common today as starvation was among our ancestors. We are trying to learn how to improve our frail vessels, but the work goes forward too slowly. We are like the early philanthropists with their soup kitchens, trying to solve basic problems by temporary palliatives.

If we are to keep widening our horizons without killing off our present version of the human race in the process, we shall first have to build ourselves physical vehicles which will be capable of doing harder work and maintaining more drastic pressures from both within and without. We have received explicit directions on how to do this. All we have to do is to read the Christmas story in the Bible. It tells us that Christ was born in Bethlehem of a virgin mother. For "Christ," read "enlightened man," *Homo sapiens* not as he now appears to be but as he has the capability to become. For "virgin," read "Virgo," the synthesizing of mind, body, and spirit in relation to the planet Earth. This is accomplished by joyfully doing whatever comes to hand, seeing the smallest physical act as a step forward in carrying out the cosmic plan. For Bethlehem, read the literal translation from the Hebrew: the House of Bread.

An old slang term for the human stomach is "breadbasket." Virgo's job is to keep the breadbasket filled by the toil of her hands, knowing that however hard she works, she deserves no more credit for what she accomplishes than our hands do for having carried out the tasks which our intelligence assigns to them. Being the goddess of the harvest, she knows good bread from bad and communicates the knowledge by how she copes with the food we eat. Wholesome food helps her to make the body strong and healthy. Worthless trash in our breadbasket can produce nothing better than a weak, ailing vehicle.

The position of Virgo in our charts gives clues to where we can begin to see the wholeness of life. What sign rules the sixth house indicates where bodily and mental weaknesses will probably show up, and planetary aspects to this house show us ways to cope with them. Above all, however, this first triple sign teaches us to give all three areas of being their due importance in terms of the life as we are leading here and now.

Once we have perceived the body as the temporary house of the immortal spirit, we understand how essential it is that all human beings get enough to eat. We are all tied together like mountain climbers on a rope, and the safety of all depends on the ability of each to do his share. We see that our primary, immediate responsibility is to the body in which we personally happen to be dwelling at this time. We begin to understand how silly we should be to indulge in excesses of either gluttony or asceticism, and how downright wicked it is to misuse the bounty which Virgo constantly lays at our feet.

We who live in the midst of plenty have no excuse whatever for not concentrating our minds on the day-to-day chore of getting the right foods into our breadbaskets so that we shall be adequately provisioned for the journey into a brighter future.

Misinterpretations of the Virgin Birth story have given rise to bizarre notions that sanctity is somehow promoted by celibacy and mortification of the flesh by fastings and scourgings. Misinterpretation of the evidence for reincarnation might cause us to speculate, "What difference does it make how well or ill I take care of this body? I can always shed it and grow another."

Let us bear in mind that those were *worldly* treasures which the Three Wise Men brought to the Child born in the House of Bread. What more precious piece of knowledge can we bring to our immortal and continually inherited storehouse of memory than the learning experience of trying to build a vehicle strong enough to carry us into a better world? If we had paid more attention to our bodies in past lives instead of alternately starving and stuffing them, we should now be more adequately equipped for the job we have to do, and Virgo wouldn't be leaning so hard on the panic button. Right now, she seems to be expending too much of her energy scolding at us for not bringing in the sheaves. How can we get her to stop talking and put those clever hands to work?

22 · Libra

Second Air Sign, Cardinal, Masculine, Dual
Venus Rules, Saturn Exalted
Color: Green; Symbol: The Scales

UNTIL now, we have been working on the lower half of the zodiacal chart, which we have found to be the realm of material coming-to-be on an individual basis. Now we take our first step upward from the physical into the realm of mind and spirit, and immediately we've got a fight on our hands.

And look who's opposing whom! Here is Venus in her own

bright green house, and there's Mars in his blazing red Aries house. Since these happen to be the colors of the Italian flag, we ask ourselves, "What would Sophia Loren and Marcello Mastroianni do in a situation like this?"

Because the seventh house is the House of Marriage, a great deal of romantic fantasy has been spun around it. Libran natures have been decorated with more hearts and flowers than a shopful of Victorian valentines. But look at the center of your chart, where Libra meets Aries. Here are two clashing colors, two lusty forces which together represent the primal urge. Here is Fire meeting Air, and when the flame is fanned, the sparks are sure to fly. Now we're beginning to understand why the ancient Jewish astrologers declared Libra to be the ruler not only of marriage but of war, and why we've been getting the two spheres of action mixed up ever since Eve said, "I do."

The symbol for Libra, we note, is a pair of scales. This has given rise to the fairytale that Libra's influence in a chart automatically bestows a calm, level-headed nature. If you should ever run across one of these "typical" Librans we hear so much about, you'd better have him stuffed and mounted, because he'll be an astrological oddity worth collecting. Most likely, he has you so bedazzled with his charming manners and physical beauty, of which this sign does often impart an entirely disproportionate share, that you'll hand him all the rest of the allegedly Libran virtues on a silver platter without noticing whether he's entitled to them or even wants them. He may even reject your offering with a brusqueness which will rock you back on your heels and leave you bruised and battered in spirit if not in person. "He doesn't know what's good for him," you'll moan. This may be true, but it's not your business to tell him so. Libra must strike his own balances.

Observation shows that, far from being the serenely peace-loving house it is often represented to be, the seventh house is the one most fraught with troubles. Wherever Libran influences show up on your chart, a balancing process is needed. If Libra happens to appear in or on its own house, a happy marriage may be the answer for you. If it is somewhere else, a partnership with relation to that position, or work connected with that house may help you to put your life in better perspective. In any event, we all have to cope with Libra somewhere, so let's explore this maddening but delightful subject further.

The opposition of Venus to Mars which we have already noted tells us in the plainest possible language that here is where we face the problem of male and female polarities. We are accustomed to think of marriage as a union—hopefully a happy one—which takes place between two persons of opposite sexes. We are also beginning to wonder whether marriage may also operate on a grander scale, in the world of spirit which determines the climate of terrestrial life.

If this is so, we see more clearly how vital it is for each of us to put our microcosmic world of body, mind, and spirit in tune with the macrocosm of which it is a necessary and finally indistinguishable part. Virgo in her earthy way has hit us squarely in the guts with the necessity to accept the triune nature of being. Now it's up to Libra to work out methods of coping with the information.

Esoterically, Libra is said to deal with *karma*, and karma simply means *work*. God told Adam, "In the sweat of thy brow shalt thou eat bread." The meaning of this allegory is plain. Work goes on incessantly, whether or not we do it consciously. Our bodies must keep on pumping air and blood through our ever-busy systems of ingestion, digestion, assimilation, excretion, locomotion, mentation. Our minds are never at rest. Choices are continually being made, whether or not we exercise our right to choose freely and wisely.

We can alter the nature of our work to some extent, but we cannot get away from the fact of work. Consequently, our best course is to adjust action to desire, to balance the Mars and Venus forces in such a way that we shall be doing the kinds of tasks we want to do, making each act a meaningful step upward.

Getting our aspirations in balance with our activities is no one-time deal. Libra's work is never done because our lives are constantly in a state of flux. Everything we learn, everything we eat, everything we do, everything we say affects the balance of positive to negative. It is right that we should be in a state of imbalance, otherwise we'd never get anywhere. "A man's reach should exceed his grasp, or what's a Heaven for?" The Kingdom of Heaven has been defined as attunement to the order of Nature. Hell could be explained as a place where you sit around letting Heaven get away from you.

It is only by continual use of the Venus power of imagination to formulate higher goals, then setting Mars in action toward the achievement of what we have dreamed that we can reconcile the need for balance with the urge to go on. If we plan noble deeds but make no effort to carry them out physically, we overload the scales on the side of passivity and fall flat on our astral faces. If we turn Mars loose in the field without first asking Venus to draw an accurate map of what he's supposed to be striving toward, we overbalance on the side of action without direction, and the same stalemate occurs.

Failure to put our spiritual accounts in balance by constructive action is what gives rise to all those karmic debts we have to keep on the books from one incarnation to the next. Our difficulties in working them off arise mostly from failure to understand precisely how much we owe to whom.

Goodness knows it's not that we haven't been told. There's always somebody around who claims to have all the answers. Our trouble is, we tend to listen with only one ear. We may hear what's being said, but not what's being meant. We're so anxious to get the albatross from around our necks that we don't pause to consider whether the preacher's answer may not be our answer. We charge off in all directions to work off what we've been told is our guilt and wind up often as not with a different but no less onerous load.

In the Biblical parable, Jacob describes Issacher (whom the Zohar equates with astrological Libra) as "a strong ass crouching down between two burdens." Aesop tells a fable of the ass who stood debating which of two equally succulent thistles to eat first until he collapsed from starvation—a typically Libran situation. Why do we see this emphasis on double trouble, and why insist on identifying Libra with the beast of burden most renowned for its stubbornness?

After having encountered a single and a triple sign, we note that we're back to a dual symbol. At a glance, however, it's obvious that here we shall encounter a different aspect of duality. Aries, Taurus, Gemini, and Cancer are all concerned with the burgeoning child spirit and child animal in relation to parents and other outside forces. Now we've moved to the upper half of the zodiac, where grownup meets grownup.

Psychiatrists define the adult personality as one who is willing and able to accept responsibility for his own life. Saturn's exaltation here tells us that Libra is going to be acutely conscious of his obligation to perform the duties which have been laid down to him so emphatically by Virgo.

The Bible tells us that there were seven foolish virgins as well as seven wise ones, and that they let the Lamp of Illumination go out because they were silly about wasting oil. If Virgo doesn't exercise her function intelligently, Libra will be left in the dark as to what's expected of him. Thus he's apt to pick up the wrong saddlebag and make an Issacher of himself in more ways than one.

Once Libra has made a choice, that exalted Saturn will make it extremely difficult for him to lay the burden down. Therefore, we can sympathize with his hesitation to make commitments, even though his backing and forthing may exasperate us beyond words. Ponder your own chart. See if the house which shows Libra ruling isn't the area where you feel most deeply the necessity and also the difficulty of making decisions with regard to the work you have to do.

If the problems seem disproportionately large, ask yourself, "Is this where I'm being too hard on myself? Is this where I've saddled myself with an unnecessary burden of guilt by blindly accepting other people's images of what I should be and do, instead of formulating my own goals and choosing my own methods of action in accordance with the principles of the Life Force?"

Other people's concepts of what character traits and behavior patterns are admirable may be far sounder than those which we ourselves have so far been able to develop. We always need teachers. We do right to listen and learn. But just as nobody else can digest our food for us, nobody except ourselves can weigh, test, and eliminate what is not good for us.

The Jewish custom of starting each new year with a Day of Atonement is a beautiful example of how we may use the Libra force constructively. It is interesting to note, by the way, that the Yom Kippur service takes place during the period, roughly between September 23 and October 23, which astrology ascribes to Libra. We cannot assume it was by accident that a people skilled in astrology chose for this rite the time when vibrations would be most favorable.

At Yom Kippur, according to Jewish theology, it is established who shall live and who shall die during the coming year, and by what means; but it is stressed that tragedy can be averted by making a stronger effort to control the positive and negative polarities in daily life. The congregation makes a mass confession of the sins committed during the past year. Each communicant takes upon himself an equal share of guilt, even though he personally may have committed no wrong.

The reasoning is, "I didn't do it, but I let it happen. I failed to set a strong enough example of righteousness. Had I been a good shepherd, according to the example set down by The Lord, instead of contenting myself with being a good little lamb, His other sheep would not have strayed. Therefore, the guilt is mine as well as theirs. Sharing my brother's guilt, I lessen his karmic burden. By contributing my acts of righteousness to the sum total of right and wrong instead of trying to keep all the credit for myself, I help the scales of justice to swing into balance, not only for me but for the entire social structure of which I am a unit. Atonement, broken down into syllables, is at-one-ment. Only when all of us together have achieved equilibrium at this point in our racial development can we take another meaningful step forward."

The rite of Yom Kippur is performed during a twenty-four hour fast. Abstinence is practiced in order that the body, which Jews understand to be the Temple of God, may cleanse itself of substances tainted by the previous year's misdeeds and be ready to start the New Year pure in flesh as well as spirit.

We can imagine no more beautiful way of wiping clean the slate and starting fresh than for all the human race to perform one Day of Atonement together. But how many of us would be able to carry the ritual through in full consciousness and sincerity? We suspect that at this stage our problem would lie less in accepting guilt than in being willing to contribute to the general absolution.

As our awareness increases, we perceive what tremendous social problems have been created by greed and shortsightedness. We have begun to face up to our personal responsibility for these crimes against our fellow beings and our planet, and to start trying to make up for what we've done. Even though we grumble at the expense of welfare programs, we keep contributing our tax money to support them. Playing on our accumulation of guilt, organized charities have become big businesses. We admit that most of the money we contribute goes to pay the organizers' salaries and subsidize their office expenses rather than to carry out their professed aims; we argue that they at least do some good, and they provide jobs for the people who work at collecting. What we aren't so ready to admit is that what we give away rids us of some of our guilt at being "haves" who occupy the same planet with these "have-nots." It is at least a token effort to achieve a balance between our wealth and their lack. If we are greatly burdened with guilt, deserved or not, we have many opportunities to work it off by joining demonstrations and getting ourselves jailed for crimes we never committed or by sacrificing ourselves in various other ways for what we conceive to be the common good.

Why are we so ready to accept guilt, and so doubtful about absolution? It is only that we're more familiar with evil, therefore better able to picture ourselves as sinners than saints? How often have we looked with compassion on some miscreant being led off to jail and murmured, "There but for the grace of God go I," and meant it. Had our circumstances been less fortunate, we might perhaps have been greater rogues than he.

But whatever we might have been, we can't help feeling rather complacent about what we are. Facts are facts. While this social outcast is doing his stretch at hard labor, we shall continue to be happy, honest, well housed, well fed, and well respected. Why has Fortune smiled so sweetly upon us at the same time that she was tipping him the Black Spot? Even as we abase ourselves, we can't help wondering, "Why am I thus blessed? Can it be that I'm *somehow rather special?*"

If Duty seems to expect sacrifice from us, we can give up our pleasant homes, our fine clothes, our tasty food, our money, everything we hold precious. We can spend our lives toiling in the service of those whom society has cast adrift. Men will call us saints and perhaps we shall accept the title. If we have already acknowledged ourselves blessed above common men, it follows that we must be uncommon. It is not hard to make Earthly sacrifices if we are thoroughly convinced that we occupy preferred positions on a higher plane of living.

But this is not how sainthood works. If we perform benign acts solely for the purpose of adding stars to our crowns, we're still loading the scales on the side of self. Our sacrifices will have been made only to enlarge that notion of specialness we call Ego, so they won't really have been sacrifices at all.

Most of us are "good people." We're willing to make reasonable efforts toward helping others. We now understand that we could have done more to prevent their remaining poor, ignorant, stupid, criminal, afflicted with mental, physical, and social ills from which Providence has set us free. We see the justice in our taking responsibility for conditions which our indifference has helped to foster. We are trying to direct our powers positively instead of negatively, but we are too often doing it on a me-above–you-below basis.

And those whom we wish to make objects of our charity know it. Welfare recipients make demands instead of taking our handouts with gratitude. Blacks speak their minds about the "Great White Goddess" taking an ego trip at their expense. If we really love, we don't notice what color our brothers and sisters are. If we really want to share, we just do it, and nobody's feelings are hurt.

After having worked so hard to establish personal identities, it is bitter for us to admit that there are some things the individual self cannot do. We can sin like anything, but we cannot grant absolution. If we try to be our brothers' keepers without first acknowledging the fact of brotherhood, we wind up acting like hypocrites.

Obviously, we still have a great deal to learn about our relationships. Somehow we have to realize ourselves not just as growing creatures, not just as mammals, not just as men and women, but as units of a larger reality. Therefore, we can see why the seventh house would logically be concerned with marriage. Wedlock is the laboratory in which we learn to unite ourselves in order to experience that sense of wholeness which seems so much greater than the sum of its parts.

Because of Libra's tendency to assume guilt to itself, we can readily understand why the House of Joy has acquired such a bad name, why the marriage bed is so often used as a torture chamber, and why subjects with strong seventh-house vibrations in their charts have a propensity to marry in haste and repent at leisure.

Astrologers often point out that people born with the Sun in Libra—and we should expand that to include a Libra Ascendant as well as other notable Libran influences—are apt to be outstandingly successful in business and spectacularly unfortunate in marriage. It is as though they felt the need to balance the books, by taking to themselves equal measures of happiness and unhappiness. This is by no means always the case. Libra's willingness to make adjustments and see the other side of the coin can function beautifully in a marriage if the partner is able to provide a stabilizing influence without leaning too hard on either side of the scales. Two Librans, in fact, may make the ideal couple.

Still, the exalted Saturn influence in this house will insist on the union's being turned into a business deal. We make the husband and wife sign a legal contract, in obedience to Saturn's proddings. Bring it down to Earth. Make it practical. Make it *binding*. This in itself is no bad thing, but our misunderstanding of the Saturnian influence has caused us to bungle grossly. We're now trying to set ourselves right in this area as in so many other aspects of our civil structure. During recent years especially, Uranus in Libra has been giving us surprising insights about the institution of marriage. Pluto, now in Libra, will prod us to evaluate our findings and make fair judgments about the family concept on which our present society is based.

It has been suggested that the system is in the process of breaking down, and that the two-by-two concept will soon give way to the commune where mates are interchanged according to the mood of the moment and children are the responsibility of all since nobody will know who is the father of whom. This is by no means a new idea, and though it may sound attractive, anthropological research indicates that it doesn't work very well.

Although many denizens of the animal kingdom mate promiscuously and some humans are not exempt from the practice, we higher primates have an inclination to cleave to the one-he–one-she principle. As we come down from the trees and out of the caves, we begin to realize what a tough job it is to relate our widening worlds of mind and spirit to the more familiar but still often intimidating world of animal, vegetable, and mineral. The harder we work toward becoming civilized, the more intensely we feel a need to replace blind copulation with a sharing of responsibilities and learning experiences. We sense that our task will be greatly eased if we can expand the external fact of cohabitation to include the whole experience of living together.

Have the wedding bells actually sounded their own death knell? Let's overlook the rhetoric for the moment and consider the facts. Immediately, we're confronted with a revolt against celibacy in religious groups. Priests want to get married. Nuns are no longer content to be Brides of Christ and wear their wedding gowns only in their coffins. Judging from the scandalous whispers of yesteryear, this is not because sex was ever entirely absent from the cloisters. It is simply that these persons have become aware that they can more efficiently perform the religious duties to which they have dedicated their lives if they are given the opportunity to become more complete human beings on the physical as well as the spiritual level.

Historically, we have thought of marriage primarily as a duty. Parents selected suitable brides or grooms for their children in accordance with established customs aimed at maintaining and strengthening the tribal unit. The object of these unions was to consolidate wealth and/or to bring forth children whose bloodline would make them acceptable family members and who could be trained to carry on the established pattern. The Old Testament makes it a most scarlet sin for a dead man's brother to refuse to impregnate the widow and thus carry on the brother's seed.

Sons and daughters of royal families have always been used as pawns and married off wherever advantageous political alliances could be formed. Most social groups have employed the same principle of child barter, though the rules vary according to the particular standards of the group involved. Selling one's daughters to the highest bidder was the norm not only in the slave markets of Istanbul but in the drawing rooms of Victorian England.

Mothers who, like Mrs. Bennett, made it the business of their lives to marry off their girls honestly believed they were performing their duty. Until she was able to break down the barricades which Cancerian solicitude had built around her and get out to earn her own bread, a spinster was an economic liability, therefore an object of scorn and often an unpaid slave in some family member's household. Even today, the term "old maid" is an insult and people who wish to be kind will ask, "How come an attractive girl like you can't find a husband?" That she might not yet have found the particular husband she wants is irrelevant. There are plenty of guys around; everybody looks good to somebody. What's she saving it for? What, indeed? Is it any wonder the Women's Liberation groups are screaming in Venusian fury and hurling their brassieres (symbols of confined duality) square in the faces of these well-meaning persecutors?

The gay bachelor has been given a great deal of lip envy by the husbands; but if his state is all that desirable, why has the adjective "gay" gradually taken on the meaning of "homosexual?" The fact is, his married brothers secretly despise any adult male who dodges the responsibilities of matrimony. He knows this and hates himself for being a coward even as he goes forth to conquer among the chicks or seeks solace in the arms of some other gay bachelor as wretched as himself.

Libra's insistence on making it legal is what galls many of us, especially those few who have been able to form a true spiritual, intellectual, and physical union and maintain it over a period of years without going through the usual formalities. If a deeply satisfying and continuing sense of oneness is not marriage, then what is? Yet the union is branded illicit because we haven't signed a contract. This may be because of religious or ethical scruples, or because one partner is still legally bound by an existing contract even though physical, intellectual, or spiritual ties have been dissolved or never really existed. What actually does constitute adultery: cohabitation without a marriage license or cohabitation without love?

This is the sort of question we've been asking ourselves lately. Attempts to define marriage on a more practicable basis have led to demands for amended divorce laws and vigorous application of the existing ways of escape. Haven't you been amazed to see how many long-standing marriages are being dissolved?

But haven't you been equally astonished at the number of these divorced persons who immediately contract marriages with more congenial mates, and still more startled to learn that dear old Aunt Henrietta has suddenly, after sixty-three years of spinsterhood, eloped with a fascinating widower? Confirmed bachelors and bachelorettes are taking the plunge in ever-increasing numbers, just when we thought we were getting rid of the whole silly business. How do you figure that one out? Now that we've eliminated sexual taboos, nobody has to get married just to have someone to go to bed with.

The fact is, people apparently feel a genuine need to select one specific mate and to solemnize the union with some sort of ceremony. Whether we personally share or approve of this need, we can't overlook the evidence that monogamous marriage is still the backbone of our social structure and will probably remain so during the foreseeable future. We shall continue to perform wedding ceremonies, though we may delay them, sensibly enough, until the union has been tested by a period of cohabitation and found to be mutually satisfying. We shall probably wish to draw up legal contracts for the protection of property and children, because we don't really believe in communism and we always drift away from it into private family units, where the one-to-one relationship can be most satisfactorily and thoroughly explored.

Now that we have produced far more children than we need and are threatened with destruction by overpopulation unless we use effective birth controls, we no longer have to exert pressure on our young to marry and propagate. Now that children are growing up so much smarter than their parents, trying to coerce them into planned marriages is a hopeless and thankless task. We'll just have to let them go their own ways until they decide to get married solely for the fun of it, and this is what Venus in Libra is all about.

Being human, young people of this or any generation can still make mistakes in choosing partners. While this no longer condemns a couple to life-long misery, it does waste their time and pile one more burden of disappointment on the negative side of the scales. This world cannot afford many more failures. To make a stupid match is irresponsible and a perversion of what we are capable of doing. In the solar ecology it's a crime, and we shall be fined in proportion to the gravity of our offense. Any two persons contemplating union should examine the possibilities for success or failure long and carefully before they involve themselves in each other's lives.

By now we realize how helpful our own natal charts can be in revealing our character traits and motivations. Therefore, a comparison of the prospective partners' charts should, and can, show the probabilities for the success or failure of any relationship. Skilled astrologers can tell almost at a glance who is likely to be attracted to whom, and why, and what's apt to be the outcome of the romance.

Please take careful note of that word "skilled." This does not include glib assertations that "Scorpios should marry Cancers because they're both water signs and they'll understand each other's devious ways and rotten tempers." By now, we know the subject is rather more complex than the newsstand publications would have us believe. Research has, however, turned up some easily spotted indications which can help us to determine whether it's the real thing at last or just the influence of a full moon on an active glandular system. To explain these in full would take another book, but some highlights will be given in the last chapter of this one. At the moment, since we've brought up the subject of Scorpio, let's find out whether the eighth house is inhabited by a character as devious and rotten as we've been led to believe.

23 · Scorpio

Second Water Sign, Fixed, Feminine, Triple
Mars and Pluto Co-rule, Uranus Exalted
Color: Blue-Green; Symbols: The Scorpion, The Eagle,
 The Phoenix (some astrologers add The Serpent)

We can see right away that the second triple sign is going to be a far different kettle of fish than Virgo's hygienically maintained laboratory. There, Mercury was in full charge. Here the three most explosive planets are all crammed into one house. Instead of one easily interpreted symbol, we have a confusing choice of three or four, none of which most people would care to have for house pets. Can you wonder why Scorpio has always been considered the most troublesome, bad-tempered, and downright nasty sign in the zodiac?

Yet of all the signs, this is the one we most need to understand. For a long time, occultists have maintained that Earth is a Scorpio planet. Pictures taken by astronauts show a predominantly blue-green planet whose surface is mostly water, visible indications that the occultists are correct in their analysis.

They also say that Earth is a hospital planet, a rehabilitation center where souls who have failed to adjust to the evolutionary process in other worlds are sent to brush up on their techniques. We can see the force of this argument, too. If we swallow our civic pride and consider our present situation in galactic terms, we have to admit that Earth doesn't amount to a row of pins compared to worlds which astrologers and astronomers now believe to exist in vast numbers.

Even within our own relatively puny solar system, we may not be as important as we think we are. We know next to nothing about the solar ecology. We can't prove that we are the only planet capable of sustaining life, because we don't know how many forms life can take. We don't know how much we're capable of seeing in terms of what there is to be seen.

We can say that a fly sees differently from a fish, and a dog better than a fly, and a human better than a dog; but there the chain of comparison has to stop. Our solar system may contain forms of life to which we should seem no more alert than the stones beneath our feet appear to us, even though we know they are made up of constantly vibrating electrical charges and are therefore as alive as we, though on a different level of vibration.

This sort of speculation is great fun. It's comforting to think that we shall some day shed this mortal coil and go to live among brighter stars. We see no logical reason to doubt the possibility, but the purpose of this book is to try to talk common sense, and common sense tells us that we ought not to be as concerned about what is out there as about what we are doing right here. What if we are constantly being visited by flying saucers bringing noble teachings from outer space? Does this mean our planet has no value except as a landing field for UFOs? To begin with, what makes us so sure every other planet is inhabited by higher beings?

Advertising people have a succinct definition for "expert"—somebody from out of town. A prophet may be without honor in his own country, but he tends to gain renown in direct ratio to the distance between him and it. We assume that any being who would take the time and trouble to come this far must have some message to impart. So what great message does a tourist take to Miami Beach? Isn't it reasonable to suppose that if some of us came here from other planets, we did so because Earth had something we couldn't find elsewhere?

All right, what do we have here? Variety, for one thing. It would be reasonable to suppose that a planet where everybody got along with everybody else would be somewhat homogeneous in its makeup, especially if its work in the solar ecology consisted of beaming one type of vibration to the rest of the system. But in this one small ovoid, we have at the time of writing a span of anthropological development ranging from early primitive to post-Batman. No matter what stage in the human life experience we have failed to handle adequately, we can find a suitable group in which to reincarnate and try again. We can experience vastly different climates and geographic conditions. We can be extremely rich or abjectly poor. Think how many different languages we can speak, what a variety of customs we can observe, what a wealth of ideas are stored in Earth's collective memory system. Whether they were brought here from other civilizations or evolved from creative activities on this planet, the fact is that they exist here and they do equip Earth to serve as a rehabilitation center. This is the most sensible explanation of why this planet is the way it is that we've struck yet, at any rate.

If we accept this hypothesis, we can get a better idea of

what we're doing here. We shall no longer be able to take the chain of apparently futile lives and deaths, the struggles, the sufferings and deprivations which we have had to undergo as proof that no higher form of existence is possible. The argument—God can't exist, because if He did, He would save me from this misery—is not valid now because it is based on the assumption that the ego is a separate unit rather than part of a continuum.

A child may whine, "Papa spanked me, so I'm going to run away." He may even retaliate by killing the old man. To him thenceforth, the father is dead; but physical removal cannot alter the fact of the man's having lived and been the driving force in bringing about the child's physical birth. Even if we succeed in manufacturing babies in test tubes, we shall have to rely on the Life Force to make them function. We can't bring about life, because life already *is*. We can't operate it, but only let it operate. We may bypass the man-woman physical relationship, but we can't do without the masculine-feminine polarities.

It strikes us as significant that the commandment, "Honor thy father and thy mother" finishes, "that *thy* days may be long in the land." If this were merely an injunction to be kind to the old folks at home, we should expect it to say, "*their* days." Therefore, we may interpret it to mean, "Give due consideration to both the positive and negative aspects of the Life Force, in order to live out this life in a way which will be productive of good."

We all know how it works. Children bouncing a ball chant, "First comes loves, then comes marriage, then comes Susie with a baby carriage." After Libra has united the male and female forces in holy wedlock, we naturally expect progeny. And do we ever get them!

The astrological meaning of Scorpio is connected with the Hebrew letter Nun, which is also a word signifying, "fish." Water teems with life. Even a drop from the kitchen faucet yields up strange secrets when we scrutinize it under a microscope. Jacques-Yves Cousteau and his crew have taken fantastic underwater motion pictures in various parts of the world. Wherever the films are exposed, they come up with the same information: here is mystery, here is action, here is abundance beyond man's imagining. Here is life endless and everlasting: little fish eating tiny shrimps, bigger fish eating the little fish, huge predators eating the big fish, then dying and falling to the bottom where the tiny shrimp feed on their carcasses and swim away to be eaten to be eaten to be eaten....

And none of this death matters because there is always that incredible spawning, spawning, spawning. Fish no longer than our thumbs lay eggs enough to fill up all the oceans and crowd us off the face of the Earth, were it not for what we now see as the blessing of physical destruction. And in death we see life. A mullet must die that a swordfish may live; a swordfish must be caught so that we may enjoy a fish dinner and go to bed strengthened to perform the act which will continue our own species. Old people die so that hopefully wiser and kinder people will have room to live and beget still better babies. If it is not presumptuous, we might hope that man must die so that God-in-Man may live.

As has been mentioned before, this act of dying is nothing to be afraid of. We have done it many times. In a real, physical sense, we do it all the time. We shall keep on repeating the act until we shan't have to do it any more because we shall have become what we desire to be.

If we die young, as we reckon life spans at this stage in human history, it may be that we feel we have learned all this particular life experience has to teach us, or that we have chosen a situation which is not likely to teach what we have to learn. If we live long, tedious, miserable lives praying for deliverance from this vale of tears but still being impelled by something inside ourselves to struggle for existence, we can be sure the Life Force is trying to pound something into us that we're stubbornly refusing to know.

People are living longer now than they used to because we have learned to build bodies capable of absorbing more wisdom. One of our troubles now is that our minds often wear out before the physical vehicle has run down, so one of our jobs is to strengthen our mental capacities.

Look at the planets which are found in Scorpio. Pluto the Redeemer is teamed with Mars the Protector. Here we have opportunities not only to judge what is wrong with us, but to set ourselves in order. How do we do that? By using exalted Uranus to start something new. Where Scorpio appears in our charts, we shall see the creative principle manifest itself in some way, whether or not we intend it to.

One of the old standbys on the vaudeville circuit went something like this:

"Zeke, I understand you and your wife have twenty-seven kids."

"Yup, but we ain't goin' to have any more."

"Why not?"

"We found out what was causin' it."

Comedians couldn't raise a snicker on that joke any more. We know too much about the birds and bees. But how many deluded innocents have fallen prey to Scorpio's lust to propagate simply because they didn't know what was happening to them? And how many of us are giving birth to monsters right now because we're not aware that sex isn't just something that happens between man and wife on Saturday night?

At the mental level, the sexual process of mating and propagating goes on constantly. The stream of consciousness never stops flowing. In sleep, relieved of controls imposed by tribal mores, habits, and preoccupation with the myriad affairs of our waking lives, our minds may allow themselves to create wild fantasies. Freud shocked and intrigued us by insisting that dreams are invariably sexual, but we had to admit finally that he was right, although not quite in the way he thought he was.

Freud's discovery is particularly interesting to Cabalists because it appears to be a case of buried astrological data working its way up to consciousness through an armor plate of scientific realism which may have been laid down over several incarnations. He recognizes the essentially triune nature of spirit but tacks on Latin names to appease the *Zeitgeist*. Superego, Ego, and Id are not different in essence from what a Jesuit would call Father, Son, and Holy Ghost and what astrology implies by this triple sign. But Freud's Superego is still the Old Testament God of Wrath, and he is too bound up in a physical concept of sex to carry his theory beyond the big-fish-eat-little-fish–little-fish-eat-shrimp–shrimp-eat-big-fish cycle. This leaves us with a full belly and a stiff upper lip, but nothing to look forward to except more of the same. We can do better than that.

The key word for Scorpio is *dissolution*. Early in our discussion, we established that the purpose of dissolving is to form a solution. Neither the most fleeting thought nor the most paralyzing neurosis can be dissolved from our minds *except by putting something else in its place*.

The only answer to death is the creation of new life. The only cure for the desperate round of death-in-life is to move on an upward-spiralling helix instead of in a closed circle. The process is the familiar one we use in developing a strain of disease-free corn or a more beautiful rose. We keep discarding any plants which do not approach the standards we have set and continuing to breed the best of what we have until we get precisely what we want.

A glance at the movie section of any daily newspaper will convince us that Earth is certainly acting like a Scorpio planet right now, as far as physical sex goes. Moreover, we have started physical hybridizing on a world-wide scale. This has come about through the death and violence with which Scorpio has traditionally been associated.

In the previous chapter, it was explained that Libra is the House of War. Wars are started by Libran statesmen and directed by Libran generals, but nobody expects the leaders to do the actual fighting any more. Carnage is now openly linked to copulation in the eighth house, which doesn't really surprise anybody, since we've known it all along. All's fair in love and war, we tell our children. It isn't how you play the game, but whether you win or lose.

Battles between husband and wife and battles between nations tend to have similar results. Any girl who has lived near an Army barracks can tell you why war has been called The Great Leveler. Since Stone Age Man learned how to fashion a war club out of a mastodon's thigh bone and liberate his neighbors, women have been considered legitimate spoils of war. Invariably, once Mars and Venus have worked off their differences, they get down to the real business of the meeting.

Thus are brought forth children in whom are blended both the physical traits and the stored memories of their respective tribes. Division has led to unification. In defeat, the weaker is impregnated by the stronger, so that the offspring tend to equalize the strengths and weaknesses of the parents. Separate pools of cultural experience are blended, thus raising the potential intelligence of the children.

Until now, we have bought such civilizing influences at too high a price. Pluto the Hanging Judge has made us pay with terrible physical suffering for wasting so much of our wealth in the effort to get more. He has torn us apart emotionally because we have failed to show respect for each other as equally valid expressions of the power-to-be.

We suggest that the jealousy, vengefulness, and violent acts which have been attributed to Scorpio are in fact responses to acts which originate in Libra. We don't seek revenge until we have conceived the ugly thought, "I'm going to get even with you. I'll make you pay for hurting me." We are not jealous unless we feel possessive. Mars won't fight, remember, until Venus gives him his orders.

Let's look at our charts again. Besides having Venus in the house next door, we see that the other Venus-ruled house, Taurus, is directly across the way. Now we understand why so many marital, as well as martial, quarrels center around money. Here is why so many of us are torn between the desire to do what will make us happiest and the notion that we must do what will bring in the highest wages. Here's Venus nagging at Mars to bring home the bacon, and there's Pluto sitting on the moneybags, threatening him with all the furies of Hades if he grabs more than his fair share. If we satisfy Scylla, we risk getting gulped down by Charybdis. How do we run the channel between being rich and being happy? Scorpio suggests that we talk to the man upstairs.

Earlier, it was stated that the eighth house deals with what we call the occult, that is, knowledge visible to anybody who is willing to learn how to look. From what we've been discussing, we might conclude that this knowledge is available to Scorpio because she needs all the help she can get.

Here's a pretty paradox, by the way. Throughout this chapter, the masculine pronoun has been used freely, because Mars, Pluto, and Uranus are all anthropomorphized as males. Still, we must not forget that this is a feminine sign; whereas Libra, where Venus the epitome of femininity rules, is masculine. Brood on this.

What ever we make of it, we still ought to find out what the gentleman upstairs has to say. There he is, Uranus, higher octave of Mercury, seated vis-à-vis Lady Moon, pale mistress of the hidden sea, the superconscious in direct gravitational pull with the subconscious.

In the early days of marine exploration, oceanographers simply let down weighted nets and hauled up whatever swam into them. When fish of unexpected shapes appeared, they began to suspect that even more curious forms of marine life might be found. They devised scoops that could be dragged along the bottom.

Now it got really exciting. All sorts of weird objects began to appear. Unfortunately, few of them reached the surface in good condition. Fragile shells would be broken by the scoops; fish accustomed to immense pressures would be burst open by the expansion of nitrogen as they reached our surface atmosphere.

Gradually, we developed diving suits, the bathysphere, submarine vehicles, aqualungs, learned to adapt our bodies to the alien atmosphere, and began to probe the depths in earnest. By now we have learned a great deal about the seas and, manwise, have exploited their treasures on a large scale. In the water as on the land, we have made bad mistakes, and Pluto has accordingly punished us. Overfishing, dumping of pollutants, oil spills have taught us bitter lessons.

Now we're trying to face up to our crimes against Nature and repair the damage before we destroy this small but often delightful laboratory which has been lent for our instruction in the facts of life. We realize that we can no longer afford the luxury of growing "too soon old and too late wise." We're men and women now, and we must face our responsibilities. We have the equipment and the training to handle the job, and Pluto will accept no excuses. We *have* to be healthy, happy, and strong in body, mind, and spirit. We *have* to learn to love so that we can learn to share. Until we do, we shall keep running the old rat race over and over again. If we mess up this planet beyond repair, we shall have to make a fresh start somewhere else, and we may not get such a charming location next time. So it will pay us to learn all that Scorpio has to teach.

Occult study seems to go in waves, like the water with which astrology associates it. White settlers' experiences on the North American continent have been typical. We started by trying to uproot the indigenous religions, which were largely involved with attempts to contact higher spirits directly by fasting, interpretation of dreams, and ceremonies which sometimes involved the use of what we now call psychedelic drugs. Among our own numbers, we conducted witch hunts and went so far as to hang some of those who were accused of having supernatural contacts. Like the early fishermen, our first reactions were, "Destroy the deep-sea monsters. They're not like us, so they must be evil."

Then we progressed to stage two: "Let's haul up the net and see what's in it, just for curiosity's sake." Table-tapping, phrenology, spiritualistic séances, ouija boards, and whatnot had their day, did their stunts, and vanished through the trap door in a whiff of sulfur. Now came more responsible attempts at psychical research. Séances were conducted under progressively more rigid controls, in the presence of skilled observers, and still found to produce paranormal phenomena, whatever that might mean. With devices such as Zener cards and psychokinetic machinery, we managed to scoop up evidence for telepathy, clairvoyance, clairaudience, thought control, precognition, and projection. We established to the satisfaction of any reasonably open-minded person that what the spaewives had been telling us all along was at least potentially feasible.

But we still didn't know how to work the machinery, so we rather brushed aside the findings until we began to realize how desperately we needed to expand our knowledge. Now, many of us are reexamining witchcraft, necromancy, satanism, working old spells, brewing old potions, on the off chance that something of value might be hidden under the rubbish. As the awkward dredges of the early oceanographers ruined more specimens than they brought up, we are causing a great deal of destruction without achieving very good results. We need to show more intelligence and refine our techniques. However, we ought not to be totally discouraged by the mess that's been made in the field of the occult sciences so far. This bungling is a necessary part of learning the craft.

As yet, we have no reason to feel complacent. We don't really know much of anything, and we're not at all sure how much we may reasonably expect to find out. Whatever it is must have something to do with the mechanics of creation at a higher level than we have operated at thus far. We know that creation is a sexual process; therefore, it seems most unwise for us to waste our natural resources on indiscriminate physical sex, as we have been doing. In the apt vulgarism, we'd better quit screwing around and try to find out what we are aiming toward.

24 · Sagittarius

Third Fire Sign, Mutable, Masculine, Single
Jupiter Rules, No Planet Exalted
Color: Blue; Symbol: The Archer

THE symbolism of the last fire sign is one of the most interesting things about the zodiac. We call it simply, "The Archer," but traditionally Sagittarius is shown as a Centaur—half man, half horse—in the act of shooting an arrow from a longbow. Here is Paul Gsell in Rodin's studio, contemplating the statue, "The Centauress":

> The human bust of the fabulous creature yearns despairingly toward an end which her longing arms can never attain; but the hind hoofs, grappling the soil, are fast there, and the heavy horse's flanks, almost crouched in the mud, cannot kick

free. It is the frightful opposition of the poor monster's two natures—an image of the soul, whose heavenly impulses rest miserably captive to the bodily clay.

Thus speaketh the Purple-Prosy Piscean. Yet what a graphic image he evokes of the joyful experience death and reincarnation can be! What a relief it is to know that we shall one day be able to liberate those "heavenly impulses" from the "bodily clay" and create a less ponderous vehicle.

However, we don't have to remain bogged down in the mud until the wheel decides to give us another whirl. The Centaur himself is shown wildly a-gallop and still trying to speed his effect on the world ahead of his physical presence, by means of a well-aimed arrow. At least we hope it's well aimed, because that bow looks powerful.

The gesture of shooting unveils the meaning of the ninth house, which astrology describes as the realm of abstract thinking, dreams, visions, religion, and philosophy. "A man's reach should exceed his grasp, or what's a Heaven for?" is what Sagittarius wants to know. This is where we outreach our physical and mental grasp of what we know as reality and aspire toward that which we can sense but cannot see.

We observe that the only planet involved here is Jupiter, the force of accepting, making it real. We notice also that this house opposes Gemini, where we learned to sort out and classify. Therefore, we understand that it is here we formulate into creeds and philosophical systems the thoughts which Scorpio fished up out of the hidden depths. The hunter's arrow transfixes the flying bird and transforms a far-off vision into the basic ingredient for duck soup. We may mourn for beauty lost, but we eat the meat and pick the bones and hope we shall soon be able to shoot another duck because we need the sustenance and we enjoy the sport of bringing it down.

Exoteric astrologers say that Sagittarians are great athletes and hunters. We can see why this might be so. Liz Tressilian, in her whimsical *Cat Horoscope Book*, draws a delightful picture of the Sagittarian cat who honestly believes himself to be a horse. Any lounge lizard who has been trapped into a country weekend with a Centaur may have reason to suspect that this case of mistaken identity affects humans as well as cats.

Ah, but the Sagittarius-influenced man or woman isn't just any horse: he's Silver and the Lone Ranger combined, and you may as well reconcile yourself to playing Tonto or Scout or both, because whether you want to or not, you'll be bullied into it. For your own good, of course. Sagittarian types always know what's best for everybody, and they're not shy about saying so. They are the sheriff, we are the posse. Ours not to question why; ours but to gallop after our dauntless leader, who is absolutely certain where he's going even if it happens to be exactly opposite to where he thinks he's going to get. The beautiful self-assurance of the misaimed Sagittarian is a phenomenon which has to be experienced to be believed.

Here is a piece of astrological common sense garnered from bitter experience: never start out on even the shortest excursion with someone born with the Sun or Ascendant in Sagittarius unless you first equip yourself with a full thermos, sandwiches, first-aid kit, sleeping bag, and several changes of clothing. You may get to your announced destination in record time, or you may wind up in Shangri-La. You won't know which until you're there. Needless to say, you won't get to drive, nor will there be any use in picking out routes in advance, because maps are for cowards. If the Centaur does ask you to navigate, he'll be past any turnoff before you can point it out, and it will be *all your fault*.

Woe unto any coward born with Venus in Sagittarius, for we are irresistibly attracted to these Horsemen of the Apocalypse and they to us. Unless we learn to take a firm stand when the dearest and best suggests a jolly spot of mountain climbing before dinner or a quick dip in the Baltic during a northeast gale, we shall spend our probably brief span of years in an aura of liniment and cough drops, wracked by sprains, pulled muscles, and fractured nerves.

Tarot represents the ninth house's activity by Key 14, which is called "Temperance." The meaning here has nothing to do with moderation in eating and drinking, but with the metallurgical process of tempering. A blacksmith tempers a horse shoe by heating it white hot, then plunging it into cold water. This makes the originally brittle iron tough and relatively flexible, able to withstand greater shocks and perform harder work. Combining this thought with the fact that Gemini is Cabalistically known as Zain, the sword, we begin to understand the heroics of Sagittarius. Here, we are testing our minds, our bodies, our spirits. Having caught a glimpse of the Great Beyond, we now believe that nothing will ultimately be impossible to us. But the question of how much we can accomplish here and now has still to be answered.

Being able to shoot beyond our reach means that we can externalize our ideas, get outside our personal selves. Hence we can see new possibilities in the creative force which we realized in Scorpio. We understand that "Go forth and multiply" may refer to many things other than the begetting and bearing of children. We can multiply skills, knowledge, abilities to make our dreams materialize.

Sagittarius has been tagged a visionary, but analysis of his planetary influences as well as a glance around the bedroom or office of any strongly Sagittarian subject would indicate that the Centaur's visions are more apt than not to be expressed in tangible forms. It has not, we think, been sufficiently emphasized that Sagittarius is a collector. He may collect Ming vases, toy trains, bits of paper scribbled over with notes for the book he may some day write, or whatever best corresponds to his fantasy life. In any event, he is sure to have a great deal of stuff around, and despite his vaunted cheerfulness, he may become extremely annoyed if you try to tidy it away.

He has these things in his possession because he needs them. That buoyant self-confidence we hear so much about in this house depends on the fact that the Archer is holding the bow. He may not be able to see the mark toward which his arrow is speeding, but he can feel between his hands the springy wooden arc, the slackened bowstring which he can pull taut at will, to shoot again and again until he hits his target.

Sagittarius

Where Sagittarius appears in your chart, you will find an interest in material success. You will surround yourself with whatever concrete symbols best express your success image. You will do this both in terms of the house which Sagittarius rules and the sign which rules your ninth house. You may not think you've done anything of the sort, but if you analyze your possessions carefully enough, you'll find some amusing proofs of this statement.

A subject with Sagittarius rising will never be satisfied until he's his own boss, in full charge of his material fortunes, directing his personal destiny. He won't be much interested in having partners, because he knows that "He travels fastest who travels alone." With the Twins opposite, he won't be averse to including others in his enterprise and will assume a degree of responsibility for their happiness and well-being, as long as it's clearly understood he's the boss.

Sagittarius ruling the fourth house will tend to make the subject king or queen of the castle. The home will be a reflection of the individual's personality, a haven of comfort and security. Friends and family will be joyfully invited to share its delights, but Heaven help any invader who tries to take over. The subject may or may not be an efficient housekeeper, depending on what other influences prevail, but he or she will strive to be a real homemaker.

The seventh house may not be the happiest place to find Sagittarius ruling. Libra places paramount importance on sharing, and this is the one thing Sagittarius can't do. This is a single sign, and a most forceful one, seeing marriage as an opportunity for Jupiterian expansion, especially at the material level. In spite of lofty ambitions to achieve the perfect marriage, he—or, more devastatingly, she—will probably insist on wearing the pants. If the partner is not willing to knuckle under, friction is bound to ensue. This would have to be a highly developed spirit indeed not to become argumentative and critical in such a position.

The unfortunate paradox is that persons with Sagittarius strongly influencing the seventh house often marry with an eye to financial security, whether they admit it or not. By their carping, they impair the efficiency of the goose that lays the golden eggs. This is a testing situation of the first magnitude. All honor is due to the subject who can overcome its negative possibilities and achieve a true union. If a real marriage does take place, we can be sure it will be on a high spiritual level.

We shan't be able to evaluate Sagittarius in relation to the tenth house until we've got that far. However, since we have identified the Midheaven as dealing with vocation, ambition, public status, employees, and superiors, we might expect to find Sagittarius reigning supreme here, the Great Dreamer united with the Great Doer. Here we might find the statesman, the inventor, the philosopher, the minister who brings our cloud castles down to Earth and installs indoor plumbing so that we may live better and thus become better. Negatively, this subject could be a tyrant.

Of course Sagittarius could have many different interpretations in terms of the twelve houses. We have particularly mentioned these four because having Sagittarius at any one of them would mean, unless there is an intercepted sign, that we are dealing with an intriguing astrological phenomenon known as the Mutable Cross. That is, we have the four mutable signs, Gemini, Virgo, Sagittarius, and Pisces, at the four key positions East, North, West, and South (Ascendant, Nadir, Descendant, and Midheaven, respectively).

Understanding what mutability means in astrology, we should thus expect anybody having a Mutable Cross in his chart to be able to adapt himself to changing circumstances and to make sure his circumstances do, in fact, change. This can be good or bad. In a chart with many fixed signs, it could be the saving grace, the extra push needed to get the Centaur's haunches out of the mire and spur him to higher ground. It can temper the willfulness of a Cardinal sign overbalance, helping the subject to be more flexible, more inclined to examine different points of view. Where preponderance of Mutable signs already exists, however, it could keep the subject spinning around so fast he'd never know where he was and might even indicate a susceptibility to mental breakdown. This could be averted by making efforts to slow down and use the forces at one's disposal to achieve a better sense of direction and balance the stresses.

It is important to emphasize over and over the complexity of our subject and the unfairness of making snap interpretations. The deeper we dig, the more clearly we realize how little we've yet turned up in terms of what vast wealth of knowledge exists. Again and again we are struck by resemblances between astrology and medicine.

To the village wise woman, it was all so easy. She gathered her roots and herbs, stewed up her teas, applied her poultices, and if the patient got better, the magic had worked. If he died, it was clearly a case of stronger witchcraft against which her little powers couldn't be expected to prevail. A century ago, the learned doctor in his blood-stained frock coat still didn't find the problem too complicated. He opened a vein or applied a leech and drew off a few pints of blood hoping the infection would thus escape. If God in His wisdom chose to take the victim to a better world, who was the doctor to question the ways of Providence?

Gradually we've learned to adjust our treatments to the ailment and have probably, although we can't be sure, begun to cure more patients than we kill. The further we explore the wondrous workings of the human apparatus, the more specialized we become. Each physician selects a specific portion of the anatomy and concentrates on learning all he can about it, and the more he finds out, the more he must narrow his field of inquiry.

A specialist has been defined as "Somebody who knows more and more about less and less." This sounds absurd, but it isn't. A learned professor of mathematics has to let his wife do the family income tax each year. Does the fact that he can't do simple arithmetic make the professor less qualified to teach calculus? Not at all, nor does the decision to specialize in Arabian Parts or the Lunation Cycle or any other single aspect of astrology make an astrologer more or less competent. The only danger would lie in attempting to apply his knowledge outside its proper frame of reference.

As a young medical doctor, for instance, Freud became acquainted with the pain-relieving properties of cocaine. Immediately he began to prescribe this perilously addictive drug for anything and everything. Some astrologers are trying to do much the same sort of thing with their pet hobbyhorses. It is earnestly hoped that all of us will come to realize, as Freud gradually came to do, that there are no cure-alls. No remedy applied from the outside is going to work. The patient himself must take an intelligent hand in both the diagnosis and the process of recovery. What the physician and the astrologer can do is point the way.

This gets us back to that fiery arrow called Sagittarius. We see that there are advantages in having zeal opposed by discrimination, and in having a self-propelled, single-minded house in which to sort out and follow up the images which have been spawned so profusely in Scorpio. In order to transcend the mundane, we must hitch our wagons of personality to a star, and we're glad to have such a definite pointer to help us decide which star.

Sagittarius is often called an exceptionally happy sign. We can see why the Archer might have cause for rejoicing. Here's Jupiter insouciantly helping himself to whatever he wants from Pluto's bottomless treasure chest, which is conveniently situated right next door. Opposite live the Heavenly Twins, always ready to come out for a frolic. This may explain the wide streak of child which is such a frequent and charming facet of the Sagittarian character.

Samuel Clemens (Mark Twain), James Thurber, Winston Churchill, Pope John XXIII are fine examples of subjects born with the Sun in Sagittarius. None ever slacked on the job of using all his abilities creatively for the benefit of the general public. None ever lost his ability to laugh and to share the joke. Yet each of these men was tested beyond what some of us would consider human endurance. Thurber struggled all his life with poor eyesight and finally went blind. Clemens educated himself to become probably the greatest novelist America has yet produced, made a fortune and lost it by trusting the wrong people, battled himself out of debt by being funny on the lecture platform while his adored wife and two of his daughters were dying. Churchill stiffened the backbone of a pathetically ill-equipped nation and was the guiding spirit in wresting victory out of certain defeat. Pope John was stuck against his will with the task of shoring up the Vatican's crumbling foundations and trying to relate his Church to a world which had left it behind. Beethoven, also born in Sagittarius, composed his greatest music after he had become stone deaf.

Have we any right to say, "I can't," when examples like these show what man can do if he tries? What triggers this kind of motivation? Since everybody has some Sagittarian influence in his life, we can't argue that they were born under a luckier star than we. The question we must face is, "How do we draw the bow?"

In Cabala, Jupiter is associated with the direction West. This could explain why Americans invented the mythos of the Wild West, and why the entire Western Hemisphere seems to be trigger-happy. Anyway, this link with the act of shooting suggests some interesting things about how Sagittarius works.

To begin with, we think of shooting as a masculine activity. The sexual symbolism is so obvious that a woman with a firearm tends to strike us as being vaguely hermaphroditic. Now, let's look again at our charts. Sagittarius, a masculine sign, opposes Gemini, also a masculine sign. This is the only opposition in the zodiac which involves only two planets, and both of these are personified as male figures, neither of whom astrology associates with the sex act. The Mercury-Jupiter opposition strikes us more as a teacher-pupil relationship, with Gemini eager to learn and Sagittarius always ready to instruct.

Another point to consider is that these are the only two signs which have something to do with weapons. There is an important difference between the sword of Gemini and the bow and arrow of Sagittarius. The sword is held in the hand. The swordsman can wield it with only as much strength as is in his own arm and stab or slash only what comes within his reach. His enemy can defeat him just by staying out of reach.

The archer stands a better chance of bringing down his prey. The bow propels his arrow with far greater force than his arm could do. Targets can be hit from a considerable distance. The one place his weapon fails is in hand-to-hand combat. The bow can't be used unless the archer has room to draw it, and the slender arrow is too weak to serve any purpose by itself. In other words, to be effective, Sagittarius must be *detached*.

Furthermore, he has to hit what he's aiming at, or his potential superiority doesn't mean a thing. The least skillful Twin whacking about with a sharp sword can do more to win a battle than an Archer who can't shoot straight. Therefore, we can see why the former is concerned with practical knowledge at the personal level and the latter with abstract knowledge on a wide-ranging mental and spiritual level. The farther away our target, the more precise our aim must be. We can't allow ourselves to be distracted. We have to concentrate on seeing our target clearly, on training and coordinating every muscle to draw the bow smoothly, with every ounce of our strength.

It's not having the best weapon but knowing how to use the one he has that makes an expert archer. It's not always the greatest talent, but the greatest ability to put his talents to work that makes the successful achiever. We start by studying ourselves to discover where our potentialities lie. Then we improve our skills in this area by persistent practice. Then we select our target. Then we employ our body muscles to draw back the bowstring, our eye muscles to line up the arrow, our minds to gauge its trajectory. *Then we let go.*

Only when we are children can we feel the thwack of the sword in our hands and think, "I am doing this." The more mature we become, the more intensely we train ourselves in using the powers which manifest themselves through our minds and bodies, the more definitely we understand what the archer knows.

Of itself, the bow has no power, the arrow no direction. Of himself, nobody has strength enough to hit a far-off target. All he can do is set up the shot as best he can, then let the weapon do its work. Even so, the arrow would fall useless to the ground were it not for some force which he cannot feel, taste, smell, hear, or see; only *trust* will drive it onward to his goal.

The more we learn, the more skills we acquire, the more we have to say with Jesus, "Of myself I can do nothing. My Father that is within me, He doeth the work." But what sort of paradox is this, "My Father that is within me?"

25 · Capricorn

Third Earth Sign, Cardinal, Feminine
Saturn Rules, Mars Exalted
Color: Blue-Violet; Symbols: The Crocodile, The Goat, The Unicorn

"I CANNOT forecast to you the action of Russia. It is a riddle wrapped in a mystery inside an enigma." Substitute "Capricorn" for Sir Winston Churchill's observation about the

U.S.S.R., and you'll have some idea of what we're up against in the tenth house. If you study the symbol, you will find a suggestion of duality in the V, singleness in the little squiggle like a lower case "e" which is tacked on at the end, and triplicity in the fact that it is made up of three different strokes. But we certainly can't classify it as single, dual, or triple as we have done with every other sign. This would give us a clue that Capricorn is going to take some special explaining, even if we hadn't already begun to suspect so from its position at the Midheaven.

Being up there all by itself, no wonder Capricorn is astrologically associated with the act of climbing. Physiologically, it is said to rule the knees. Symbolically, it is most often called the Sign of the Goat, the animal which can scramble to heights no other quadruped dares attempt and nibble sustenance from what appears to be bare rock. Hence Capricorn is pictured as unswerving in his drive to achieve material success, spartan in his habits, not the handsomest creature imaginable, but a respectable, hardworking soul whom we ought to respect for his solid virtues even if we don't find him very interesting.

Since this is an Earth sign, Capricorn is concerned with earthly wealth. People strongly influenced by this vibration may amass tremendous fortunes by sheer dogged digging. They won't use it as Taurus does, to keep them in comfort. The Goat wants power and prestige. One of the ways to obtain these is to have more money than other people.

Glancing across the wheel, we notice that Capricorn is opposed by Cancer, which as we know is the shell builder, the container, the fencer-off, staking our claim on a particular segment of life experience. We may infer that Capricorn is the carpenter who fills that space and builds a house for the Earth Mother and her brood to live in.

"In my Father's house are many mansions." Perhaps this statement by a carpenter born under Capricorn can help us to clarify this enigma. The tenth house has been described as the house of vocation, ambition, public status, employers, and superiors; but it is more than that. This is the house of the

Heavenly Birth, of God, or whatever we choose to think of as God.

We have been passing through a phase of unbelief. Not long ago, somebody got the idea that God is dead, but since he was unable to produce the body, he failed to prove his case. Even atheists who welcomed the attempt to get rid of this bourgeois religion myth wriggled uncomfortably. If God is now dead, then He must at one time have lived, which rather messes up their thesis. On the other hand, if God never existed, then how can we evolve a concept of God in which to disbelieve?

Voltaire said, "If God did not exist, it would be necessary to invent him." Thereupon arguments were raised that man had done just that. This idea found credence among many intelligent people, with good reason. The gods in which the greater part of humanity believes are indeed gods of their own making. A man-made god is an idol. An idol is a false god. The Tarot card attributed to Capricorn is Key 15, The Devil, or Baphomet. It shows a hideous creature with the head of a goat, the ears of an ass, the wings of a bat, the legs of an eagle, and an adrogyne human torso with one breast and arm female, the other male. The gods we create are apt to be just such mixed-up bogeymen as this, because in trying to assemble our ideas of theology we are frequently dealing with forces we don't understand and assuming a power which is not ours.

We are trying to create God in the image of Man, and relate to this image as we might to a flesh-and-blood parent. "If God is supposed to be Love, how can He make me so miserable? How can I believe in a Supreme Being who lets the world get into such a rotten mess?"

In the first place, who says you're miserable, and who sees the world as a rotten mess? The sufferer does, obviously, but he'd have to be a supreme egotist to assume everybody else shared his view. To his neighbor, the world may be a glorious place with a few messy corners that need tidying up. The sufferer's complaints may evoke in the neighbor any emotion from warm sympathy to mild compassion to complete indifference to wonder that anybody could let himself get into such a predicament when he could have used his head and stayed out of trouble, to anger at being made to assume responsibility for somebody else's problem.

Mark Twain once wrote that in every conversation between two people, six different personalities are involved. There is the real John, known only to his Maker; the John whom John himself thinks he is; and the John whom the other fellow believes him to be. John may be a dull, stupid person but fancy himself a sparkling wit. His neighbor believes him to be an artful rogue. So any silly remark John makes in trying to be funny will be taken by the neighbor as an attempt to deceive. The neighbor will project an equally false image of himself, which will be misunderstood by John in terms of his own false notions about the other.

When we consider how many misunderstandings of this nature we're involved in every day, we can take it as a tribute to our ability to love that we don't all wind up despising each other as cheats and liars. Being so often unsure of the personal image we wish to project and of what our closest friends are really like, how can we form an accurate image of an unseen Supreme Being? Cabalistic astrologers call Capricorn the House of Illusion and ascribe to it the letter Ayin, or "eye." This is where we must try to see what we've been doing wrong and face the responsibility to start putting it right.

Occultists point out that although we celebrate Christ's birthday in Capricorn, He was actually born in Leo. If we translate Christ accurately as "enlightened man," we find new meaning in Alexander Pope's apparently smug injunction, "Know then thyself. Presume not God to scan. The proper study of mankind is Man." Christ is a person who has achieved complete awareness of his or her identity as a working unit of the Life Process. We here on the planet Earth have known few such beings, and we may doubt whether any of the self-styled Messiahs operating today have in fact reached this stage of enlightenment. Nonetheless, the possibility of Christhood exists within us all. Please take careful note of that word "within."

If this is so, why do we have to be covering up for ourselves? Why do we need all these false identities? Why can't we simply accept ourselves and each other for what we are?

Deception is based on fear. That frightful image on the Tarot card represents the devils we conjure up out of our subconscious minds. When we are unwilling to take control of our own destinies, we turn the Goat into a Scapegoat. In the Mosaic ritual of Yom Kippur, one of two goats was chosen by lot to be sent alone into the wilderness, having the sins of the congregation symbolically laid upon it. The other, sinless goat was sacrificed on the altar.

This seems a strange ritual. The "good" goat is put to death while the "bad" goat is set free. Neither goat is in fact better or worse than the other but has had its fate determined by chance. Still, isn't this what we see happening every day? If we trust to some sort of blind luck, or to a God who seems as far beyond our reach as the high priests were above the goats, our fates do seem to be determined by trivialities like the turn of a card or the toss of a die. The wicked go free while the good perish for their sins. You laugh a little, cry a little, you die, you're buried. What can you do?

For one thing, we can make up our minds not to be the goat. We can refuse to accept responsibilities which are not properly ours and concentrate on minding our own business. We can quit shrugging our shoulders and murmuring. "That's the way it is;" and resolve, "This is the way it's going to be," and stick to our resolutions. We can open our eyes and find out ways to scale the mountains which seem to be blocking our paths.

Any Capricorn-inspired person reading this book is probably operating at this level, or trying to. Not many persons interested in finding a philosophy to live by are still at the "crocodile" stage, though we do find traces of that outmoded reptile in some heavily Capricorn-influenced personalities.

A crocodile is not a lovesome thing, except perhaps to another crocodile. It spends its life lolling around in stagnant waters and noisome swamps, prefers its food rotten, refuses to take care of its babies, and never exerts itself except to kill, which it accomplishes by treacherously posing as a floating log or sneaking up on its victims under cover of murky waters. Crocodiles live many years, but they do not mellow with age. They are popularly supposed to shed crocodile tears as they devour innocent babes and beautiful virgins and sweet little old ladies, but they aren't a bit sorry, really, and we shouldn't be taken in by them.

At the lowest level, this sign is the most coldly materialistic and greedy that we have to cope with. The Crocodile will get hold of anything that's going and bury it in his private mudhole to rot rather than share with anybody. This is the sort of character who is found frozen to death in one squalid room, stretched out on a filthy mattress stuffed with thousand-dollar bills. Physical comfort, beauty, music, light, laughter—none of the things which add up to happiness for most humans seem to mean anything to him. He is totally in the grip of Saturn, interested only in turning all the gold he can get to base lead.

At this level, when Mars comes into the picture, he shows himself at his most brutish. Here we find the fanatics, the paranoiacs who can only think of relationships in terms of, "I'm going to get you before you get me." Sexuality becomes gross physical lust. In fact, we have made the Goat a symbol of lust. Pan and his satyrs have goatlike haunches, horns, and hooves. The Oxford Dictionary defines "goatish" as "lascivious."

Because Saturn's restraining influence inclines Capricornian subjects toward ultraconservatism, this Mars-Saturn clash causes some unevolved subjects to develop a double standard of ethics. "Do as I say, not as I do," is their motto. "You must be virtuous and honest, but I am privileged to exercise my goatish proclivities as well as to grab all I can get because I am in some way better than you—richer, whiter, blacker, taller, shorter, more exalted by political office, executive rank, noble birth—anyway, I'm *different*. And furthermore, I'm clever enough not to get caught."

Of course they're not really fooling anybody but themselves. Novelists and feature writers have gotten rich on daring exposés of goatishness in high places. Judging from what we've read lately, we might get the impression that the higher the subject's rank, the ranker his moral standards. This is far from the truth; it's just that the wicked ones are better copy. Still, we can see how Capricorn might operate here. The determination which drives a subject to scale the heights could result from an imbalance of what Freud calls libido and astrologers call Mars. Once he's got to the top, what's he going to do with this superabundance of masculine aggressiveness?

Persons in high places are generally surrounded by subjects who are only too willing to become victims. The temptation to work off excessive libido by physical encounters would be constantly dangled in front of them. No exchange of emotion would be demanded. The Goat could pay off in money, jewels, mink coats, better jobs, added prestige, or whatever recompense the willing victims exacted. In other words, if he consented to "play the goat," Capricornus would then be "made the goat." Successful people are often too wise, humble, and genuinely virtuous to become involved in such spurious deals. They know that at the spiritual level nothing would be exchanged but pain and guilt, which brings us back to Baphomet.

The more deeply we explore astrology, the more emphatically we believe in the fundamental goodness of the Life Force. Accepting the concept of goodness and the law of polarity, we find that we also have to believe in the existence of evil. We've been going around for years chanting, "Nothing is either good or bad; thinking only makes it so," but what do we mean by thinking? And how can we think anything into being good or bad unless we first accept goodness and badness as realities which are directly antithetical?

Trying to straighten out this concept, we might define God as the personification of good, and the Devil as the personification of evil. This is how most people would define them. But an old saying that must have come out of some alchemist's attic gives us a more interesting definition: "The Devil is God as He is misunderstood by the wicked."

Mulling this over, we begin to wonder about that crocodile.

Did he perform his contemptible acts out of malice, or because he honestly believed this is the way God wants all good crocodiles to behave? Did our Puritan divines jail adulterers and hang witches out of spite or honest conviction that they were protecting their other parishioners from falling into the trap of wickedness by showing what horrible punishments are visited on all who stray? We may ask how they reconciled these terrible judgments with the Biblical injunction, "Judge not, lest ye also be judged." It's simply that the Devil thinks he's God.

We don't have to go far back in history to find appalling crimes being committed in the name of religion. Even as these words are being written, Protestants and Catholics are slaughtering each other in Ireland, a country which was the highest seat of learning in the Western world, before the Christians arrived. This same division between the faithful followers of the Prince of Peace has, so far, kept Canada from becoming the great nation she ought to be. The grim confrontation between India and Pakistan, not long ago a single nation, is basically a clash between Hindu and Moslem. Is it any wonder so many of us turn sick at the mention of words like God and Church and refuse to have any part of such wickedness?

Yet the Goat continues to climb. We stumble, skin our knees, are caught in avalanches, swept into ravines. We pick ourselves up, shake off the debris, and start again the painful struggle toward the peak. How can we show such magnificent courage when we are such abject failures as human beings?

We are not failures, since we do not admit defeat. We may sometimes act stupid and perform silly acts of devilment. We may set up false gods for others to knock over or destroy what our brothers have set up, congratulating ourselves that we are doing God's work as we slit the throats of God's other children. We are all guilty of having done wicked things, and we have been punished over and over again. We still have penalties against us, but we're beginning to understand what we've done wrong. Seeing how the system operates, we shall be able to work off our debts.

Whatever we do, we cannot escape the necessity to work within the solar ecology. We know that this operates in only one way. Therefore we have only one reality, which is above, below, around, and within us. Good and evil are only the opposite poles of the same one thing. The Devil is only a shadow cast by our getting in the way of the one light. When we can see life as an orderly continuum instead of a heap of unrelated fragments, we shall know that we have, in truth, nothing to fear except fear itself.

Nobody can make us afraid of what doesn't exist. Only our own imaginations can people the dark corners with ghosts and specters, and nobody but ourselves can laugh them away. *Mirth* is another key word for Capricorn. This is the great clue to separating God from the Devil. Where Capricorn shows up in our charts is the place where we must tear off the masks and find out that what passed for reality is nothing but sham, that life is a glorious joke in which everybody can share.

Think back to what we learned about Saturn. Remember what a jolly old soul he used to be until we loaded him with the woes of the world? He hasn't changed, no matter how different he looks without the vine leaves in his hair. Take away the chains of deception, see what responsibility really means, and you'll find that assuming your share is the greatest fun in the world.

To love the struggle for its own sake, to work for the joy of the task instead of for what you think you might get out of it, is to put yourself into harmony with the flow of life. Once you realize there is only one world, one task in which all of us are equal sharers, you will find a tranquility of body, mind, and spirit which cannot be explained but can only be experienced. That's when the Goat's rough coat turns to dazzling white, his two clumsy, curled horns straighten out to blend into one of shining gold, and the Unicorn lays his head in the lap of the Virgin.

26 · Aquarius

Third Air Sign, Fixed, Masculine, Dual
Saturn and Uranus Co-rule, No Planet Exalted
Color: Violet; Symbol: The Water Carrier

THE eleventh house holds special interest at this time. Not only for students of astrology, but for everybody who is at all alive to what's happening around him. A popular song tells us that this is the Age of Aquarius—which it isn't, quite yet. Aquarian bookshops, theaters, organic food restaurants, and Uranus knows what else are springing up everywhere. How can we keep from wondering what this Aquarian Age thing is about?

Putting together what we've learned so far, we see that we already know a good deal about Aquarius. This is the house of friends, social life, hopes and fears, wishes and aspirations. Some astrologers call it simply the House of Brotherhood (which naturally includes sisterhood).

On our charts, Aquarius opposes Leo, the sign of self-realization. We may, then, deduce that eleventh house activities would involve amplifying the concept of self into that of group member, seeing the individual as part of a society which, like himself, is a continuum transcending time and space. Where this influence appears in our natal charts, we should expect to find ourselves more concerned about people in general than ourselves in particular.

If the influence is strong, as in an Aquarius Ascendant, Sun, Moon, or a group of two or more planets in this sign, we should be inclined to choose forms of self-expression which involved the group more than the individual. It has been said that seventy-five percent of the names in the Hall of Fame are of persons born with the Sun in Aquarius. Immediately, we think of Abraham Lincoln, Franklin D. Roosevelt, and Adlai Stevenson.

What did these men have in common? They were all brilliant thinkers. They were all willing to employ unorthodox methods. They were all forceful communicators. They were all prompted by a sincere desire to serve humanity. They were all visionaries, and they all got carried away by their visions sometimes. And they each had trouble with his wife.

With all respect to the ladies involved, let's consider the records. Mary Todd Lincoln must have been an extremely difficult woman to live with. Some said she was mentally unbalanced. She was called recklessly extravagant, although not enough credit has been given her for the taste and flair with which she redecorated the White House. She was bad tempered and domineering. She was not Lincoln's first love, and he may not have loved her at all. Yet without her tyrannizing, Lincoln might have given way to the moodiness, vacillation, and lack of confidence he often showed in his early years. She was the one who prevented him from escaping responsibility by flight, as his father had done, and prodded him into making effective use of his inestimable powers of leadership.

On the other hand, Adlai Stevenson's divorce may have cost him the Presidency. His relationship with his wife could not have been amiable, judging from a book of verse called *The Egghead and I* which she later published, yet he himself did not want the divorce. Had she been willing to stick with him, the wife-and-family image would have made him appear less the visionary and more the practical man of affairs, and a real leader might have been elected at a time when, as history has taught us, vision and leadership were most needed.

The picture of Eleanor Roosevelt hounding her exhausted and dying husband to perform what she saw as his public duties is hardly one of domestic felicity. Yet nobody can say that she was not an effective First Lady, or that she didn't know what her relationship with FDR was about. Her autobiography, *This I Remember*, gives us a succinct picture of what it's like to be married to a strongly Aquarian personality:

> He might have been happier with a wife who was completely uncritical. That I was never able to be, and he had to find it in other people. Nevertheless, I think I sometimes acted as a spur, even though the spurring was not always wanted or welcome. I was one of those who served his purpose.

Obviously, this was no ideal masculine-feminine relationship. The wife had to *act as a spur*, to assume the role of the dominant partner, and we cannot suppose that a man as astute as Roosevelt selected her and hung on to her for any other reason than that she was capable of nagging him into action. As we now know, he refused her offer to divorce him so that he could marry a more passively feminine woman. The reason given is that he was afraid of being disinherited by his mother, who appears to have been a far greater bully than his wife. Evidently the courageous leader who steered the United States out of the worst depression in history and through World War II did not trust himself to function without at least one really tough woman backing him up.

There seems to be this curious hint of the androgyne about any predominantly Aquarian personality. Tallulah Bankhead with her deep voice; Gertrude Stein, close-cropped, squat, dressed in mannish tweeds; Wolfgang Amadeus Mozart, unable to earn a living with his glorious genius because he wasn't aggressive enough to demand what was owed him—thousands of such examples could be cited, but why bother? Study Aquarius-influenced subjects among your acquaintances. You're bound to find evidence that Aquarius, although a masculine sign opposing a masculine sign, with masculine personifications present in all the four planets in both his own and the opposing house, doesn't always seem to know or care which sex he belongs to.

This air of detachment is what Aquarians' mates always bring up to excuse their take-over operations. "If I didn't make the decisions, they'd just never get made. John is so wrapped up in his work that he wouldn't notice if the roof fell on him."

What these hard-driving spouses don't realize is that they have been carefully chosen for the jobs they're doing. While they think they're pulling the strings, they are being subtly manipulated into doing all the things Aquarius doesn't care to be bothered with. The meek shall probably inherit the Earth, because the meek are using their meekness as a weapon to make the strong fetch and carry for them.

Aquarius has gone a step beyond illusion. He understands that this masculine-feminine–Red Work-White Work about which we're making so much ado is only the same force working in ways which appear to be at odds but are in fact complementary. Why should he exert himself to take sides, when there's a good possibility that both sides are the same side?

Abraham Lincoln kept a private diary. During the Civil War, he wrote:

> The will of God prevails. In great contests each party claims to act in accordance with the will of God. Both may be, and one must be, wrong. God cannot be for and against the same thing at the same time. In the present civil war it is quite possible that God's purpose is something different from the purpose of either party; and yet the human instrumentalities, working just as they do, are the best adaptations to effect His

purpose. I am almost ready to say that this is probably true; that God wills this contest and wills that it shall not end yet. By His mere great power on the minds of the now contestants, He could have either saved or destroyed the Union without a human contest. Yet the contest began. And, having begun, He could give the final victory to either side any day. Yet the contest proceeds.

Who, reading these words, can doubt that Lincoln was one of the great mystics? Here in one paragraph is a summation of all we have been trying to explain. It is an avowal of faith in a Supreme Power. It acknowledges that human will is under the supervision of a greater will. It describes the human being as a useful instrument in carrying out the divine plan.

Lincoln does not presume to know what the plan may be. He is confident that a plan exists, that he is taking a meaningful part in its operation, and that the struggle, however dreadful and futile it may appear to his limited vision, is not for nothing. This was all he had to know. It was enough to keep him doing his duty as he saw it, and it should be enough to inspire us to do the same.

It is important to remember that these are the private thoughts of the President who shocked the Congress by telling dirty jokes during the most desperate phases of the war, who made some spectacular blunders as Commander-in-Chief, and finally had to get a Taurean to win it for him, just as Roosevelt had to rely on Truman later in a similar circumstance. Lincoln may have been a saint, but he was also a neurotic human being with pronounced manic-depressive tendencies. He could envision peace but was never able to achieve it within his home, his administration, or the country which rewarded his efforts with public revilement and an assassin's bullet.

The Age of Aquarius is supposed to bring us peace and understanding. We can at least hope to increase understanding, since this appears to be the motive for our presence on a hospital planet. Since we are constantly adding to our memory pool, we can't very well diminish our knowledge.

A cynic might say, "What's to diminish?" But such deprecation is cheap and silly. We must appraise ourselves fairly. As individuals, as a nation, and as members of the world community, we know a great deal more now than we did in Lincoln's time. We have learned that civilization does move, slowly but inexorably, toward the light. We shall become better people. We are in the process of transformation. How fast we move depends on how hard we try.

Astrological influences can create a more favorable climate for the development of harmonious relationships; but if we have apocalyptic visions of the Water Bearer dousing us with love and goodwill more or less the same way as drunken conventioneers drop paper bags filled with water out hotel windows on the heads of passers-by, we'd better revise our expectations. We must remember that we *are* the Water Bearer, and the life-giving fluid we pass from one to another is human self-consciousness.

Lincoln described humans as "the best instrumentalities to carry out His purpose." Whatever we may think he meant, or whatever we ourselves may mean, by "His," we cannot now doubt that we are in fact instruments. It would be great if we could see the triumph of the new technology not as more efficient electronic devices, but as thoroughly humanized men and women, helping each other to reach a higher awareness of our potentialities.

We found out earlier that Uranus can put weird ideas into our heads, and we're seeing this happen. The talk of environmental conditioning which has been filling our newspaper feature sections lately seems to be straight out of Huxley's old horror story, *Brave New World*. From the same source comes the concept of cloning, or producing entire colonies of identical humanoids under laboratory conditions. No doubt this has been tried in previous civilizations here or elsewhere, else why would the idea persist in our group unconsciousness?

The question is, why should we want to do such things? We've already got the plastic bottles shaped like Frankenstein and Dracula. Being nonbiodegradable, these are creating problems of disposal. What should we do with whole cities full of such creatures which would have the added disadvantages of being able to walk, talk, defecate, and require to be fed, housed, and kept in repair? Undoubtedly, peace and understanding would exist in such a society, since everybody would have the same concepts programmed into his brain mechanism. Nobody would compete, nobody would fight against his brother, because everybody would be everybody. Isn't this what we are striving toward?

In Haiti creatures called Zombies are said to exist. These are human bodies, from which the souls have departed and which have been mechanically reactivated by witchcraft. Being without mind or spirit, they work in blind obedience to the person who has been able to project his will into them. Since the story is so persistent and so many people claim to have seen Zombies at work, we suppose there must be something to it, though we don't know what. Perhaps they are exactly what they're said to be. Perhaps they are persons who are supposed to have died but were actually drugged or put under hypnotic trance, then lobotomized or kept under drugs. Perhaps they are low-grade morons incapable of self-direction but capable of functioning under supervision.

We have found that children with IQs so low as to be unmeasurable can be taught to perform simple tasks. They may be more capable at these than brighter workers whose attention is more easily diverted. Even Epsilons have their uses, we find. Many a harassed housewife might find it convenient to have a Zombie at her beck and call. Then what's wrong with Zombies? Why does the very word evoke a mixture of pity and loathing?

We have reason to doubt how far environmental changes can affect response to the rhythms of the solar ecology. Dr. Frank Brown of Northwestern University did an interesting experiment which fortified this doubt. He transplanted some live oysters from Chesapeake Bay to a Chicago laboratory for a different experiment and was surprised to observe that the mollusks continued for an extended period to open and shut their shells in strict rhythm with the Chesapeake Bay tides which would have brought them food in their native habitat, performing the act an hour later each day. Since tides depend on the Moon's gravitational pull and release, he had to conclude that the oysters' daily time adjustment must be conditioned by the lunar rhythms under which they had been born.

In other words, no matter where we happen to be, we are what we are and we respond to the cosmic forces in our own way. Here was a laboratory illustration of what astrologers had been saying down through the ages. Interesting as Dr. Brown's oysters are, they bring to mind one of the maxims of Baloo:

> If you find that the bullock can toss you,
> Or the heavy-browed sambhur can gore,
> Ye need not stop work to inform us.
> We knew it ten seasons before.

Since we're so new on this planet, we're often tempted to snatch up each new bit of knowledge we acquire and rush about shouting, "Eureka!" Like the blind men who went to see the elephant, we can all be right and all be wrong if we stop exploring before we've found out that the tail, the tusks, the ears, the trunk, the hooves, the torso are all parts of something bigger. In order to understand even the possibility of a greater plan for life, we have to keep improving our sending and receiving apparatus, so that the Life Force can broadcast more clearly to us and we can pass on the message without distortion.

This is why we can't afford to create any more Zombies. The master-slave society has been tried any number of times, but it has never worked and it always leaves us with a mess to clean up. Saturn in Aquarius ought to be able to define our responsibilities more clearly than that. Why is Uranus up there snapping, crackling, popping off rockets that explode with dazzling brilliance to show us new heights which can be reached if we exert our ingenuity to devise new ways of climbing? Why is the Sun beaming straight into Saturn's face, showing us the reality behind the mask, illuminating the dark corners so that we shan't be disturbed by ghosts of the past? Why is Neptune opposing Uranus, turning his mirrors into a heliograph that can broadcast our most exalted thoughts and transform them into realities? Surely it's not so that we can trot out a rack of test tubes and whip up a batch of babies made to the same recipe, like a housewife baking muffins. What sort of pompous jackasses must we be to try to form anybody else in a mold of our devising, whether we do it by environmental controls, education, or fiddling around with genetics?

The one horrendously wrong thing about many idealistic projects for the betterment of the human race is that they tend to leave out the one vital element, human love on a person-to-person level. It is not enough for a child to be warm, fed, and sheltered. Somebody has to kiss it and talk to it and make it feel important enough to start using its ability to become a real person who can pass love on.

We might accept the theory of choosing auspicious dates for having babies by astrological principles, because having babies whose temperaments were in harmony with our own would make it easier for us to love them. Since we should all be choosing on different levels, there would appear to be no danger of our breeding a race of stereotypes.

Still, it behooves us to tread warily and be sure of our ground before we start trying to reform society in any way, however sensible it may appear. Hitler tried to create a Master Race by setting up breeding camps where members of his elite guard mated with hand-picked Nazi Youth girls. The Fuehrer was such a firm believer in astrology that the British High Command hired astrologers of their own in the hope of learning what the Nazi leader's soothsayers might be telling him. Therefore, it may be that astrological factors were taken into account in the breeding process. If so, we ought to know about it, and to do follow-up studies on the offspring of these unions before we advocate any further mass breeding experiments.

We can only operate effectively if we focus that opposing heliograph system sharply enough to show what Uranus the Magician has up his sleeve. Otherwise, eleventh-house influences in our charts can send us on endless and fruitless travels in search of identity. The curiosity which is so valuable in scientific research can lead us to poke our noses into other people's business. Yearning for the new and different, we could become restless and stir up trouble just to relieve our boredom. We might use our manipulative powers not to adjust better to our fellows, but to get things out of them. The mental power which makes highly developed Aquarian subjects superb mathematicians, statesmen, and social workers can also be used in devising high-flown schemes which never amount to anything.

We should be well advised to enter the Aquarian Age not with the notion that Santa Claus is at last coming to town, but with the expectation that we are going to be stretched far above and beyond our present concepts of human existence. We shall be faced with responsibility tests greater than any we have taken before, and we shall know if we flunk them, which wasn't always made plain to us in the past. With Uranus blinking like a lighthouse overhead and the Sun in Leo shining from across the way, we shan't be able to use the excuse that we weren't able to see clearly what was happening. Our great problem will be to make use of the light without being dazzled by it. We must be sure that we pour out our precious water of consciousness where it will do the most good.

27 · Pisces

*Third Water Sign, Mutable, Feminine, Dual
Jupiter and Neptune Co-rule, Venus Exalted
Color: Red-Violet; Symbol: The Fish*

MORE accurately, the symbol for Pisces is two fishes swimming in opposite directions but bound together—and this is important—by a slender cord. The sea in which they swim is Neptune, the Universal Solvent, bringer of mists, fogs, and hallucinations. Where does this description lead us? It looks as though in the twelfth house we shall be paddling around in circles, always confused and never getting anywhere. With Neptune roiling the waters, those poor fish can't see where they're going and couldn't get there if they knew, because one is pulling against the other. This is as good a description as any for some of the actions which heavily Pisces-influenced subjects have been known to commit.

Astrologers often have as much trouble trying to understand this sign as its subjects do. Here's a typical example of what we're likely to find in popular works on astrology: ". . . usually has little worldly ambition, cares nothing for rank and power, seldom succeeds in making money, and rarely accumulates it."

So whom does this same writer, in this same chapter, list as "typical Pisceans?" George Washington, Elizabeth Taylor, Rudolf Nureyev, the Earl of Snowdon . . . we *are* talking about the same sign, aren't we?

The truth of the matter is, those fish are not such self-sacrificing creatures as we think. Pisces may succeed in deluding others, and even himself, about the altruism of his motives, but when the chips are down it's apt to be our finny friends who scoop up the pot. Because of that Neptunian haze which pervades the twelfth house, we just don't see them doing it. If you've ever tried to catch a fish in your hands, you know not only what slippery characters they are, but also how hard it is to hold on to them after you think they're securely in your grasp.

Furthermore, have you noticed how quickly their iridescent beauty fades when they are drawn out of their watery element? Perhaps this is why Pisces-influenced subjects tend to be superb actors. On the goldfish-bowl stage, separated from what we call the real world, standing in the artificial gleam of the spotlight and the footlights, they can make their glittering scales reflect colors and patterns which dazzle us by their brilliance and charm. The Fish can transform themselves into whatever will please us most, without having to disappoint us in the end by turning out to be quite different from what we thought we loved and admired.

The trouble is, not all Piscean subjects get to perform on the stage. They have to put on their shows wherever they happen to be, and the outcome can be disenchanting. Not realizing we're only the audience, we take their play-acting for sincerity. We submit poor Pisces to the firm Saturnian grip of Libra in attempting a genuine relationship, then wonder why the exquisite creature grows cold and stiff. Even when the situation begins to smell a bit fishy, we may enter into the act rather than allow our illusions to be shattered. Pisces has a knack of involving others in his fantasies, which, thanks to exalted Venus, may be on the grand scale. The case of Piscean George Washington is a case in point.

America's first President undoubtedly had many genuinely fine qualities. Whether or not he can be classed as a truly great man, in the sense that Lincoln achieved greatness, is debatable. Our evaluations are confused by time, sentiment, and that roseate Neptunian glow which still hangs about the tall, big-bodied, small-headed figure with the ill-fitting false teeth. Does it matter? What counts to us now is that Washington was able to act the part of a leader at a time when the newly united thirteen colonies needed strong leadership to survive and emerge as an independent nation.

Like so many of those unworldly Pisceans, Washington managed to fall in love with a rich girl. In fact, he courted two others before persuading Martha Custis, a widow with two children, to join her considerable fortune to the one he had recently inherited from his brother. He was a good businessman and continued to accumulate wealth all his life, although he was such an inept general that only the still greater incompetence of the British forces enabled him to achieve a costly and long-overdue victory. He was kind to his own slaves. (Yes, dear reader, slaves. Although he opposed slavery on social and economic grounds, he made no move to free those whom he had inherited as part of his brother's estate.) But he let his troops go barefoot in the snow at Valley Forge while he chiselled the Continental Treasury out of enough expense money to have equipped every ragged man in the field with sound boots and a warm coat.

When he was elected President, he generously offered to serve without salary as he had as Commander-in-Chief, provided the Congress would continue to pay any bills he incurred in pursuit of his duty. Instead, the Congress begged him to accept a fixed stipend, on the grounds that the country was too poor to finance any more of its leader's self-sacrifice.

But the father of his country did look impressive on his white charger, and he cut a dashing figure in his fine clothes, especially at the routs and revels he (like most Pisceans) so much enjoyed. As President he set a standard which even Herbert Hoover never attained. He returned no calls, even refused to shake hands with anybody, acknowledging salutations with a formal bow. He rode out in a coach drawn by four or six smart horses, surrounded by lackeys and outriders in elegant livery. He attended receptions dressed in a black velvet suit with gold buckles, yellow gloves, powdered hair, a cocked hat with an ostrich plume, and a sword in a white leather scabbard. Except for a weekly public levée, he saw nobody except by appointment.

In short, Washington the hero of the Revolution became George the First. The atmosphere of artificial pomp and circumstance he insisted on maintaining brought shocked protest from statesmen who had thought they were founding a democracy, but he spurned their criticisms and became even more aloof.

History has tried to excuse his behavior as due to shyness, but this does not seem plausible. Washington had always loved socializing and had been accustomed since a youth to move in the Colonies' most aristocratic circles. Even while he was having horses shot out from under him on the frontier in Braddock's War, we find him yearning for the assembly balls back home. He was a rich man with an impressive estate, at which he loved to entertain lavishly. Why should he suddenly become paralyzed with diffidence on being elected President? No, common sense tells us that he was just playing it the way he saw it. He had no precedent to follow, because nobody had ever held the position before. Therefore, he fell back on what he had heard about reigning monarchs abroad. *Noli me tangere* seemed a reasonable motto. A President of the United States is not as other mortals.

This thought may have given him private satisfaction. A propensity to hug the secret feeling, "I am a creature apart from the common herd," may be one of the mistaken notions

Pisces has to get rid of. Twelfth-house influences in our charts do tend to inspire bizarre ideas. Not for nothing has Pisces been associated with secrets, spying, prisons, hospitals, and illness both physical and mental. Paranoiac and/or schizophrenic tendencies may be manifested among persons who have failed to see the dangers in letting those two bewildered fish swirl about uncontrolled in the waters of subconsciousness.

Those who do have this vibration under some degree of control are often skilled at conjuring up Neptunian mists which obscure what's actually happening. It may be next to impossible for other people to figure out what the Fish are up to. They may be deceiving themselves; at least, one half of the Piscean personality may be tricking the other half. This is the most dualistic of the dual signs. A Piscean can give the impression of being two entirely different people, adjusting his behavior and conversation to either role with such facility that both are equally convincing, even though Piscean A may act and talk like the direct antithesis of Piscean B. Yet it is not safe to assume that this duality of behavior will always produce a stalemate. Either Fish A or Fish B is sure to take over sooner or later. One way or the other, Pisces will get to where the feeding is richest.

Because Pisces has talked so much about self-sacrifice, we have been too easily convinced that this actually takes place. Astrologers associate Pisces with the feet. Feet are given us to walk with. If a subject is inspired by the Piscean vibration to walk into a situation of apparent self-immolation, we can be sure she is not going quite so unrewarded as she appears to be.

We say "she" because Pisces is a feminine sign, not because sex has anything in particular to do with Piscean behavior. In fact, the virginity we did not find in Virgo, the opposing house, has often turned up here. Celibacy was easily accepted as a tenet of Piscean Age religion because these "cold fish" may prefer sexual fantasy to sexual fact. Dreams and visions of wild orgies from which the dreamer could awaken triumphantly inviolate and primed with some interesting subject matter for his next sermon on the Evils of the Flesh were favorite indoor sports of Piscean Age divines.

Pornography in the forms of paintings, drawings, books, strip-tease shows, and whatnot has been popular entertainment during the age now closing. In its last flurries, we are being treated to such a surfeit of sexy magazines, filthy novels, nude stage shows, X-rated movies, and public copulation that we are heartily sick of the subject and ready to retch at the sight of one more silicone-inflated bosom. This probably has been a necessary catharsis, but we shall feel relieved when it's over.

Comparison of the symbol for Pisces with that for Aquarius gives us a hint of how our attitudes toward physical sex may change as we get into the Aquarian Age. In Pisces, we see two crescents facing in opposite directions, held together by a line which is placed at the center, or self-conscious level. And we have indeed been self-conscious about sex. Physical intercourse has been grudgingly allowed under certain circumstances ("It is better to marry than to burn") and for practical reasons of maintaining the species ("Shut your eyes and think of the Empire, dear"). Submission to the husband and the bearing of children was the duty, not the joy, of the wife. Providing material comforts for his wife and children was the duty, not the joy, of the husband.

In such a setup, each partner would be apt to see his or her survival as an individual as dependent on keeping the line pulled tight by getting the most he can and giving the least possible amount in return. We have used the Piscean vibration as a fisherman uses his tackle. He can't see what's under the water's surface. He baits his hook as attractively as he knows how, casts his line, waits for a nibble, then tries to land what he's hooked. Doing this takes some skill. He can't allow the line to grow slack or it will get snarled and he won't be able to reel in. He can't put too much strain on it or it will snap. He has to play it out the least possible amount, let the fish run a bit, haul it back, keeping up the subtle but relentless tension until he's worn it out and can bring it to the net.

When Christ told His disciples, "Be no longer fishers of fish.

Be ye fishers of men," He may have been giving them precise instructions on how to go about making converts in terms of the then prevailing zodiacal influences. We don't know if this is so, but we are able to see how the Piscean idiom has involved itself with our familiar concept of courtship and marriage.

A girl who gets married has "hooked a husband," whom his male friends refer to as "the poor fish." If their sexual relationship is not good, it's usually because one partner is a "cold fish." If one succeeds in getting possessions or sexual favors out of the other without giving up something of equal value in return, it's because he's "handing her a line" or she's "playing him for a sucker" (a fish which is easily caught because it will take almost any bait).

It is regrettably true that many of those meek, self-abasing Pisceans we hear so much about are particularly clever at this sexual fishing. Once they've landed their catch, they may surprise us by their ruthlessness in either devouring their prey or deciding they don't want it after all and flinging it to the cat. Strong Piscean subjects may be the best possible spouses, parents, and friends, or the worst. They seldom do things halfway, and they never do the same thing twice. You either get both fish on a silver platter or you get no fish at all, depending on how they happen to be feeling at the moment.

Pisceans see themselves as angels of benevolence,* but too often they rush to our aid like the would-be rescuer who brains the drowning swimmer with a life preserver. In trying to be kind they can perform acts of horrendous cruelty, because they don't seem to have the knack of putting themselves in the other person's place.

The Fish can only do what they imagine to be the right thing. With Venus exalted in this house, the imagination may

---

* A charming exception is the subject with the Moon in Pisces, who loves to visualize his friends as the lofty souls he would like to be. This may result in beautiful relationships, since his open admiration can inspire them to live up to the images which that glamorizing Piscean Moon reflects. This subject may show more of the sweet, gentle, retiring qualities usually associated with the twelfth house than one born with a Pisces Sun or Ascendant.

be overpowerful. The diffusing power of Neptune coupled with Jupiter's expansiveness can lead to self-deception on the grand scale. Therefore, Pisces seems to work best when she doesn't have to think at all but can let that bossy Virgo across the street tell her exactly what to do under every circumstance. She may talk a great deal about freedom, but she manages every time to maneuver herself into a box. The key word for this house is *reorganization*.

Trying to cope with so vast a subject as astrology in a single volume is like being a conscientious teacher in charge of a group doing a ten-day economy tour of Europe. We know we can't possibly get it all in, so we do our best to whet the student's appetite in the hope that he'll go back and cover the ground more thoroughly another time. Brief as our glimpse of the twelve houses has been, however, we cannot have escaped discerning that we do organize our lives.

That we do not yet see the pattern of a life cycle doesn't mean that none exists. Spectators who know nothing of football see nothing but a lot of men in odd-looking costumes being rude to one another as they try to control a ball which obviously refuses to be controlled. To the initiated eye, each man is expertly carrying out his individual role in a carefully thought-out strategy. The outcome of the game depends not on chance, as it may look to the ignorant one, but on which team can make more effective use of the strength and skill at its disposal. If neither team is very good, they won't put on much of a show and they'll make many errors, but they will still be operating within the structure of organized football.

Being last man up in the zodiacal cycle, Pisces knows that the Great Scorer will soon be coming to mark against his name, and that it won't matter if he won or lost, but if he played the game. Twelfth house subjects thus tend to be especially concerned with operating inside the rules. Look at George Washington, given a brand-new country to do pretty much as he liked with and squeezing his concept of the Presidency into the stiffness of European courts, leaning so heavily on the conservative Hamilton for counsel that the liberal Jefferson quit his Cabinet in disgust, and quitting himself when his sensibilities were wounded by criticism of his rigidity. Look at some of our glamorous Piscean actresses and see how businesslike they can be even about their love affairs, manipulating the legal processes of marriage and divorce to their material advantage.

Look at the religious movements which have been developed into elaborate organizations during the Piscean Age; Islam, Catholicism, the many variations of Protestantism, all the isms that boil down to one thing: an attempt to reduce abstract concepts to a set of concrete rules which, rigidly observed, may assure one a place in a rigidly organized afterworld. The important thing about these theologies is that they give each of us an opportunity to keep trying to be slightly holier-than-thou, so that the tension does not slacken, and our sense of identity is maintained.

The Organization Man is no mid-twentieth-century phenomenon. This game has been played all through the Piscean Age. We are now aware of how much suffering has been caused by our insistence on trying to erect a social structure solid enough to stay put once we got it arranged to our liking. The theory has been that we should be happier when everybody knew exactly who he was and what he was supposed to do. Lopping off the hands and feet of those who refused to adjust to the Procrustean bed seemed justified because of the glorious end we had in view.

The failure of the organization as we have seen it, of course, lies in our imagining that bliss is stasis. By the time we've finished driving in the last nail, the tide has turned. What we thought would be an ivory tower turns out to be nothing but a sand castle which gets washed away. Our cruelty to ourselves and our fellows has been for nothing. Our children don't want that lavishly furnished home we tried to build for them. Had we been more alert to each other's needs instead of concentrating so hard on paying our fire insurance by going through the established rituals, we should not be winding up the Piscean Age in karmic debt up to the elbows.

Aquarius's symbol of two parallel wavy lines will, we hope, inspire us to adjust better, to maintain our identities without having to set up situations of tension. Whether we can achieve all the song-writers have promised remains to be seen. Detachment can be carried too far. The androgyne vibration in Aquarius gives rise to troubled speculation as to whether a race of boy-girls and girl-boys will lose the magic of romantic love. This was one of the real gains we made in Pisces, even though not enough of us have yet been able to enjoy it to the extent of which we are capable.

We fervently hope that sexual union will not be reduced to a gymnastic exercise, as Huxley has suggested it may. We hope we shan't forget that babies need cuddling as well as hygienic cribs and vitamin-enriched pablum, that men and women need a sense of self-respect far more than they need colored refrigerators.

Aquarians are susceptible to fine-sounding theories like, "From each according to his ability, to each according to his need." But who determines the need? And how do we get people to exercise their abilities unless they are either driven by material ambition or determined to be martyrs? The Piscean Age has shown us the pitfalls in both these motivations. How can we promote the performing of work not out of a sense of duty to society and a determination to be holier, or richer, than somebody else, but from a joyful sense of personal involvement with the Life Force itself? We must not expect too much too soon. We still have a long way to go and a great deal to learn before Utopia emerges on this small but intriguing planet.

By now it will have dawned on the reader that, although we have been working counterclockwise at the personal level, from Aries to Pisces, society as a whole is working clockwise, from Pisces to Aries. It would be an interesting exercise to sit down with a sheet of paper and trace each of the symbols in its shorthand form, starting with the two fish, back to back and tied together, progressing backward through the various single, dual, and triple forms, noting how each relates to the ones before and after it and how at last Aries emerges as exactly the same sign as Pisces, only with the cord of tension gone and the two crescents joined together at the bottom. As we now know, this is the level of the subconscious, which astrology links with the Universal Solvent and the element Water, in which the living creatures from whom we are said to be evolved first developed—as fish!

So Pisces is both an end and a beginning. In this house on our natal charts are revealed our leftover karmic debts. Here is where we see what we have to work off this time around, where we need to organize a more relevant structure of body, mind, and spirit. This is the secret diary in which we have written things we don't want other people to know about us. Perhaps we don't want to realize them ourselves but are still carrying them around like those hideous family relics to which we attach ourselves because Uranus hasn't yet managed to wake us up to the fact that they're nothing but dust catchers and prodded us into throwing them out. Those secrets we're so guilty about ought to be brought out into the light and dusted off so that we can benefit from what they have to teach us.

The process of transforming hidden guilt to conscious knowledge is one of Neptune's jobs. It is interesting to notice that Pisceans, like Leo-influenced subjects, are great antique collectors, probably because these are the two signs where Neptune is active. As the Piscean Age draws to a close, there seems to be a mass movement to save all we can of a vanishing era. Old potato mashers, carpet beaters, chamber pots—utensils Grandma was delighted to get rid of—are being rescued from the trash heaps and put to uses over which Granny would have laughed herself sick.

If we can't find enough of the original articles, we make plastic replicas and advertise them for sale in words like, "Bring the cozy warmth of colonial days into your home." What was so cozy about a mud-chinked log cabin with a puncheon floor and no heat but a fieldstone fireplace? Of course it's ridiculous. It's more of that moonbeam spinning that Venus and Neptune are so clever at. But it's also darn good business. Let us not forget that Jupiter co-rules in Pisces. As Leto, Io, et al., found out, what Jupiter wants, Jupiter gets.

We should never waste pity on a Piscean, and we ought not to sit around feeling sorry for ourselves for having made a mess of the Piscean Age. In the first place, we can't tell yet how much of it has been bad and how much good. Events which now appear to have been disasters may have contributed more to the overall good of our planet than those we look back on with pride. Christ was crucified in Pisces, but Christ died to erase our karmic debt of accumulated sin and was born again on a higher plane. If we did not die to misery, how could we be born to joy?

The Piscean creed is "I believe." Living in the twelfth house, we have often been gullible, easily led, easily confused, yet incredibly stubborn in clinging to our mistakes. As the Yom Kippur service reminds us, the sin of one is the sin of all. We take the error upon ourselves and sacrifice ourselves. Each one of us is the crucified Christ. We are not yet what we are capable of being, so we must die out of our old, faulty selves even as this age is dying. We must be born again, and again, until we learn to believe in beauty and goodness and in our ability to love and be loved, not for anything we can get out of it, but purely for the fun of it. Then we shall really be living.

The stars are not going to maneuver us into this happy state. If we rely blindly on outside influences, we shall get stuck this time just as badly as we've been stuck before. Astrology is not a network of strings by which human puppets are pulled about. It is a method of learning how to take our own lives under firmer control and steer them toward higher achievements in terms of bodily, mental, and spiritual fulfillment. Astrology is not mumbo jumbo or mysticism, but ordinary common sense; and it's high time we called it so.

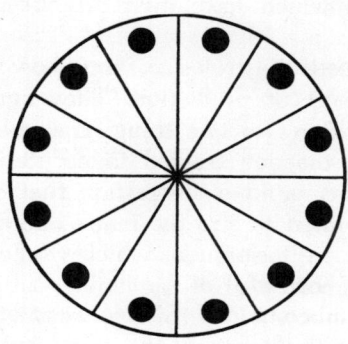

28 · A Note on the Reading of Charts

LIKE Einstein's theory of relativity, astrology is easy enough to apply once you've grasped the basic principles. An astrologer needs to be well grounded in the fundamentals before he can read a chart with any degree of accuracy, and even an expert will constantly be discovering new things in a chart, since each one is drawn up on many levels of existence. Still, we don't have to be professional geographers to make practical use of a road map, and anybody who applies himself can gain helpful insights from his chart.

It is true that a competent astrologer, of whom there are many now practicing, can look at a chart and say, "On August 2, 1976, you are going to marry a tall girl with red hair and have six children. The marriage will turn out unhappily and you will be divorced within ten years." And precisely that will happen to you, *if you allow it to happen*. On the other hand, you can refrain from marrying a tall, red-haired girl and thwart the fate which has apparently been laid down for you.

To do them justice, astrologers who know their business do not make this sort of prediction. They know too well the power of suggestion, for one thing. It would be easier than you realize for someone trained in occult work to plant in your subconscious mind a suggestion that you are *fated* to marry this girl, *fated* to sire too many children, and *fated* to give way to the disillusionment which would be likely to follow on having a houseful of screaming babies. If you didn't know that the subconscious mind *always* obeys instructions, you could fail to countermand the astrologer's prediction and the Moon would dutifully make the prediction come true. Thus the onus of causing you to form a marriage that was not going to work would rest in some measure upon the astrologer, leaving him as well as yourself with a karmic debt to pay.

Let this be a warning. If you pursue the study of astrology, you are sure to be pestered by friends and acquaintances for readings. The best advice is, don't do it until you have had enough training to feel sure of your ground. Even then, you will be wise to weigh your words carefully. Make your friends understand that astrology is not fortunetelling, but a way of evaluating strengths and weaknesses and learning how to tackle problems in the most effective way, by working with instead of against the cosmic forces.

A reputable astrologer takes his work seriously. One does not show a chart to anybody but the person concerned or discuss it except with someone who is honestly interested in working out a better relationship with that person. The better way is to pass on what you've learned so that others can work out their own charts and discover for themselves how astrological analysis can help them to lead more fruitful lives.

Setting up a chart is rather simple and great fun. If you wish to learn, there as a number of texts available which explain the process. However, there also seem to be many young astrologers about these days who will do it for less than the price of an ephemeris. Computerized charts may be obtained for as little as three dollars, although the one this writer got as a test was not very accurate. Increased demand for natal charts accurate to the minute will probably result in more competent programming, but computing a chart is really the easiest part of astrology.

An accurate natal chart is drawn up on the basis of the subject's place, date, year, and hour of birth. Having obtained one, place it in front of you along with the colored chart of the twelve houses you have drawn, and the ten little colored spots which represent the planets. Place each spot in its appropriate house on the colored chart according to your natal chart, and see what sort of pattern you get. Are the spots all bunched together? Are they scattered all over the chart? Is there a "seesaw" arrangement? Do you feel comfortable with the pattern or rather puzzled by it?

Think what the colors mean. Note which spots are on Fire, Water, Air, and Earth signs; which are Cardinal, Fixed, or Mutable; how many masculine, how many feminine. Write down all this information and analyze it in terms of what you've learned. You see, already you've gained some fascinating insights about what those odd-looking squiggles and numbers are trying to tell you.

In *The Guide to Horoscope Interpretation* (Sabian Publishing Society), Marc Edmund Jones offers an approach to understanding charts by means of such patterns as you now have in front of you. While it is by no means a final answer, his system is especially helpful in giving beginners a general idea of what they're likely to find in a chart.

Briefly, he describes the "Bundle," where all ten planets occur in three or four adjoining houses, as denoting the one-track-mind sort of person who will limit his span of interest to his own immediate concerns and pursue a single objective with amazing perseverance.

The "Bowl" has all planets within a span of six houses. This is obviously a one-sided character. Jones maintains that the "Bowl" always has something to give, and we should also suppose this subject had a great deal to take since the law of polarities would lead him to transfer some of the full bowl's contents to the empty bowl. The tilt of the bowl is said to indicate the general character of the subject: e.g., an upper-hemisphere bowl would be more concerned with mental activity; a lower-hemisphere bowl with physical things.

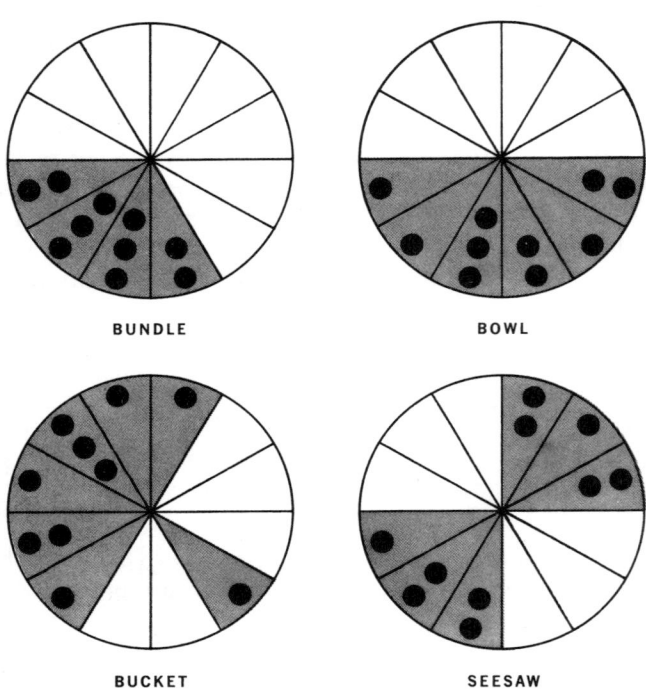

BUNDLE

BOWL

BUCKET

SEESAW

The "Bucket" resembles the "Bowl" but has one planet in a house outside the semicircle. This is the handle by which the subject can carry his bowl, thereby rendering it a more effective receptacle for collecting what he wants from life. In terms of modern communication, this outside influence seems to function like an antenna and may play an extremely important role in helping the subject to relate to the world around him.

If instead of one, we find two or three planets bunched

together in the "handle" position, Jones calls the formation a "Splay." Here, the subject would be more emphatic about receiving as well as giving. His attitude is a definite "Me-to-you, you-to-me," which could tend to make him pugnacious and insistent on getting what he saw as his rights.

On the other hand, approximately the same number of planets in two opposing "Bundles" would constitute a "Seesaw." This may or may not result in a give-and-take situation, depending on how objective the subject can be about what to give and what to take. Sometimes this denotes a disposition which swings noticeably from one mood to another, changing its mind suddenly and radically for no apparent reason.

If the planets are spread all over the chart, Jones calls it a "Splash." This subject would tend to be extremely versatile

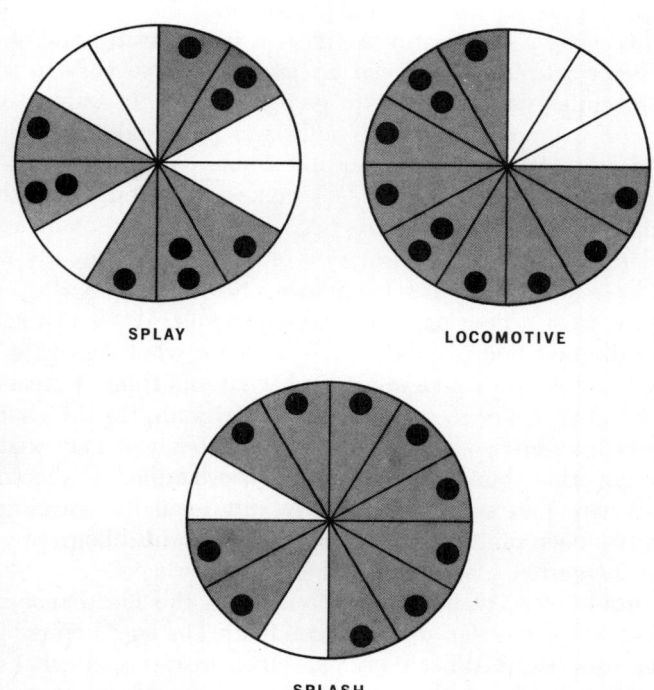

SPLAY LOCOMOTIVE

SPLASH

and flexible in his attitudes but might lack strength of will and determination in carrying his projects to completion.

Not so the "Locomotive," as Jones calls a chart which has a blank span of three adjoining houses, with the planets fairly well dispersed through the other nine. This, he maintains, is an exceptionally powerful setup. It imparts great drive and determination in fulfilling a goal, which is more apt to be social or intellectual than personal.

Each of these categories would naturally be modified by the findings in the individual case. A "Bundle" composed mainly of Air and Fire signs would behave far differently from a soggy lump of Earth and Water. A preponderance of Mutable signs would make this subject less mulish than a great many Fixed signs, less of a driver than a heavy load of Cardinal signs. We should be careful to find out all we possibly can before we start making judgments.

This system, clever and useful as it is, illustrates one of the problems astrology has been up against. It's so easy to work out formulas which appear to give a grip on the subject that we tend to apply them willy-nilly and to mistake the partial information thus obtained for the whole truth. However, we have to start somewhere, so let's make a decision as to which of the categories listed here best applies to the chart we're working on. Add this information to what you've already written down about elements, triplicities, etc.

Now, start a new page for the Ascendant. Write at the top what the first house stands for. Put down what sign is at the Ascendant on your own chart, and what you think it means in this context. Refer to the chapter on Aries and to the chapter which describes your first house sign. Later, you may wish to examine other sources for additional information. (It should be noted here that a great deal of readily available astrological data has been omitted from this text. See the Bibliography for some suggested source material.)

Consider any planets you may find in the first house. Are they in the same sign as the Ascendant? The sign before? The succeeding sign? What does this mean in terms of what you now know? Add all the information you can glean, then start

A Note on the Reading of Charts

a fresh page for the second house. If you have no planet in a house, make a page anyway. You'll want it later.

By the time you've been all around your chart, you will have compiled some fascinating notes, but there's more to come. Having pondered each planet and its position individually, we begin relating them to one another. Astrological relationships are called *aspects*, and we determine them by measuring the number of degrees between planets. Since each house represents a 30° segment of a 360° circle, it is easy to count by houses, then note whether two planets come within the range of an aspect.

For example, a *sextile* is an aspect of 60° (astrologers generally allow a variance of 4° on either side). That is, any difference within a span of 56–64° between two planets would constitute a sextile, but a larger or smaller discrepancy would not. In the sextile or any other aspect, an extra 2° difference may be allowed if the Sun or Moon is involved. Here are the aspects you most need to know about:

☌ *Conjunction:* Exact difference, 0°; allowable difference, 8° either side. This may best be interpreted as a Mercury vibration, the beginning of something. It usually indicates a personal concern which the conjunct forces are working as a team to bring about.

∥ *Parallel:* Exact difference, 0°; allowable difference, 1°. This is the same as a conjunction but even stronger because of the exact juxtaposition of the forces.

☍ *Opposition:* Exact difference, 180°; allowable difference, 8° either side. This is a Moon vibration which may create tension and misunderstanding. A need to balance the forces is evident here. However, it can also establish communication at a deep level. Tricky and sometimes difficult, but by no means always a "bad" aspect.

△ *Trine:* Exact difference, 120°; allowable difference, 8° either side. This is a Venus vibration and is generally regarded as an extremely favorable aspect, bringing ease and helpfulness. However, we know Venus is not always that easy to cope with. A more exact interpretation of the trine would be a free

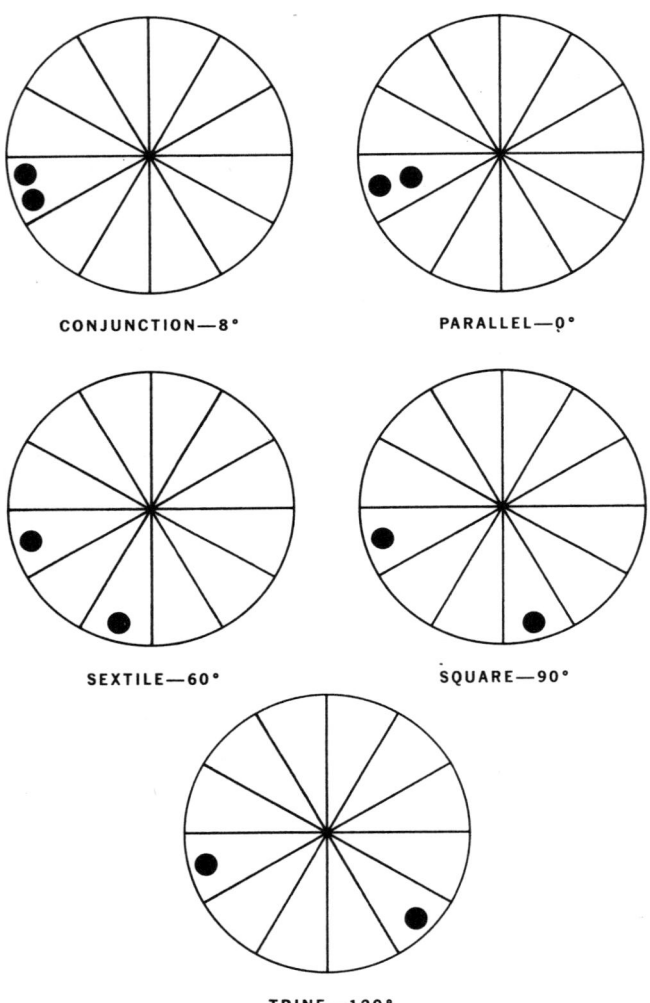

CONJUNCTION—8°

PARALLEL—0°

SEXTILE—60°

SQUARE—90°

TRINE—120°

flow of creative activity, which could be used constructively or not, as the subject chooses.

☐ *Square:* Exact difference, 90°; allowable difference, 8° either side. This is a Saturn vibration which many astrologers flatly

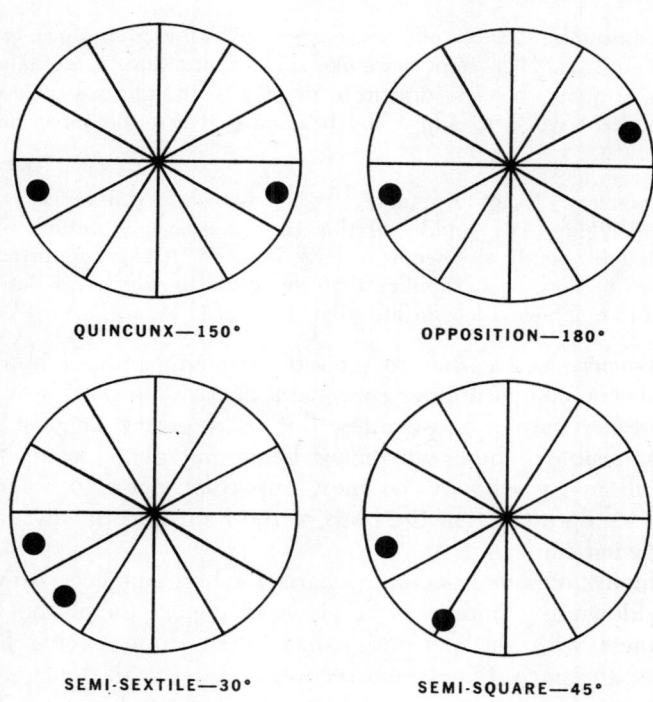

label "malefic." It need not be so. We can make the square a stumbling block or a building block, turning adversity to good account in constructing a more desirable life structure.

✳ *Sextile:* Exact difference, 60°; allowable difference, 4° either side. All astrologers (as far as we know) agree that this is a delightful aspect to find in any chart. A Jupiter vibration, it is never a problem but always brings opportunities for harmony, friendship, and attunement to the rhythms of the life cycle.

⌄ *Semisextile:* Exact difference, 30°; allowable difference, 2° either side. This is an Aries vibration and may therefore be rather stressful; however, it brings benefit from less apparent sources such as latent talents and unexpected wealth. It indicates an urge to move on.

∠ *Semisquare:* Exact difference, 45°; allowable difference, 2° either side. This seems more like a Libra vibration. It is similar to a square, but less drastic in its effects. It indicates a need for hard work, to adjust the balance between the forces involved.

⚻ *Quincunx:* Exact difference, 150°; allowable difference, 3° either side. We could call this the Capricorn vibration, although nobody else seems to have done so. It is a comforting sign to find, as it signifies that the goals to which it relates will be achieved late in life, that the best is yet to be.

We promised earlier to mention something about how to determine compatibilities from natal charts. We do this not to set down hard-and-fast rules, but as a protest against the irresponsible notions which are being put about as to who should marry whom. The most important point to make is that we do *not* go on the basis of the Sun signs or any other single indication.

Having obtained accurate charts for both subjects, draw a line down the middle of a piece of paper. Label the two columns with the persons' names, then draw twelve lines across the page. Label each section in order with the signs of the zodiac. Now, transfer whatever information you find in the charts to its appropriate position on your list. Include the Ascendant and Descendent for each, with their degrees. In this way, you can easily work out the aspects and draw logical conclusions.

If you fail to observe any significant aspects, it's safe to assume that the relationship is a figment of somebody's imagination and that disillusionment will soon follow. The more aspects you find, the more intense the relationship is likely to be, although it may or may not be a harmonious one.

A Sun-Sun or Sun-Moon trine, sextile, or conjunction would be considered favorable. Almost any Venus aspect, especially to the partner's Sun, Moon, Venus, Ascendant, or Descendent would be excellent, although a square would mean they'd have to work at building their relationship. His Mars making a favorable aspect to her Venus is a sure sign of sexual satisfaction, but her Mars on his Venus could indicate a tendency to use sex as a weapon for domination.

A Mars-Saturn square or opposition could mean constant battles. There would have to be many favorable aspects or great determination on both sides to keep this marriage from being a living nightmare. A Saturn-Saturn or Jupiter-Saturn square or opposition would probably indicate divergence of interests and unwillingness to compromise.

Any trine, sextile, or conjunction of a planet, Ascendant, or Descendent with the partner's Moon would tend toward strong emotional ties. A Moon square or opposition could lead to misunderstandings and hurt feelings through lack of communication. That double Moon in the opposition would expect so much love and sympathy that the partner might find the constant drag on his emotions difficult to endure.

Any Sun-Saturn aspect is extremely binding, although it may be hard to cope with. The Sun-Saturn square, being a Saturn vibration, is probably the strongest tie possible. If you find yourself involved with this aspect, try to relax and enjoy it or prepare yourself for a long tug-of-war. Intense and sustained effort will be required to dissolve such a bond. This may be an indication that the partners have a karmic debt to pay or an important task to accomplish together; therefore, it is usually best to handle this as a building block.

We have not space to pursue this subject any further. This book is already too long. It has been intended to give some idea of how fascinating astrology can be as an intellectual exercise, and how valuable a study in terms of human growth. Little has been said in terms of what there is to say. We have probably exasperated some and satisfied few. This is as it should be. No written word can accomplish much in the teaching of astrology. We need person-to-person instruction in this as in every aspect of human existence.

It is a maxim that when the student is ready, the teacher will appear. When you find your guru, remember that he or she is only a vehicle for the communication of information.

No writer, teacher, or student possesses knowledge, any more than we possess sunshine. We use it, refine it as best we can, and pass it on. As far as we have been able to learn, our purpose here and now is to step up the refining process by making ourselves more effective instruments to perform the work of the Sun. The sooner we get on with the job, the better for all concerned. The more clearly we learn to read our astral blueprints, the more enjoyable our work will be.

Appendix
A Note on the Use of Computer Data

HOROSCOPE information can be obtained in tabular form from computers. You will find this material easier to interpret if you set it up as a twelve-house chart. Names of signs and planets may be written out in full, as on the computer data sheet, but the shorthand symbols are more convenient to use.

The information you receive will probably look something like the following. (Symbolic equivalents do not generally appear on data sheets. These have been inserted by the author to save the reader's having to look them up, and to demonstrate more fully how the transferral may be done.)

POSITION OF PLANETS

Planet	Position	Symbol
Sun	13 degrees Pisces	☉ 13° ♓
Moon	4 degrees Scorpio	☽ 4° ♏
Neptune	27 degrees Cancer	♆ 27° ♋
Uranus	13 degrees Aquarius	♅ 13° ♒
Saturn	25 degrees Gemini	♄ 25° ♊
Jupiter	7 degrees Pisces	♃ 7° ♓
Mars	26 degrees Aquarius	♂ 26° ♒
Venus	28 degrees Capricorn	♀ 28° ♑
Mercury	23 degrees Aquarius	☿ 23° ♒
Pluto	0 degrees Cancer	♇ 0° ♋

Position of Houses

I	Ascendant	22 degrees Taurus	22° ♉
II		18 degrees Gemini	18° ♊
III		8 degrees Cancer	8° ♋
IV	Nadir	29 degrees Cancer	29° ♋
V		24 degrees Leo	24° ♌
VI		1 degree Libra	1° ♎
VII	Descendent	22 degrees Scorpio	22° ♏
VIII		18 degrees Sagittarius	18° ♐
IX		8 degrees Capricorn	8° ♑
X	Midheaven	29 degrees Capricorn	29° ♑
XI		24 degrees Aquarius	24° ♒
XII		1 degree Aries	1° ♈

Having constructed a circle divided into twelve equal sections, we begin by labeling the houses, beginning with the Ascendant. Note that in this particular chart the Sun is in an intercepted sign, that is, no house is ruled by Pisces (♓). However, the Sun must go somewhere, so we insert the sign for Pisces (in parentheses) in its usual sequence, halfway between Aquarius and Aries and put any planets which are joined to Pisces on our list in the house where Pisces now appears. Intercepted signs, and any planets associated with them, do not influence a chart as strongly as they would if they were not intercepted.

Since Pisces is intercepted, Virgo (♍) will automatically be intercepted, too. As you will see on Figure A-1, and on any chart, opposing houses are always ruled by signs which appear in the same degree.

With the houses labeled, we can easily see where each planet should be inserted. Note that a planet may belong not in the house ruled by its sign, but in the preceding house. In Figure A-2, the Moon is in Scorpio but must be placed in the house ruled by Libra, as its degree of progression is less than that of the Scorpio house. This is easy to understand if you remember that the zodiac never stands still. Like the hands of a watch, those twelve "spokes" merely indicate where the planets and constellations happened to be at the particular moment in time for which this chart is drawn.

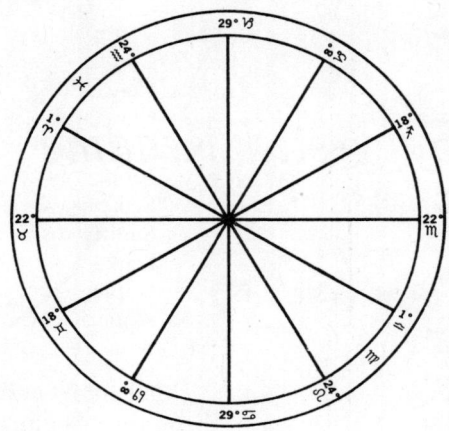

FIGURE A-1

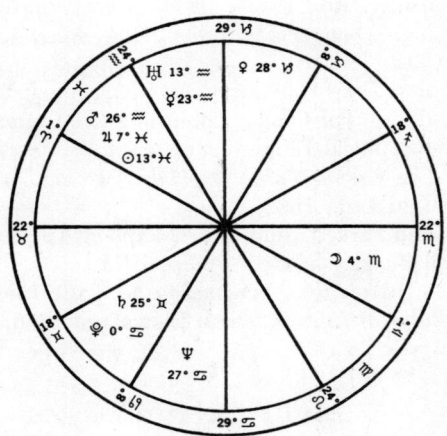

FIGURE A-2

Suggested Reading

ASTROLOGY

Adams, Evangeline. *Astrology: Your Place in the Sun.* London: Fred. Muller Ltd., 1971.
———. *Astrology: Your Place Among the Stars.* London: Fred. Muller Ltd.
DeVore, Nicholas. *Encyclopedia of Astrology.* New York: Bonanza Books, division of Crown Publishing Co. Copyright 1947 by the Philosophical Library, New York.
Lynch, John. *The Coffee Table Book of Astrology.* London: Geo. Weidenfeld Ltd., 1963.
Parker, Derek and Parker, Julie. *The Compleat Astrologer.* London: Mitchell Beazley & Geo. Philip, 1971.
Rudhyar, Dave. *Astrology of Personality.* St. Paul: Llewellyn, 1970.
———. *The Pulse of Life.* St. Paul: Llewellyn, 1968.

ASTRONOMY

Brown, Peter Lancaster. *Astronomy in Colour.* London: Blandford Press, Ltd., 1972.
Sullivan, Walter. *We Are Not Alone.* London, Penguin Books, 1970.

GENERAL

Case, Paul Foster. *The Tarot*. London: Fowler & Co. Ltd.
Frazer, Felix. *Parallel Paths to the Unseen Worlds*. Los Angeles: Builders of the Adytum, Ltd., 1967.
Ostrander, Sheila, and Schroeder, Lynn. *Psychic Discoveries Behind The Iron Curtain*. New York: Bantam, 1971.
Pauwels, Louis, and Bergier, Jacques. *Morning of the Magicians*. London: Mayflower Books Ltd., 1971.
Teilhard de Chardin, Pierre. *The Phenomenon of Man*. London: Wm. Collins Sons.

Index

Index

Absolution, 220
Acceptance, 49, 51
Actors, 270
Aesop, 217
Aggressions/aggressiveness, 78, 256
Air, 101, 121
Air people, 137
Alchemists, 34, 119, 120
Aleph, 101
Alvan Clark & Sons, 147
Anarchy, 43
Animal Farm (Orwell), 187
Aquarius
   Age of, 98, 100, 263, 268
   opposes Leo, 260
   Saturn in, 266
   symbol for, 277
Aries
   and clairvoyance, 147
   dealing with, 158
   duality of, 157
   equated with seeing, 145
   head ruled by, 157
   houses ruled by, 142–146
   Jupiter in, 151
   Mars in, 153
   Mercury in, 152
   Moon in, 154
   the Ram, 141
   Saturn in, 151–152
   in second house, 151
   and the subconscious, 154
   Sun in, 155–156
   Uranus in, 157, 158
   Venus in, 152–153
Armstrong, Neil, 147
Ascendant, 134, 178
Asceticism, 212
Aspects, 287
Assimilation, 205
Astrology/astrologers
   aims of, 8, 27, 40
   esoteric, 26, 114
   Jewish, 98
   and medicine, 245
   negative uses of, 50
   and personal relationships, 25
   and polarities, 13
   quack, 25
   study of, 282
   symbols of, 26
   terminology, 25
   understanding, 7
   use of
      in mating, 16
      in timing birth, 267
Astronomy, 139
Athletes, 240
Atomic bomb, 169

INDEX

Babies, 156
Bachelors, 152, 225
Bankhead, Tallulah, 261
Bannister, Roger, 147
Baphomet, 256
Beauty, 65
Bible, the, 211
Birth, 161
   astrological timing of, 267
Birth control, 16–17, 226
   mental, 69
Bisexuality, 64
Black magic, 102
Bode's law, 72
Body, human, 8–9, 40, 41, 212
Brave New World (Huxley), 264
Breathing, 101
Brotherhood, 45
Brown, Frank, 265
Brown, Peter Lancaster, 47
Bull, Myth of the, 162
Bullfights, 162
Busybodies, 144

Callisto (Jupiter satellite), 48
Cancer
   duality of, 192
   Jupiter exalted in, 188
   primary function of, 185
   related to speech, 185
Capitalism, 116
Capricorn
   House of Illusion, 253
   key word for, 258
   materialism of, 255
Cardinal signs, 126
Carlyle, Thomas, 24
Catholic Church, 16
Celibacy, 152, 212, 273
Chardin, Teilhard de, 94, 181
Chastity, 65
Chart
   analyzing of, 122–124, 129, 136, 178, 281
   computerized, 282–283
   drawing up, 31
   individual, 27
   natal zodiacal, 27
Children/childhood, 155, 166
Christ, Jesus, 92, 280
Christmas tree, 34
Chromosomes, 11
Church, Catholic, 16
Churchill, Winston, 246, 247
Clairaudience, 164
Clairvoyance, 147, 164
Clark, Alvan, & Sons, 147
Clemens, Samuel, 246
Clothing, 199
Collective
   subconscious, 84, 148
   unconscious, 86
Color(s)
   associated with planets, 135
   preferences, 137
   reactions to, 138
   vibrations, zodiacal, 134
Communication, 186
   telepathic, 164
Compatibility, 290
Computer technologists, 174
Conception, 16–17
Conjunction, 287, 290
Constant, Alphonse Louis. *see* Levi, Eliaphas
Constellations, astronomical, 139
Contraction, 52
Control, 46
Copulation, 66
Cosmic
   forces, 64, 82, 92, 140, 192
   laws of order, 38
Cousteau, Jacques-Yves, 231
Crabs, 183–184
Crime, 175–176
Crocodiles, 254–255
Cruelty, 173
Cyborgs, 174, 175

David-Neel, Alexandra, 164
Day of Atonement, 219–220
Death, 9, 39, 232, 234, 240

INDEX

Decanates, 36, 124–126
Deception, 254
Depression, Great, 157
Deprivation, human, 209
Descendent, 134
Desire power, 58
Devil, 256
Discrimination, 173
Dissolution, 234
Don Juan, 153, 167
Drugs, 107–108
Duality, 218
Duty, Piscean interpretation of, 42

Earth, 121
  people, 137
  as Scorpio planet, 229–230, 234
  signs, 204
Ecology
  global, 24
  solar, 20, 22, 88, 113, 140, 147, 175, 181, 226, 229, 230, 258
Economy, 158
Eggs, 208
Ego, 221, 234
Elements, 34, 122
  air, 101, 121
  Earth, 121
  fire, 114, 121
  water, 108, 121, 279
Embryo, 65
Emotion, 84
Energy, 9, 21, 38
  impulses, positive and negative, 56
  magnetic, 28
  positive use of, 51
Ephemeris, understanding, 129
Esoteric astrologers, 26
Evil, 256
Evolution, 11, 28
Expansion, 52

Failure, fear of, 60
Faith, 52
Family planning, 17

Fashion, 199
Father-figures, 197
Fear, 150
Feet, 273
Feminine signs, 121
Fetus, 65
Fidelity, 149, 198
Fire, 114, 121
Fish, 231
Fixed signs, 128
Food, 208, 212
Fraunhofer lines, 20
Free love, 67
Freud, Sigmund, 61, 233, 246, 256
Fuller, Margaret, 24

Ganymede (Jupiter satellite), 48
Gemini
  as criminal, 175
  cruelty of, 173
  Neptune in, 158
  Pluto in, 158
  Sun in, 175
  as taker, 177
  Venus in, 178
Genes, 11
Gestation, 64–65, 161
Global ecology, 24
Gluttony, 212
Goals, choosing of, 61
God, 39–40, 48, 55, 231, 252, 256
Gold, 195
Goodness, 95
Grant, Ulysses S., 168
Growth process, 10, 150, 204–205
Gsell, Paul, 239
Guide to Horoscope Interpretation (Jones), 283
Guilt, 219, 220, 222

Hall, Asaph, 147
Haruspicy, 162
Harvard Observatory, 147
Health, 205
Hearing, 162
Hebrew Flame Alphabet, 98

Hipparchus (astronomer), 139
Higher octave forces, 98
History, 200–201
Hitler, Adolph, 70, 157, 267
Holmes, Oliver Wendell, 39
Homosexuality, 65–66, 180–181, 225
Horoscope
  computers used for, 293
  as map, 26
  natal, 31
Hostility, female, 64
House(s)
  of Children, 196
  zodiacal, 145
Human
  body, 8–9, 40, 41, 212
  psyche, 24
Hunters, 240
Hypochondria, 143

Id, 234
Ideas, 100
Imagination, 65, 70, 84, 194, 217
Incarnation, 156
Industry, unionization of, 116
Inner voice, 162
Insanity, 24
Intuition, 162, 163

Jewish astrology, 98
John XXIII, Pope, 246
Jonas, Eugen, 16
Jones, Marc Edmund, 283
Jupiter
  in Aries, 151
  associated with direction West, 247
  exalted in Cancer, 188
  force, misuse of, 51
  key word for, 49
  radiation from, 48
  satellites of, 48
  size of, 47

Karma (work), 86, 216

Karmic debt, 37
Knowledge, 10–11, 165

Labor movement, 116
Landy, John, 147
Lead, 34
Lenin, Nicolai, 168
Leo
  father-figures, 197
  opposed by Aquarius, 260
  rules the heart, 197
Levi, Eliphas, 1, 23
Libido, 256
Libra
  duality of, 218
  Pluto in, 223
  Saturn influences in, 222
  Sun in, 222
  symbol for, 215
  Uranus in, 223
  Venus in, 226
Life
  cycle, 13, 18–19, 67, 161
  Force, 87, 165, 200, 204, 206, 231, 232, 256, 266
Lincoln, Abraham, 260, 262–263
Lincoln, Mary Todd, 260
Love, 66, 110, 181, 182, 197
  concept of, 179
  knowing and sharing, 44
  responsibility to, 45
  self, 41
Luna, goddess, 82
Lust, 255

MacDonald, Ramsay, 157
Magic, 100
  black, 102
Magnetic field, 145
Marriage, 215, 222–227, 244
  Venus as protectress of, 64
Mars
  aggressive side of, 77
  in Aries, 153
  force of, 76
  key word for, 74

INDEX

as lover, 79
opposed by Venus, 216
punishes, 78
size of, 71
surface, 72
and Venus, 77, 78
Mascons, 82
Masculine signs, 121
Masturbation, 181
Materialism, 255
Mating
  astrology used in, 16
  sexual process of, 233
Medicine, 25, 245
Memory, 84, 167
Menstrual cycles, 8, 163
Mercury
  in Aries, 152
  as patron of travelers, 173
  power of, 57
  size of, 54
  temperatures of, 55
Mind, human, 30, 61
Mirth, 258
Money, 195
Monogamy, 65
Moon
  in Aries, 154
  cosmic force of, 82
  gravitational pull of, 83
  key word for, 84
  orbit of, 82
  in Pisces, 275n
  position of, in natal chart, 85
  workings of, 7
Mother Letters, 98, 101
Motivation, 60
Mozart, Wolfgang Amadeus, 262
Murphy, Bridie, 31
Mutability, 244
Mutable
  Cross, 244
  signs, 128–129

Nadir, 134
Natal zodiacal chart, 27

Moon's position in, 85
Pluto in, 118
Uranus in, 99
Nature
  balance of, 17–18
  crimes against, 237
  evolutionary process of, 28
  order of, 217
Necromancy, 238
Neptune, 98, 194
  character of, 106
  co-ruler of Pisces, 107
  discovery of, 104
  in Gemini, 158
  reversing power of, 108
  rotation of, 105
  satellites of, 105
  as universal solvent, 109
Nereid (satellite of Neptune), 105
Neurotics/Neurosis, 70, 181
New York Times, 67
Noblesse oblige, 196
Noise pollution, 24
Nun (Hebrew letter), 231
Nutrition, 209

Occultism/occultists, 143, 236, 237, 253
  fad of, 2
Old Testament, 224
Opposition, 287
Order, cosmic laws of, 38
Overpopulation, 226

Parallel, 287
Paternalism, 196
Personality, 58
  adult, 218
  characteristics, 16
  influence of Saturn on, 41
Phenomenon of Man, The, (Chardin), 94
Philosophy, 165
Photosphere, 88

Physical
  action, 158
  processes, 13
Pisces
  Age of, 30, 36, 45, 107, 277–279
  creed, 280
  duality of, 273
  duty interpretation, 42
  key word for, 276
  Moon in, 275n
  symbol for, 269, 274
Planned obsolescence, 158
Plumbum, 34
Pluto, 98
  the builder, 118
  discovery of, 112, 114
  in Gemini, 158
  the Hanging Judge, 235
  in Libra, 223
  in natal chart, 118
  rotation of, 113
  in Virgo, 200, 206, 208
Polarities, 122, 152
  cosmic law of, 34, 283
  dealing with, by astrology, 13
  in the houses, 160
  Jupiter-Saturn, 34
  male-female, 68, 80, 179, 216
  positive-negative, 46, 92, 219
Pollution, noise, 24
Pomegranate, 114
Population explosion, 54
Pornography, 274
Possessions, 59
Pragmatic scientism, 11
Privacy, 198
Propagation, 233
Prophecy, 162
Psyche, human, 24
Psychiatry, 30, 157
Psychic Discoveries behind the Iron Curtain, 16
Psychic wounds, 68
Psychical research, 237
Psychometry, 164

Psychosis, 69, 70
Psychotherapy, 157
Puberty rites, 199
Punishment, 78
Puritans, 34
Pygmalion (Shaw), 188, 190

Quacks, astrological, 25
Quincunx, 290

Reality, 7
Rebellion, 59
Rebirth, 39
Reformers, 144
Reichnitz, Kurt, 16
Reincarnation, 11–12, 45, 212, 240
Reorganization, 276
Responsibility, 13, 34, 35
  accepting, 192
  dealing with, 44
  to love, 45
  to others, 42
Righteousness, acts of, 219
Roosevelt, Eleanor, 261
Roosevelt, Franklin D., 157, 168, 261
Rudhyar, Dane, 139

Sagittarius
  as athlete and hunter, 240
  heroics of, 242
  houses ruled by, 243–244
  self-assurance of, 241
  Sun in, 246
  symbolism of, 239
  Venus in, 241
Satanism, 238
Saturn
  in Aquarius, 266
  in Aries, 151
  astrological function of, 33
  climate, 33
  as father-figure, 34
  fun side of, 42
  key word for, 46
  in Libra, 222

mythology about, 34
orbit, 32
personality influences of, 41
in polarities, 46
rotation period, 32
satellites of, 33
Scientism, pragmatic, 11
Scorpio
  key word for, 234
  planets found in, 233
Scott, Sir Walter, 195
Seeing, 145
Self, attitudes to, 94
Self-assurance, 241
Self-discipline, 207
Self-love, 197
Semisextile, 289
Semisquare, 290
Sensibilities, blunting of, 21
Sex/sexual, 181
  intercourse, 66
  physical, 234
  process, 233
  symbolism, 247
  as weapon, 291
Sextile, 287, 289, 290
Sharing, 196
Shaw, George Bernard, 188, 190
Shomroni, Reuven, 98
Signs
  Cardinal, 126
  Earth, 204
  Fixed, 128
  Mutable, 128–129
Solar, ecology, 20, 22, 88, 113, 140, 147, 175, 181, 226, 229, 230, 258
Solitude, 198
Sound, 186
Spectrum, 20, 140
Speech, 187
Spirit, 30, 212
Spiritual power, 60
Square, 288, 290
Stein, Gertrude, 262
Stevenson, Adlai, 261

Stock market, 157
Subconscious, 30, 56, 279
  collective, 84, 148
Suggestion, power of, 282
Sun
  in Aries, 155–156
  Cardinal, 127
  elements of, 20
  energy of, 7
  Fixed, 128
  in Gemini, 175
  in Libra, 222
  rotation of, 89
  in Sagittarius, 246
Sunspots, 89
Superego, 234
Superstitions, 49
Swift, Jonathan, 147
Symbols, astrological, 26, 129

Tarot, 64, 241, 252, 254
Taurus
  associated with hearing, 162
  in cabalistic context, 165
  nature of, 171
Telepathy, 164
Temper, 144
Temperance/tempering, 241–242
Terminology, astrological, 25
Theologies, 29
Thermodynamics, 9
Thurber, James, 246
Titan (Saturn satellite), 33
Titius of Wittenberg, 72
Transcendental Magic (Levi), 1
Traumas, 24
Tressilian, Liz, 240
Trine, 287, 290
Triplicities, 126
Trismegistus, Hermes, 21
Triton (satellite of Neptune), 105
Truman, Harry S., 168–171
Twain, Mark, 246
Twins, 179
Tyrants, 144

INDEX

Ultraconservatism, 255
Unconscious, collective, 86
Unionization, 116
Universal solvent, 109, 279
Uranium, 102
Uranus
   Aries in, 157, 158
   discovery of, 96
   as door to freedom, 99
   in Libra, 223
   as magician, 99
   in natal chart, 99
   rotation of, 96
   satellites of, 97

Venus, 194
   in Aries, 152–153
   beauty of, 62
   force, misuse of, 68
   in Gemini, 178
   in Libra, 226
   "the mother," 70
   opposition of, to Mars, 216
   as protectress of marriage, 64
   rotation of, 73
   in Sagittarius, 241
   in the Tarot, 64
   temperature of, 73
Victoria, Queen of England, 168
Violence, 234
   and assimilating, 205

Moon's influence on, 8
Pluto in, 200, 206, 208
preoccupation with health, 205
symbol for, 204

War, 78, 215, 235
Washington, George, 271–272, 276
Washington, Martha Curtis, 271
Water, 108, 109, 121, 279
Wealth, 115, 118
Weapons, 247
Wells, John Wellington, 99–100
Wilde, Oscar, 66
Witchcraft, 166, 238, 265
Women's liberation, 206
Work, 216
Wylie, Philip, 77

Yod, 207
Yom Kippur, 219–220, 280

Zain, 173, 242
Zeitgeist, 234
Zodiac/zodiacal
   as charting device, 26
   color vibrations, 134
   definition of, 139
   houses of, 124, 142
   signs of the, 120, 129–130
Zombies, 265, 266